ALSO IN THE *FOLGER GUIDE* SERIES

The Folger Guide to Teaching *Romeo & Juliet*

The Folger Guide to Teaching *Macbeth*

(2025)

The Folger Guide to Teaching *Othello*

The Folger Guide to Teaching *A Midsummer Night's Dream*

THE FOLGER GUIDE TO TEACHING *HAMLET*

The Folger Guides to Teaching Shakespeare Series
— Volume 1 –

Peggy O'Brien, Ph.D., General Editor

Folger Shakespeare Library

WASHINGTON, DC

Simon & Schuster Paperbacks

NEW YORK   LONDON   TORONTO   SYDNEY   NEW DELHI

1230 Avenue of the Americas
New York, NY 10020

First Simon & Schuster trade paperback edition November 2024

SIMON & SCHUSTER and colophon are registered trademarks
of Simon & Schuster LLC.

For information about special discounts for bulk purchases,
please contact Simon & Schuster Special Sales at 1-866-506-1949
or business@simonandschuster.com.

The Simon & Schuster Speakers Bureau can bring authors to your
live event. For more information or to book an event, contact the
Simon & Schuster Speakers Bureau at 1-866-248-3049
or visit our website at www.simonspeakers.com.

Manufactured in the United States of America

1   3   5   7   9   10   8   6   4   2

Library of Congress Cataloging-in-Publication Data is available upon request.

ISBN 978-1-9821-0565-5
ISBN 978-1-6680-0563-7 (ebook)

THE FOLGER SHAKESPEARE LIBRARY

The Folger Shakespeare Library makes Shakespeare's stories and the world in which he lived accessible. Anchored by the world's largest Shakespeare collection, the Folger is a place where curiosity and creativity are embraced and conversation is always encouraged. Visitors to the Folger can choose how they want to experience the arts and humanities, from interactive exhibitions to captivating performances, and from pathbreaking research to transformative educational programming.

The Folger seeks to be a catalyst for:

Discovery. The Folger's collection is meant to be used, and it is made accessible in the Folger's Reading Room to anyone who is researching Shakespeare or the early modern world. The Folger collection has flourished since founders Henry and Emily Folger made their first rare book purchase in 1889, and today contains more than 300,000 objects. The Folger Institute facilitates scholarly and artistic collections-based research, providing research opportunities, lectures, conversations, and other programs to an international community of scholars.

Curiosity. The Folger designs learning opportunities for inquisitive minds at every stage of life, from tours to virtual and in-person workshops. Teachers working with the Folger are trained in the Folger Method, a way of teaching complex texts like Shakespeare that enables students to own and enjoy the process of close-reading, interrogating texts, discovering language with peers, and contributing to the ongoing human conversation about words and ideas.

Participation. The Folger evolves with each member and visitor interaction. Our exhibition halls, learning lab, gardens, theater, and historic spaces are open to be explored and to provide entry points for connecting with Shakespeare and the Folger's collection, as well as forming new pathways to experiencing and understanding the arts.

Creativity. The Folger invites everyone to tell their story and experience the stories of and inspired by Shakespeare. Folger Theatre, Music, and Poetry are programmed in conversation with Folger audiences, exploring our collective past, present, and future. Shakespeare's imagination resonates across centuries, and his works are a wellspring for the creativity that imbues the Folger's stage and all its programmatic offerings.

The Folger welcomes everyone—from communities throughout Washington, DC, to communities across the globe—to connect in their own way. Learn more at folger.edu.

IMAGE CREDITS

© Research and Cultural Collecwtions, University of Birmingham
PICTURES FROM HISTORY / BRIDGEMAN IMAGES

John Smith. Map published in *The generall historie of Virginia, New-England, and the Summer Isles . . .* (second edition, 1631), map of Virginia.
CALL # STC 22790C.2. USED BY PERMISSION OF THE FOLGER SHAKESPEARE LIBRARY

Wenceslaus Hollar. *Head of a Black Woman with a Lace Kerchief Hat* (1645) no. 46.
CALL # ART VOL. B35 NO.46. USED BY PERMISSION OF THE FOLGER SHAKESPEARE LIBRARY.

Wenceslau Hollar. *Head of a Black Woman in Profile to Left* (1645).
CALL # ART 237212. USED BY PERMISSION OF THE FOLGER SHAKESPEARE LIBRARY.

Wenceslaus Hollar. *Head of a Young Black Boy in Profile to Right* (17th century).
CALL # ART 236023. USED BY PERMISSION OF THE FOLGER SHAKESPEARE LIBRARY.

Ira Aldridge's first appearance at Covent Garden in the role of Othello—a playbill dated 1833 plus two small engraved portraits and an article in German, mounted together (early to mid-19th century).
CALL # ART FILE A365.5 NO.5. USED BY PERMISSION OF THE FOLGER SHAKESPEARE LIBRARY.

William Shakespeare; Pablo Neruda. *La tragedia de Romeo y Julieta.* Buenos Aires, Editorial Losada, S.A., 1964.

Paapa Essiedu as Hamlet and Mimi Ndiweni as Ophelia in *Hamlet*, 2018, directed by Simon Godwin.
PHOTO BY MANUEL HARLAN © RSC.

Samuel Stevens Smith. Hamlet and Ophelia, *"I loved you not"* . . . *"I was the more deceived,"* Act III, Scene 1 [graphic] / J.D.W. 1874; S. Smith sculpt. (London, England: Cassell, Petter & Galpin, 1874).
CALL # ART FILE S528H1 NO.16. USED BY PERMISSION OF THE FOLGER SHAKESPEARE LIBRARY.

/ Image Credits

H. Bencke. *Hamlet* and Ophelia, Mr. Edwin Booth as Hamlet in Shakespeare's *Hamlet*, Act III, Scene 1 [graphic] (New York, N.Y.).
CALL # ART VOL. B1, NO.184. USED BY PERMISSION OF THE FOLGER SHAKESPEARE LIBRARY.

Michelle Terry as Hamlet in *Hamlet* (2018), directed by Federay Holmes and Elle While.
PHOTOGRAPHER—TRISTRAM KENTON.

Byron Company. *Hamlet* [5 photographs of a production starring Edmund Russell as Hamlet, Miss Jane Schenck as Ophelia, Miss Louise Morewin as Gertrude, and William Hazeltine as Claudius] / Byron, N.Y. (New York, 1903).
CALL # ART FILE R963 NO. 1 PHOTO. USED BY PERMISSION OF THE FOLGER SHAKESPEARE LIBRARY.

[8 photographs of a production of] *Hamlet* [starring E. H. Sothern as Hamlet and Julia Marlowe as Ophelia]. (New York, 1904).
CALL # ART FILE S717.5 NO.12. USED BY PERMISSION OF THE FOLGER SHAKESPEARE LIBRARY.

Actors perform a scene from *Hamlet* at Shakespeare's Globe theatre Globe-to-Globe production.
AP IMAGES/ LEFTERIS PITARAKIS.

Paul Girardet. *Hamlet et Ophélie* (Paris, 19th century).
CALL # ART FILE S528H1 NO.158. USED BY PERMISSION OF THE FOLGER SHAKESPEARE LIBRARY.

Charles A. Buchel. Hamlet, Act III, Scene 1 (early 20th century).
CALL # ART BOX B919 NO.4. USED BY PERMISSION OF THE FOLGER SHAKESPEARE LIBRARY.

William Shakespeare. *Hamlet, Prince of Denmark: a tragedy. As it is now acted by His Majesty's Servants* . . . (London, 1747), pages 72–73.
CALL #: PROMPT HAM. 16. USED BY PERMISSION OF THE FOLGER SHAKESPEARE LIBRARY.

William Shakespeare. *Hamlet*. Promptbook for an E. H. Sothern–Julia Marlowe production (early 20th century).
CALL #: PROMPT HAM. 34. USED BY PERMISSION OF THE FOLGER SHAKESPEARE LIBRARY.

William Shakespeare. *Tragedy of Hamlet Prince of Denmark* (East Aurora, N.Y., 1902), finis page verso and opposite.
CALL #: PROMPT HAM. 30. USED BY PERMISSION OF THE FOLGER SHAKESPEARE LIBRARY.

Ruth Negga as the title character in *Hamlet* at St. Ann's Warehouse in Brooklyn, Jan. 31, 2020.
(SARA KRULWICH/*THE NEW YORK TIMES*)

If you are a teacher,
you are doing the world's most important work.
This book is for you.

CONTENTS

THE FOLGER GUIDE
TO TEACHING *HAMLET*

PART ONE

Shakespeare for a Changing World

Why Shakespeare?

Michael Witmore

You have more in common with the person seated next to you on a bus, a sporting event, or a concert than you will ever have with William Shakespeare. The England he grew up in nearly 400 years ago had some of the features of our world today, but modern developments such as industry, mass communication, global networks, and democracy did not exist. His country was ruled by a monarch, and his days were divided into hours by church bells rather than a watch or a phone. The religion practiced around him was chosen by the state, as were the colors he could wear when he went out in public.

When Shakespeare thought of our planet, there were no satellites to show him a green and blue ball. The Northern European island where he grew up was, by our standards, racially homogeneous, although we do know that there were Africans, Asians, Native Americans, Muslims, Jews, and others living in London in the early 1600s—and that Shakespeare likely saw or knew about them. The very idea that people of different backgrounds could live in a democracy would probably have struck him as absurd. What could an English playwright living centuries ago possibly say about our changed and changing world? Would he understand the conflicts that dominate our politics, the "isms" that shape reception of his work? What would he make of debates about freedom, the fairness of our economies, or the fragility of our planet?

The conversation about Shakespeare over the last 250 years has created other obstacles and distance. Starting around that time, artists and promoters put Shakespeare on a pedestal so high that he became almost divine. One such promoter was an English actor named David Garrick, who erected a classical temple to Shakespeare in 1756 and filled it with "relics" from Shakespeare's life. Garrick praised Shakespeare as "the God of our idolatry," and in his temple included a throne-like chair made of wood from a tree that Shakespeare may have planted. Today, that chair sits in a nook at the Folger Shakespeare Library. The chair's existence reminds us that the impulse to put Shakespeare in a temple has been at times overwhelming. But temples can exclude as well as elevate, which is why the Folger Shakespeare Library—itself a monument to Shakespeare built in 1932—needs to celebrate a writer whose audience is contemporary, diverse, and growing.

While Shakespeare was and is truly an amazing writer, the "worship" of his talent becomes problematic as soon as it is expected. If Shakespeare's stories and poetry continue to be enjoyed and passed along, it should be because we see their value, not because we have been told that they are great. Today, if someone tells you that Shakespeare's appeal is "universal," you might take away the idea that his works represent the experience of everyone, or that someone can only be fully human if they appreciate and enjoy his work. Can that possibly be true? How can one appreciate or enjoy the things in his work that are offensive and degrading—for example, the racism and sexism that come so easily to several of his characters? What about such plays as *The Merchant of Venice*, *Othello*, or *The Taming of the Shrew*, where the outcomes suggest that certain kinds of characters—a Jew, an African, a woman—deserve to suffer?

When we talk about Shakespeare, we have to confront these facts and appreciate the blind spots in his plays, blind spots that are still real and reach beyond his specific culture. In acknowledging such facts, we are actually in a better position to appreciate Shakespeare's incredible talent as a writer and creator of stories. Yes, he wrote from a dated perspective of a Northern European man who was a frequent flatterer of kings and queens. Within those limits, he is nevertheless able to dazzle with his poetry and offer insights into human motivations. We are not *required* to appreciate the language or dramatic arcs of his characters, but we can appreciate both with the help of talented teachers or moving performances. Memorable phrases such as Hamlet's "To be or not to be" are worth understanding because they capture a situation perfectly—the moment when someone asks, "Why go on?" By pausing on this question, we learn something at a distance, without having to suffer through everything that prompts Hamlet to say these famous words.

Had Shakespeare's plays not been published and reanimated in performance over the last few centuries, these stories would no longer be remembered. Yet the tales of Lady Macbeth or Richard III still populate the stories we tell today. They survive in the phrases that such characters use and the archetypal situations in which these characters appear—"out, out damned spot" or "my kingdom for a horse!" Marvel characters and professional politicians regularly channel Shakespeare. When a supervillain turns to the camera to brag about their evil deeds, we are hearing echoes of King Richard III. When the media criticizes a leader for being power-hungry, some version of Lady Macbeth is often implied, especially if that leader is a woman.

While they are from another time, Shakespeare's characters and situations remain exciting because they view life from a perspective that is both familiar and distant. The better able we are to recognize the experiences described in Shakespeare's plays in our lives, the broader our vocabulary becomes for understanding ourselves. We see and hear more when the plays dramatize important questions, such as:

- What does a child owe a parent and what does a parent owe their child? Why must children sometimes teach their parents to grow up? *King Lear*, *Hamlet*, and *Henry IV, Part 1* all ask some version of these questions.

- Are we born ready to love or is the capacity to love another something that is learned? Shakespeare's comedies—*Twelfth Night*, *As You Like It*, *Much Ado About Nothing*—are filled with characters whose entire stories are about learning to accept and give love.

- How does one deal with an awful memory or the knowledge of a brutal crime? Hamlet is burdened with both, just as many are today who are haunted by trauma.

These questions get at situations that anyone might experience at some point in their life. If you are a teenager whose mad crush is turning into love, you will have to go out on that balcony, just like Juliet. Will you be confident or afraid? If a "friend" who knows you well is feeding you lies, you will be challenged to resist them—as Othello is when faced with Iago. Will you be able to think for yourself? These questions come up in any life, and the answers are not predetermined. A goal in any humanities classroom is to improve the questions we ask ourselves by engaging our specific experiences, something very different from looking for "timeless truths" in the past.

Do not believe that you must master Shakespeare in order to appreciate literature, language, or the human condition. Do, however, be confident that the time you and your students spend with these plays will result in insight, new skills, and pleasure. Shakespeare was a deeply creative person in a deeply polarized world, one where religious and economic conflicts regularly led to violence. He used that creativity to illustrate the many ways human beings need to be saved from themselves, even if they sometimes resist what they need most. He also understood that stories can change minds even when the facts cannot. If there was ever a time to appreciate these insights, it is now.

The Folger Teaching Guides are the product of decades of experience and conversation with talented educators and students. The Folger continues to offer teachers the best and most effective techniques for cultivating students' abilities in the classroom, starting with Shakespeare but opening out on the great range of writers and experiences your students can explore. We invite you to visit the Folger in person in Washington, DC, where our exhibitions, performances, and programs put into practice the methods and insights you will find here. And we extend our gratitude to you for doing the most important work in the world, which deserves the dedicated support we are providing in these guides.

Good Books, Great Books, Monumental Texts—Shakespeare, Relevance, and New Audiences: GenZ and Beyond

Jocelyn A. Chadwick

"People can find small parts of themselves in each character and learn what it may be like to let the hidden parts of themselves out. Regardless of personal background, everyone can relate to the humanity and vulnerability that is revealed in Shakespeare's works." (Student, 2023)

" 'To me, there is no such thing as black or yellow Shakespeare,' Mr. Earle Hyman, a celebrated African-American actor said. 'There is good Shakespeare or bad Shakespeare. It's simply a matter of good training and opportunity.' " ("Papp Starts a Shakespeare Repertory Troupe Made Up Entirely of Black and Hispanic Actors," *New York Times*, January 21, 1979)

"The question for us now is to be or not to be. Oh no, this Shakespearean question. For 13 days this question could have been asked but now I can give you a definitive answer. It's definitely yes, to be." (President Volodymyr Zelenskyy's speech to the UK Parliament, March 8, 2022)

"I, at least, do not intend to live without Aeschylus or William Shakespeare, or James, or Twain, or Hawthorne, or Melville, etc., etc., etc." (Toni Morrison, "Unspeakable Things Unspoken: The Afro-American Presence in Literature," *The Source of Self-Regard*, 2019)

How have William Shakespeare's brilliant and probing plays about the human condition come to an *either/or* to some contemporary audiences? The preceding quotes reveal appreciation, understanding, and metaphorical applications along with definitions of the playwright's depth and breadth. And yet, a misunderstanding *and* sometimes *conscious cancellation* of the man, his work, and his impact have undergone substantial *misunderstanding and misinterpretation*.

For as long as any of us can or will remember, William Shakespeare has continued to be with us and our students. True, this is a bold and assertive declarative statement; however, in the 21st century, is it and will it continue to be accurate and still *valid*?

In 1592, playwright Robert Greene, a contemporary of William Shakespeare, did not think much of Shakespeare's work or his talent:

> There is an upstart Crow, beautified with our feathers that with his Tygers hart wrapt in a Players hyde, supposes he is as well able to bombast out a blank verse as the best of you: and being an absolute Johannes factotum is in his owne conceit the onely Shake-scene in a country. (Robert Greene, *Greene's Groats-Worth of Wit*, 1592)

Clearly, Greene was jealous of Shakespeare's popularity and talent.

Interestingly, what Greene objects to parallels some 21st-century perspectives that at this writing recommend removal of Shakespeare's plays and poetry from curricula throughout the country—*just because*. For Greene, the objection was Shakespeare's talent, his appeal to his contemporary audience, his rising popularity, and cross-cultural exposure—not only angering Greene but also resulting in his undeniable jealousy.

Today, however, the primary argument is that Shakespeare's texts are old and dated; he is white and male—all of which from this perspective identify him, his time, and his work as disconnected from the realities of 21st-century students: antiquated, anachronistic, even racially tinged. These arguments persist, even though without doubt, Shakespeare's London was metropolitan, multicultural, and influenced by the city's international trade—imports as well as exports.

And further, to be clear, as Toni Morrison and so many other scholars, writers, *and* readers have asserted, the *durability of* a text lies with its present *and* future audiences. I should add here that Morrison was engaging with, and "talking back to," Shakespeare's play *Othello* when she wrote her play *Desdemona* in 2011.

At this writing, there are a number of contemporary catalysts pointing out the necessity of rethinking, reflection, and consubstantiation of such texts that have long been a part of the canon. We are experiencing not only that resurgence but also a book-banning tsunami in schools and public libraries. The result of such movements and actions indeed causes us to rethink; they have also compelled educators at all levels, parents, librarians, writers, and GenZ students to speak up and out.

To illustrate concretely students' responses, this introduction necessarily includes the perspectives and voices from some high school students (grades 9–12), who attend Commonwealth Governors School (CGS) in Virginia. I asked a number of them what they thought about Shakespeare, and they told me. Their statements are in *their own words*; I did no editing. In addition, the students within the CGS system represent the panoply of inclusion and diversity.

> It's the big ideas that make Shakespeare relevant to myself and other students. Everyone loves, and everyone feels pain, so while we each might experience these feelings at different points in our lives, in different degrees, and for different reasons than others, I think Shakespeare's work is enough out of our times so that all students can connect to his themes and imagine themselves in the positions of his characters. (Student, May 2023)

And . . .

> I feel his general influence; I feel like he created a lot of literary words, and musicians like Taylor Swift draw from the works of earlier people, and Shakespeare continues to be relevant. (Student, 2023)

Interestingly, students *tapestry* what they read and experience in Shakespeare's works into their contemporary world, concomitantly, reflecting Umberto Eco's assertion about the import, impact, and protean qualities of a text's life: students create their own meaning and connections—building onto and extending Shakespeare's words, expression, characters, and challenges, ultimately scaffolding into their present realities, experiences, and challenges.

With all of these developments and conversations in mind, this Folger series of teaching guides provides that crossroad and intersection of analysis and rethinking. The central question that joins both those who see at present limited or no redeemable value in Shakespeare and those who view these texts as windows of the past, present, and, yes, the future is *"Do William Shakespeare's plays resonate, connect, and speak to 21st-century readers of all ages, and especially to our new generations of students?"*

Let us consider Eco's assertion: each time playwrights, directors, and artists reinterpret, every text undergoes a disruption, thereby reflecting new audiences. To *re-see* a character or setting when producing Shakespeare's plays is with each iteration a kind of disruption—a disruption designed to bring Shakespeare's 16th-century texts to audiences from multiple perspectives and epochs. The term *disruption* here takes on a more modern definition, a more protean and productive definition: Every time a reader enters a text—one of Shakespeare's plays, to be specific—that reader can meld, align, interweave experiences, memories, thoughts, aspirations, and fears, and yes, as the first student quote alludes, empower the reader to *identify* with characters, and moments and consequences. This reading and/or viewing is indeed a positive kind of disruption—*not to harm or destroy*; on the contrary, a positive disruption that expands and interrelates both reader and viewer with Shakespeare and each play. Past *and* present intersect for each generation of readers. In this positive disruption texts remain relevant, alive, and *speak verisimilitude*.

Similarly, we ask 21st-century students studying Shakespeare to bring their *whole selves* to the work, and to come up with their own interpretations. Allowing and privileging 21st-century students to compare and contrast and then examine, inquire, and express their own perspectives and voices remains the primary goal of English language arts: independent thinking, developed voice, and ability to think and discern critically for oneself. Both the primary text and adaptations are reflections *and* extended lenses:

> *The man i' th' moon's too slow—till new-born chins*
> *Be rough and razorable; she that from whom*
> *We all were sea-swallowed, though some cast again,*
> *And by that destiny to perform an act*
> *Whereof what's past is prologue, what to come*
> *In your and my discharge.* (The Tempest 2.1, 285–89)

Just as the past continuously informs and reminds the present, the present—each new generation—brings new eyes, new thoughts, new perspectives. Of course, each generation sees itself as unique and completely different; however, the echoes of the past are and will always be ever-present.

In so many *unexpected* ways, the 21st-century Shakespeare audience in school—students, teachers, and others—share far more with William Shakespeare and his time than we may initially recognize and acknowledge. From his infancy to his death, Shakespeare and his world closely paralleled and reflects ours: upheavals and substantial shifts culturally, sociopolitically, scientifically, and religiously, as well as the always-evolving human condition. Each of the plays represented in this series—*Hamlet, Macbeth, Othello, Romeo and Juliet*, and *A Midsummer Night's Dream*—illustrates just how much William Shakespeare not only observed and lived with and among tragedy, comedy, cultural diversity, challenges, and new explorations, but also, from childhood, honed his perspective of both past and present and—as Toni Morrison expresses—*rememoried* it in his plays and poems. Tragedy and Comedy is rooted in the antiquities of Greek, Roman, and Greco-Roman literature and history. William Shakespeare uniquely crafts these genres to reflect and inform his own time; more importantly, the plays he left us foreshadow past and future connections for audiences to come—audiences who would encounter cross-cultures, ethnicities, genders, geography, even time itself.

More than at any other time in our collective history experienced through literature, the past's ability to inform, advise, and even "cushion" challenges our students' experiences today. It will continue to do so into the foreseeable future and will continue to support and inform, and yes, even protect them. Protecting, meaning that what we and our students can read and experience from the safe distance literature provides, allows, even encourages, readers to process, reflect, and think about how we respond, engage, inquire, and learn.

> The play . . . *Macbeth* . . . is about pride; there are lots of common human
> themes. He's the basis for a lot of literature like *Hamlet* is just the *Lion King*;
> it is just *Hamlet*, but it's lions. (Student, May 2023)

One fascinating trait of GenZ readers I find so important is *the how* of their processing and relating canonical texts with other contemporary texts and other genres around them: TV, movies, songs, even advertisements. What I so admire and respect about *students' processing* is their critical thinking and their ability to create new and different comprehension pathways that relate to their own here and now. In this new instructional paradigm, we *all* are exploring, discovering, and learning together, with William Shakespeare as our reading nucleus.

Although many writers and playwrights preceded William Shakespeare, his scope and depth far exceeded that of his predecessors and even his peers. His constant depiction and examinations of the human condition writ large and illustrated from a myriad of perspectives, times, cultures, and worlds set Shakespeare decidedly apart. The result of his depth and scope not only previewed the immediate future following his death, but more profoundly, his thematic threads, characters, settings, and cross-cultural inclusions continue to illustrate *us to us*.

The pivotal and critical point here is GenZ's continued reading and experiencing of William Shakespeare's plays. As they experience this playwright, they take bits and pieces of what they have read and experienced directly into other texts they read and experience in classes and daily living. In fact, in the "tidbits" they experience initially through Shakespeare, students will connect and interpret *and make their own meaning and connections*, even *outside* of textual reading. Malcolm X, in fact, provides us with an example of how that works:

> I read once, passingly, about a man named Shakespeare. I only read about him passingly, but I remember one thing he wrote that kind of moved me. He put it in the mouth of Hamlet, I think, it was, who said, "To be or not to be." He was in doubt about something—whether it was nobler in the mind of man to suffer the slings and arrows of outrageous fortune—moderation—or to take up arms against a sea of troubles and by opposing end them. And I go for that. If you take up arms, you'll end it, but if you sit around and wait for the one who's in power to make up his mind that he should end it, you'll be waiting a long time. And in my opinion the young generation of whites, blacks, browns, whatever else there is, you're living at a time of extremism, a time of revolution, and now there has to be a change and a better world has to be built, and the only way it's going to be built—is with extreme methods. And I, for one, will join with anyone—I don't care what color you are—as long as you want to change this miserable condition that exists on this earth. (Oxford Union Queen and Country Debate, Oxford University, December 3, 1964)

Like Malcolm X, GenZ students turn toward the wind, staring directly and earnestly into their present and future, determined to exert their voices and perspectives. Their exposure to past and present literature, sciences, histories, and humanities allows, even empowers, this unique generation to say, "I choose my destiny." And the myriad texts to which we expose them informs, challenges, and compels them to always push back and move toward a truth and empowerment *they* seek. Some of us who are older may very well find such empowerment disconcerting—not of the "old ways." But then, just what is a comprehensive education for lifelong literacy supposed to do, if not expose, awaken, engage, even challenge and open new, prescient doors of inquiry, exploration, and discovery? This is the broad scope of not just education for education's sake but of reading and experiencing for oneself *devoid of outside agendas—whatever they may be or from wherever they may emanate.*

A student put this succinctly:

> Elements of his writing are still relevant in today's films and books, like his strong emotional themes, tropes, and character archetypes. Shakespeare's works are quoted often by common people [everyday people] and even by more influential individuals, including civil rights leader Martin Luther King Jr., who was known to quote Shakespeare often. I believe the beautiful and unique work by William Shakespeare is still greatly relevant and appreciated now and will go on to remain relevant for centuries more. (Student, May 2023)

The plays comprising this series represent curricula inclusion around the country and also represent the angst some parents, activists, and politicians, even some fearful teachers, have about our continuing to include Shakespeare's works. That said, there are many, many teachers who continue to teach William Shakespeare's plays, not only allowing students from all walks of life to experience the man, his time, and the sheer scope of his thematic and powerful reach, but also privileging the voices and perspectives GenZ brings to the texts:

> We can see in Shakespeare our contemporary and sometimes frightening range of humanity today—I am specifically thinking of our current political turmoil—is not unique, and that just like the evil monarchs such as Richard III appear in Shakespeare's plays, they are always counterbalanced by bright rays of hope: in *Romeo and Juliet*, the union between the Montagues and Capulets at play's end restoring peace and civility . . . It is impossible for me to watch any performance or read any Shakespeare play—especially the tragedies—without leaving the theatre buoyed up by hope and respect for humankind, a deeper appreciation of the uses of the English language, and a feeling that I have been on a cathartic journey that leaves my students and me enriched, strengthened, and hopeful. (Winona Siegmund, Teacher, CGS)

> I'm going to be honest, I'm not very knowledgeable on the subject of Shakespeare . . . I never really went out of my way to understand and retain it. All I know is that I can't escape him. No matter how hard I try, and trust me, I try, he will always be somewhere, running through the media with his "art thous" and biting of thumbs. Perhaps people see themselves in the plays of Shakespeare. Maybe Shakespeare is a dramatization of the hardships we experience every day . . . Shakespeare has stained my life. One of those annoying stains that you can't get out. A bright, colorful stain that's easy to notice. But who cares? It was an ugly shirt anyway; might as well add some color. (Student, May 2023)

> Taylor Swift's "Love Story." I LOVE the STORY of *Romeo and Juliet*. See what I did there? But in all honesty, there are so many Shakespeare-inspired works (*Rotten Tomatoes, West Side Story, Twelfth Grade Night*, etc.) that I liked and remained relevant to me, and prove that Shakespeare will always be relevant. The first Shakespeare play I read was *Macbeth* when I was twelve and going to school in Azerbaijan. And even as a preteen studying in a foreign country, I loved the story and found it morbid, funny, and wise all at the same time. My Azerbaijani classmates liked it, too. Due to this unique experience, I think that anyone can enjoy and identify with Shakespeare's works, no matter their age or country of origin. (Student, May 2023)

The five plays in this Folger series represent the universal and social depth and breadth of all Shakespeare's poetry and plays—verisimilitude, relevance, *our* human condition—all writ large in the 21st century and beyond. Through characters, locations, time periods, challenges, and *difference*, William Shakespeare takes us all into real-life moments and decisions and actions—even into our *not yet known or experienced*—to illustrate the human thread joining and holding us all as one.

> Despite being several hundred years old, Shakespeare's works have yet to Become antiquated. There are several reasons for this long-lasting relevance—namely the enduring themes. Shakespeare's themes on humanity, morality, loss, and love remain relatable for people across all walks of life. (Student, May 2023)

In sum, a colleague asked me quite recently, "Jocelyn, why do you think students just don't want to read?" To add to this query, at this writing, I have tracked an increasing, and to be honest, disturbing sentiment expressed on social media: some teachers positing, essentially, the same perspective. My response to both is the same: our students—elementary through graduate school—*do* read and write every day. They will also read what we assign in our classes. However, this generation of students first thinks or asks outright—*Why?* What do I *get* if I invest the time and effort? Most assuredly direct inquiries with which many veteran teachers *and* professors are unfamiliar—perhaps even resentful. But let's be honest. Our students of a now-patinated past most likely felt the same way. Remember the plethora of *CliffsNotes* and *Monarch Notes*? I know I threw my share of students' copies in the trash—wanting them to read for themselves.

Just like adults, our students, especially today, have a right to ask us *Why?* What *do* they *get* if they invest their time in reading assigned texts? Umberto Eco brilliantly answers why our students *must* continue reading and experiencing texts—for this series, William Shakespeare's plays—and learning through performance:

> Now a text, once it is written, no longer has anyone behind it; it has, on the contrary, when it survives, and for as long as it survives, thousands of interpreters ahead of it. Their reading of it generates other texts, which can be paraphrase, commentary, carefree exploitation, translation into other signs, words, images, even into music. ("Waiting for the Millennium," *FMR* No. 2, July 1981, 66)

To illustrate Eco's assertion, I will leave it to one student and two people with whom all teachers and many students are familiar:

> Shakespeare's work is relevant because his legacy allows people from all walks of life to understand that they can make a difference. Although people from all walks of life may not always relate to his works, the impact that he made on modern literature and theater is undeniable. The lasting dreams that his works have provided for young people lay the groundwork for our future. Shakespeare's living works are proof that one small man with one small pen can change the future of everything around him. (Student, May 2023)

I met and fell in love with Shakespeare . . . It was a state with which I felt myself most familiar. I pacified myself about his whiteness by saying after all he had been dead so long it couldn't matter to anyone anymore. (Maya Angelou on her childhood introduction to and love of Shakespeare in *I Know Why the Caged Bird Sings*, 1969)

and, as Malcolm X proclaimed:

I go for that. (Oxford Union Queen and Country Debate, Oxford University, December 3, 1964)

Why This Book?

Peggy O'Brien

First, let's start with YOU: If you are a schoolteacher, know that you are the **most** precious resource in the world. In every school, town, city, state, country, **civili**zation, solar system, or universe, there is none more valuable than you. It is **hard,** hard work and yet. . . you are doing the most important work on earth. Period.

At the Folger Shakespeare Library, we know this well and deeply, and that's **why** you are a clear focus of our work. If you teach Shakespeare and other complex liter-ature—and particularly if you are a middle or high school teacher—it is our **mission,** passion, and honor to serve you. Therefore . . . welcome to *The Folger Guides to Teaching Shakespeare* and our five volumes on teaching *Hamlet, Macbeth, Othello, Romeo and Juliet,* and *A Midsummer Night's Dream.*

Here's why this book: our overall purpose. We know that many of you find **your**selves teaching plays that you don't know well, or that you've taught so often that **they** are beginning to bore you to death. (You talk to us, and we listen.) So, these books **give** you fresh information and hopefully meaningful new ideas about the plays you **teach** most frequently, along with a very specific way to teach them to *all* students—highfliers, slow readers, the gamut. We see the Shakespeare content and the teaching methodology as one whole.

We often get these questions from y'all. You may recognize some or all of them:

- How on earth do I even begin to think about teaching a Shakespeare play? No **one** has really ever taught me how to teach Shakespeare and my own experience **with** Shakespeare as a high school student was . . . not great.

- How can Shakespeare possibly make sense in this day and age? In this changing world? Old dead white guy?

- Shakespeare can't possibly be engaging to *all* my students, right? I mean, it's **true** that really only the brightest kids will "get" Shakespeare, right?

- SO . . . what's the Folger Method and how does it fit into all of this?

- I have to teach the "10th-grade Shakespeare play"—whatever it is—and I haven't read it since high school, or maybe I have never read it.

- I'm a schoolteacher and don't have extra time to spend studying up before I **teach** this stuff.

- Doesn't using those watered-down, "modernized" Shakespeare texts make it easier? Aren't they the most obvious way to go?

- Can learning and teaching Shakespeare really be a great experience for my kids and for me too?

Our *Folger Guides to Teaching Shakespeare* are hopefully an answer to these questions too.

Here's why this book: the Folger Method. At the Folger, not only are we home to the largest Shakespeare collection in the world but we have developed, over the last four decades or so, a way of teaching Shakespeare and other complex texts that is effective for *all* students. We're talking well-developed content and methodology from the same source, and in your case, *in the same book.* Imagine!

The Folger Method is language-based, student-centered, interactive, and rigorous, and provides all students with ways into the language and therefore into the plays. Our focus is words, because the words are where Shakespeare started, and where scholars, actors, directors, and editors start. Shakespeare's language turns out to be not a barrier but *the way in.* The lessons in this book are sequenced carefully, scaffolding your students' path. They will find themselves close-reading, figuring out and understanding language, characters, and the questions that the play is asking. All of this when they may have started out with "Why doesn't he write in English?" It's pretty delicious. If you want to know more about the Folger Method right this minute, go to the chapter that starts on page 37.

A couple of things I want you to know right off the bat:

- Because the Folger Method involves lots of classroom work that is interactive and exciting (and even joyful), sometimes teachers are tempted to pull a few lessons out of this book and use them to spruce up whatever they usually do. Oh resist, please. Take the whole path and see what your students learn and what you learn.

- There is no "right" interpretation of any play (or work of literature, for that matter).

    In working with the Folger Method principles and essentials, your students come up with their own sense of what's going on in *Hamlet*. Their own interpretation. Not yours, or the interpretation of famous literary critics, but their own. And then they bring it to life. Exciting! That's what we're after, because the skills that they'll develop in doing this—close-reading, analysis, collaboration, research—they will use forever.

- The Folger Method may call on you to teach differently than you have before. Be brave! You are not the explainer or the translator or the connector between your students and Shakespeare. You're the architect who sets up the ways in which Shakespeare and your students discover each other . . . and we'll show you very explicitly how to do that.

Here's why this book: parts of the whole. Each of these guides is organized in the same way:

- **Part One is the big picture:** Folger director Michael Witmore and Jocelyn Chadwick both take on the "Why Shakespeare?" question from very different angles. And Jocelyn brings students into the conversation too. Delicious!

- **Part Two is *YOU* and *Hamlet*.** Through a set of short takes and one delicious long take, you'll get a stronger sense of the play. The shorts are some speedy and pretty painless ways to learn both the basics and a few surprises about both *Hamlet* and Shakespeare.

  The long take is "Who's/Whose Hamlet?" an essay written for you by Rubin Espinosa, an accomplished and celebrated Shakespeare scholar. We know that you have no "extra" time ever, but we also know that schoolteachers find connecting with new scholarship to be enlivening and compelling. New ways to look at old plays—new ways most often sparked by the changing world in which we live—continue to open up many new ways to look at Shakespeare. What you take away from Rubin's essay may show up in your teaching soon, or maybe at some point, or maybe never—and all of those are good. You may agree with or grasp his perspective on *Hamlet*, or you may not; he will get you thinking, though—as he gets us thinking all the time—and that's what we're about.

- **Part Three is you, *Hamlet*, your students, and what happens in your classroom.**

  - The Folger Method is laid out clearly—and bonus: with the kind of energy that it produces in classrooms—so that you can get a sense of the foundational principles and practices before you all get into those lessons, and your own classroom starts buzzing.

  - A five-week *Hamlet* unit, day-by-day lessons for your classes, with accompanying resources and/or handouts for each. We know that the people who are the smartest and most talented and creative about the "how" of teaching are those who are working in middle and high school classrooms every day. So, working schoolteachers created all of the "What Happens in Your Classroom" section of this book. They do what you do every day. While these writers were writing, testing, and revising for you and your classroom, they were teaching their own middle and high school kids in their own. And I am not mentioning their family obligations or even whispering the word "pandemic." At the Folger, we are in awe of them, and for many of the same reasons, are in awe of all of you.

  - Two essays full of practical advice about two groups of students whom teachers ask us about often. The first details and demonstrates the affinity that English Learners and Shakespeare and *Hamlet* have for one another. The second focuses on the deep connections that can flourish between students with intellectual and emotional disabilities and Shakespeare and *Hamlet*. No barriers to Shakespeare anywhere here.

  - The last essay is packed with information and examples on pairing texts—how we make sure that students are exposed to the broad sweep of literature while at the same time are busy taking Shakespeare right off that pedestal and into conversations with authors of other centuries, races, genders, ethnicities, and cultures. This is where magic starts to happen!

This is Why You, and Why This Book, and now . . . **back to YOU!** As Polonius says in Act 1, "Go to, go to!" A joyful and energized journey of mutual discovery is at hand—for you and your students. Get busy in Elsinore! And tell us how it all goes. Get online with us! Follow us at folger.edu! Come visit our newly expanded building and new programs right near the Capitol in Washington, DC. You belong here! We will always leave the light on for you.

PART TWO

Getting Up to Speed, or Reviving Your Spirit, with *Hamlet*

Ten Amazing Things You May Not Know About Shakespeare

Catherine Loomis and Michael LoMonico

The basics: Shakespeare was a playwright, poet, and actor who grew up in the market town of Stratford-upon-Avon, England, spent his professional life in London, and returned to Stratford a wealthy landowner. He was born in 1564—the same year Galileo was born and Michelangelo died. Shakespeare died in 1616, and Cervantes did too.

1. In the summer of 1564, an outbreak of bubonic plague killed one out of every seven people in Stratford, but the newborn William Shakespeare survived.

2. In Shakespeare's family, the women were made of sterner stuff: Shakespeare's mother, his sister Joan, his wife, Anne Hathaway, their daughters, and granddaughter all outlived their husbands. And Joan lived longer than all four of her brothers. The sad exception is Shakespeare's younger sister, Anne. She died when she was seven and Shakespeare was fifteen.

3. Shakespeare appears in public records up until 1585, when he was a 21-year-old father of three, and then again in 1592, when he turns up in London as a playwright. During those lost years, he may have been a schoolmaster or tutor, and one legend has him fleeing to London to escape prosecution for deer poaching. No one has any idea really, but maybe there is a theatrical possibility: An acting company called the Queen's Men was on tour in the summer of 1587, and, since one of their actors had been killed in a duel in Oxford, the town just down the road, the company arrived in Stratford minus an actor. At age 23, did Shakespeare leave his family and join them on tour?

4. Shakespeare wrote globally: in addition to all over Britain, his plays take you to Italy, Greece, Egypt, Turkey, Spain, France, Austria, Cyprus, Denmark and, in the case of *The Tempest*, pretty close to what was to become America.

5. Shakespeare died of a killer hangover. The Reverend John Ward, a Stratford vicar, wrote about Shakespeare's death on April 23, 1616, this way: "Shakespeare, [Michael] Drayton, and Ben Jonson had a merry meeting, and it seems drank too hard, for Shakespeare died of a fever there contracted."

6. On Shakespeare's gravestone in Stratford's Holy Trinity Church is a fierce curse on anyone who "moves my bones." In 2016, archaeologists used ground-penetrating radar to examine the grave, and . . . Shakespeare's skull is missing.

7. Frederick Douglass escaped slavery and as a free man became a celebrated orator, statesman, and leader of the American abolitionist movement—and he was a student and lover of Shakespeare. Visitors to Cedar Hill, his home in DC's Anacostia neighborhood, can see Douglass's volumes of Shakespeare's complete works still on his library shelves and a framed print of Othello and Desdemona on the parlor wall. In addition to studying and often referencing Shakespeare in his speeches, Douglass was an active member of his local Anacostia community theater group, the Uniontown Shakespeare Club.

8. Shakespeare is the most frequently produced playwright in the U.S. Despite this, *American Theatre* magazine has never crowned him America's "Most Produced Playwright," an honor bestowed annually based on data from nearly 400 theaters. He always wins by such a large margin—usually there are about five times more Shakespeare productions than plays by the second-place finisher—that the magazine decided to just set him aside so that other playwrights could have a chance to win.

9. While Nelson Mandela was incarcerated on South Africa's Robben Island, one of the other political prisoners retained a copy of Shakespeare's complete works, and secretly circulated it through the group. At his request, many of the other prisoners—including Mandela—signed their names next to their favorite passages.

> *Cowards die many times before their deaths;*
> *The valiant only taste of death but once.*
> *Of all the wonders that I yet have heard,*
> *It seems to me most strange that men should fear,*
> *Seeing that death, a necessary end,*
> *Will come when it will come.*

These lines from *Julius Caesar* were marked "N. R. Mandela, December 16, 1977." Nelson Mandela was released from prison in 1990.

10. The Folger Shakespeare Library is in Washington, DC, and houses the largest Shakespeare collection in the world, just a block from the U.S. Capitol. We are Shakespeare's home in America! We are abuzz with visitors and audience members from our own DC neighborhoods, from across the country and around the world: teachers and students, researchers and scholars, lovers of the performing arts, all kinds of learners, and the curious of all ages and stages. Find us online at folger.edu/teach—and do come visit our beautiful new spaces. Be a part of our lively and accessible exhibitions and programs, explore rare books and other artifacts, join a teaching workshop, and enjoy the magic of theatre, poetry, and music. We're waiting for you, your classes, and your families!

Ten Amazing Things You May Not Know About *Hamlet*

Catherine Loomis and Michael LoMonico

1. Shakespeare named his son, born in 1585, Hamnet. Hamnet and his twin sister, Judith, were probably named after Shakespeare's Stratford neighbors Hamnet and Judith Sadler (who named one of their sons William). Hamnet died in 1596 at age 11; the parish register records his burial, but not his cause of death.

2. In December 1579, when Shakespeare was 15, a young woman from a village two miles from Stratford drowned in the River Avon under doubtful circumstances. The coroner then—as Laertes does with Ophelia's death—made considerable efforts to show that the death was not a suicide. The young woman's name was Katherine Hamlett.

3. *Hamlet* was first published in 1603 in a small book called the first quarto, or Q1. We believe that it was not printed from a written manuscript. Instead, the printer may have listened to actors who had played minor roles in the play as they recited the parts they remembered. Q1 may have been printed from their memory of the play. The Q1 *Hamlet* is very different from the one we have come to know. There is no "To be or not to be, that is the question" anywhere. In Q1, Hamlet says, "To be or not to be, I there's the point!"

4. As far as we know, the earliest recorded performance of *Hamlet* outside England happened near the coast of West Africa. The crew of the ship the *Red Dragon*, anchored off Sierra Leone in 1607, performed the play.

5. One near-contemporary source claims that Shakespeare himself played Hamlet's father's ghost at the Globe Theatre. We have also learned from a contemporary play featuring a ghost—Francis Beaumont's *The Knight of the Burning Pestle*, 1607—that the actor playing the ghost in *Hamlet* likely wore makeup made of grease and flour.

6. Women have been playing Hamlet pretty regularly at least since the 1780s. French actress Sarah Bernhardt played Hamlet to great acclaim onstage in 1899 and in a two-minute film adaptation a year later. In a 1920 German-made silent film, Danish actress Asta Nielsen played him as a woman raised as a boy. More recently, Ruth Negga and Cush Jumbo played Hamlet in theaters in Ireland, England, and the U.S.

7. President Abraham Lincoln was a student of *Hamlet*. In an 1863 letter to American actor James Hackett he wrote, "I think the soliloquy in Hamlet commencing 'O, my offence is rank' surpasses that commencing 'To be, or not to be.' " Lincoln died less than two years later, assassinated as he sat in a theater watching a play. His assassin, John Wilkes Booth, was an actor who, a few months before he murdered Lincoln, played Mark Antony in a New York production of *Julius Caesar*.

8. In 1951, Owen Dodson, chair of the Drama Department at Howard University—one of America's most prestigious historically Black universities—was staging *Hamlet*, obviously with an all-Black cast. During their rehearsal period, Dodson and Earle Hyman, the actor who was playing Hamlet, reached out to British actor and director Sir John Gielgud, who was on tour in Washington, DC, at the time. They were unable to meet at Gielgud's hotel because DC's segregation laws prevented them from doing so. Gielgud joined Dodson and Hyman at the Greyhound bus station lunch counter to discuss the play. The Howard production of *Hamlet* was reviewed very favorably in the *New York Times*.

9. *Hamlet* has been staged countless times, but never with the geographic range of the Globe to Globe *Hamlet*, a tour produced by the Globe Theatre in London to celebrate Shakespeare's 450th birthday. Over the course of two years, twelve actors and a stage crew of five traveled over 186,000 miles to perform *Hamlet* in 197 countries. The role of Hamlet was played alternately by Ladi Emeruwa, who was born in Nigeria, and Naeem Hayat, whose family is from Pakistan.

10. The Folger Shakespeare Library is heavy into *Hamlet*! The Folger has over 500 printed copies of *Hamlet* solo—in manuscript, promptbooks, numerous translations, and even a copy in the original Klingon. We have produced *Hamlet* six times on our Elizabethan stage, offered a wide range of humanities programs with a *Hamlet* focus, and worked with hundreds of thousands of schoolteachers on ways to teach *Hamlet*. Since 1992, 3.5 million *Hamlet* fans have purchased copies of the Folger Shakespeare edition, and during the 12 months prior to this writing, *Hamlet* was downloaded 500,000 times from the free online Folger Shakespeare. In 2016, the Folger *First Folio! The Book That Gave Us Shakespeare* tour sent First Folios—Shakespeare's plays collected for the first time and printed in 1623—to be exhibited in all 50 states, Puerto Rico, and the District of Columbia. More than 600,000 people came to see these magical books. And in every location, the Folio was opened to "To be or not to be, that is the question."

What Happens in This Play Anyway?

A Plot Summary of *Hamlet*

Events before the start of *Hamlet* set the stage for tragedy. When the king of Denmark, Prince Hamlet's father, suddenly dies, Hamlet's mother, Gertrude, marries his uncle, Claudius, who becomes the new king.

A spirit who claims to be the ghost of Hamlet's father describes his murder at the hands of Claudius and demands that Hamlet avenge the killing. When the counselor Polonius learns from his daughter, Ophelia, that Hamlet has visited her in an apparently distracted state, Polonius attributes the prince's condition to lovesickness, and he sets a trap for Hamlet using Ophelia as bait.

To confirm Claudius's guilt, Hamlet arranges for a play that mimics the murder; Claudius's reaction is that of a guilty man. Hamlet, now free to act, mistakenly kills Polonius, thinking he is Claudius. Claudius sends Hamlet away as part of a deadly plot.

After Polonius's death, Ophelia goes mad and later drowns. Hamlet, who has returned safely to confront the king, agrees to a fencing match with Ophelia's brother, Laertes, who secretly poisons his own rapier. At the match, Claudius prepares poisoned wine for Hamlet, which Gertrude unknowingly drinks; as she dies, she accuses Claudius, whom Hamlet kills. Then first Laertes and then Hamlet die, both victims of Laertes's rapier.

What Happens in This Play Anyway?

A PLAY MAP OF *HAMLET*

Mya Gosling and Peggy O'Brien

What happens in HAMLET?

Art by Mya Lixian Gosling
of goodticklebrain.com
Concept by Peggy O'Brien

When **Hamlet**, Prince of Denmark, went away to school, his family looked like this:

But, when he came home, it looked like this:

What happened?
Who is to blame?
What should he do now?

Who's Who in Denmark

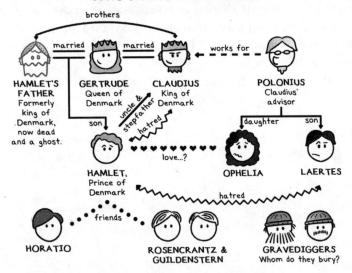

There's Just So Much Going On!

Who's/Whose Hamlet?

Ruben Espinosa

The experience of approaching *Hamlet* for the first time was once described to me as something akin to the feeling of seeing, also for the first time, Michelangelo's *David* in person—of walking down the corridor in the Galleria dell'Accademia in Florence, Italy, and arriving at the well-lit room that holds in it the iconic sculpture only to look up at it and wonder, "What do I do with it?" The *David* looms over you and is overwhelming, as does, it seems, *Hamlet*. I find the symbolism behind this comparison to be perfect. *Hamlet* is a work that is so often imagined as beyond our reach, awe inspiring, and meant for a particularly privileged audience. What, then, are we asking our students to behold when they come to *Hamlet* for the first time?

In this essay, I want to draw attention to the dominant assumptions regarding the value of *Hamlet* to our students and to our society, and then I want to scrutinize why such assumptions simply work to uphold an unnecessary reverence both for the play and for Shakespeare. To my mind, we can't teach this play with the mere idea of building an appreciation for Shakespeare or his dramatic work that is so often imagined as quintessential. Instead, when approaching a text like *Hamlet*, we need to recognize in that experience an opportunity to see Shakespeare as a vehicle that allows us to bring important conversations to the fore. We simply can't imagine ourselves as a docent guiding our students through the corridors of a museum that upholds elitist perspectives. Sure, there is much to admire, but there is also so much more that can be accomplished as we look at this art with a critical eye. To that end, I want to highlight how this play, in its attention to notions of belonging and alienation, offers present-day students and audiences something beyond a beautiful work that we are invited to stare at quietly.

The monumentalizing of Shakespeare is all too often an act that goes unexamined, and his perceived greatness is generally taken as a given. If this is true of Shakespeare, it is also true of *Hamlet*. Take, for example, Douglas Bruster's first chapter, "In the Shakespeare Museum," from his book *To Be or Not to Be* (London: Continuum, 2007). Bruster says to the reader, "Imagine finding yourself in the Shakespeare Museum" (1). This imagined museum—with "vast marble hallways" and manifold galleries containing within them "artefacts" from various plays and poems, and also auditory experiences with visitors "listening to Shakespeare's words"—is clearly meant to highlight Shakespeare's greatness (1). After some experience with plays like *Macbeth*, *Romeo and Juliet*, and *The Tempest*, Bruster describes the feeling of arriving at *Hamlet*:

> Just ahead, though, you catch the sight of the most arresting thing of all. For here, off the Museum's expansive *Hamlet* wing, you come across an entire gallery devoted to the "To be or not to be" speech. Walking past rows of skulls, rapiers, and portraits of Hamlets gone by, you step into this shadowy room set aside for Hamlet's famous soliloquy. (1)

Given that Bruster's book is entirely about the soliloquy in question, one can understand this setup—these dramatic imaginings hold within them the speech that deserves sustained attention in his mind. I will, perhaps predictably, return to the speech later in this essay, but here I draw on Bruster not only to highlight the elements that monumentalize both the author and this speech, but also to see how easy it is to lead readers to arrive at the conclusion that *Hamlet* and its parts are worthy of our sustained attention—they are worthy of an entire gallery in a museum. I urge you not to take that as a given.

When we stop to consider why *Hamlet* has enjoyed such popularity among critics and readers over time, we begin to see a different picture emerge. As Ian Smith says of Horatio's task "to tell Hamlet's story" at the play's end, it "has become" not only Horatio's "assignment" but also "the business of literary criticism" ("We Are Othello: Speaking of Race in Early Modern Studies," *Shakespeare Quarterly* 67.1 [2016]: 106). This is to say, literary critics are often much too eager to imagine Hamlet speaking for us all. Smith goes on to say, "Critics identify with Hamlet personally and see in his doubt and skepticism a philosophy that resonates with their world view" (106). What, then, are the implications of such a desire to identify with Hamlet? "One obvious but too often underappreciated answer," Smith says, "is that this claim of identification has been nurtured by an academic industry in which white, male interests were historically epitomized, reflected, and affirmed" via Hamlet (107). Like Smith, we must recognize that the play's imagined value, over the centuries, has been tethered to a particularly privileged, white readership, but this reality has gone largely unnoticed. If approaching *Hamlet* is like approaching Michelangelo's *David*, as I mention at the outset, then what one ultimately beholds is something distinctly white. As Smith suggests, Hamlet's whiteness is something we should be acknowledging, because not all readers can nor will want to identify with Hamlet in a way that they are often encouraged to do so.

It is best if we, as educators, question the long tradition of propping up this play because of the perception that Hamlet's worldviews are somehow universal. They are not, and as such we need to look beyond him. Indeed, there is so much more to *Hamlet* than Hamlet. This is not to suggest, though, that we need to ignore Hamlet altogether. On the contrary, I think much of what he introduces is important for us to consider, but we should also consider other provocative issues that this play puts forward without needing to explore what those issues reveal about his character. Instead, we should consider what they reveal about us and our own experiences. What I would encourage us to think about in our teaching are the play's energies when it comes to challenging oppressive structures of power—and there are many in this play. Gender, race (as Smith reminds us, whiteness is a race, too), patriarchal structures, religious division, and social hierarchies are all themes that this play explores in important detail. From where I stand, though, *Hamlet* offers us an opportunity to think through with our students why we often subscribe to social conventions that devalue the lives of so many. The play's interrogation of such issues is a generative place to begin. In what follows, then, I want to highlight three separate concepts that the play puts forward—all engage with issues of belonging and alienation, topics that resonate in our present moment and that open the door to meaningful classroom discussions: hospitality, voices of subversion, and vulnerable bodies.

Before I arrive at these topics, I want to outline briefly the play's relatively straightforward plot. When the play opens, Hamlet's father has already died, and we learn that in the aftermath of that death his uncle Claudius has married Hamlet's mother, Gertrude. In the process, Claudius secures his role as King of Denmark—a role Hamlet clearly believes belongs to him when he says of Claudius later in the play, "He that hath killed my king and whored my mother, / Popped in between th' election and my hopes" (5.2.72–73). Hamlet hoped that he would be king. Shortly after the play opens with all of this baggage for us to unpack, a ghost who seems to be Hamlet's father appears to Hamlet to reveal that Claudius murdered him, and the ghost encourages Hamlet to get revenge. For the remainder of the play, Hamlet struggles with making the decision to avenge his father's murder. It is worth noting that *Hamlet* is a revenge tragedy that, in the iteration that we have come to know and admire, came after the revenge tragedy had been in vogue in Shakespeare's England. Shakespeare seems to have revisited this genre to contemplate what happens if the eponymous hero is not willing to enact revenge. What happens if one resists that call from the spirit of the father, and instead seeks to understand all that is rotten in Denmark? What happens if patriarchal expectations and other structures of oppression are scrutinized? That should be a roadmap that we follow.

Indeed, the first line of the play offers its readers a key moment to scrutinize how to approach the play. When Barnardo asks, "Who's there?" (1.1.1) at the onset of the play, he is literally asking the person he is approaching (Francisco) to identify himself. He wants to know if he is a Dane, if he is a citizen of Denmark, and if he is loyal to the same king. It is Barnardo's desire to know that the man he cannot see in the darkness of night is like him and not some foreign threat. But the question could loom as large as the more famous "To be or not to be?" question, because the play deals quite forcefully with a desire to understand oneself. In the process of being asked to identify oneself, we are also invited to contemplate who we are. In other words, the question could be posed to the play's audiences—including our students—as well.

More provocatively, perhaps, this question also presents us with the distinct opportunity to think about hospitality. The question, "Who's there?" demands that the other identify himself/herself/themself. I am reminded here of Jacques Derrida's view of hospitality when he writes,

> To put it in different terms, absolute hospitality requires that I open up my home and that I give not only to the foreigner (provided with a family name, with the social status of being a foreigner, etc.), but to the absolute, unknown, anonymous other, and that I *give place* to them, that I let them come, that I let them arrive, and take place in the place I offer them, without asking of them either reciprocity (entering into a pact) or even their names. (Jacques Derrida and Anne Dufourmantelle, *Of Hospitality*, trans. Rachel Bowlby [Stanford, CA: Stanford UP, 2000], 25)

According to Derrida, true hospitality demands that we *do not* ask that question. It requires us to accept the stranger without reservation or need for identification. If only we were so welcoming of strangers in our nation.

With this play's opening question in mind, then, I want to trace through the moments in *Hamlet* where hospitality is more explicitly explored before I get to why this theme matters. After Hamlet interacts with the ghost of his dead father, he is seemingly energized in his desire to follow the ghost's request for Hamlet to remember him. When Horatio expresses his rather famous response to the surreal events at hand, "O day and night, but this is wondrous strange," Hamlet responds, "And therefore as a stranger give it welcome. / There are more things in heaven and earth, Horatio, / Than are dreamt of in your philosophy" (1.5.185–88). The latter part of Hamlet's rejoinder is often underscored, as it falls in line with Hamlet's larger philosophical inquiries asking us to think beyond what we know. But Hamlet's immediate response is critical—"And therefore as a stranger give it welcome." Hamlet seems to be saying that it is one's obligation to give welcome to strangers, and as such these strange events should receive the same hospitable reception. Be open to it, he seems to suggest to Horatio, just as you should be open and hospitable to strangers.

Later in the play, Hamlet is more straightforward in his call for hospitality. When the actors arrive at Elsinore, and after introductions have been made and passages from plays have been recited, Hamlet requests that Polonius take these men in and give them lodging: "Good my lord, will you see the players well bestowed? Do you hear, let them be well used" (2.2.548–49). Polonius responds, "My lord, I will use them according to their desert" or deserving (2.2.553–54). Hamlet responds: "God's bodykins, man, much better! Use every man after his desert and who shall 'scape whipping? Use them after your own honor and dignity. The less they deserve, the more merit is in your bounty. Take them in" (2.2.555–59). Hamlet's directive to Polonius is clear—treat these men not in the way they deserve to be treated, but much better. When he tells Polonius to treat them with the honor and dignity Polonius would want for himself, he acknowledges that these actors deserve kindness and hospitality *because* they come to Elsinore as strangers.

We should, perhaps, be wondering why, in a play seemingly focused on revenge, hospitality is a reoccurring theme. When we think about transgressions that occur in the play, and the grief that is consistently underscored, why is *Hamlet* gesturing at the law of hospitality? What does it have to do with such oppressive structures? Whether it is ghosts or strangers who visit Denmark, the idea is that they should be welcomed with dignity. But we know that not all in Denmark are afforded such dignity. I want, then, to look beyond Hamlet at my last, and perhaps most significant, example of the play's attention to hospitality.

When Ophelia suffers madness as a result of the murder of her father, she speaks freely in the court in what is commonly dubbed her "mad speech." When Claudius asks her how she is doing, Ophelia responds, "Well, God dild you. They say the owl was a baker's daughter. Lord, we know what we are but know not what we may be. God be at your table" (4.5.47–49). Ophelia's reference is to a bit of folklore that would have been familiar to Shakespeare's audience, and one that I think is critical to locating in her response subversive potential. The story surrounding the baker's daughter is squarely about hospitality. The Christian folktale is about Jesus disguised as a beggar, and it is as follows:

> Our Saviour went into a baker's shop where they were baking, and asked for some bread to eat. The mistress of the shop immediately put a piece of dough into the oven to bake for him; but was reprimanded by her daugh-

ter, who insisting that the piece of dough was too large, reduced it to a very small size. The dough, however, immediately afterwards began to swell, and presently became of a most enormous size. Whereupon, the baker's daughter cried out, "Heugh, heugh, heugh," [Who, who, who] which owl-like noise probably induced our Saviour for her wickedness to transform her into that bird. This story is often related to children, in order to deter them from such illiberal behavior to poor people. (Quoted in Robert Tracy, "The Owl and the Baker's Daughter: A Note on *Hamlet* IV.v.42–43," *Shakespeare Quarterly* 17.1 [1966]: 84)

The story is not uncommon, as it imagines Jesus in disguise as a beggar to keep Christians honest. The baker's daughter, it seems, fails the test, as she casts aside the law of hospitality to mistreat the stranger. As a result, when she expresses, "Who, who, who"—as in "who is responsible for this?"—she is transformed into an owl. Because Ophelia is a daughter to a recently murdered father, we might read into this her own position or transformation. But within the play, she is in no position to afford nor deny hospitality, and thus such an assumption makes little sense. So I am interested in investigating the subversive energies behind this allusion, which are much too often ignored.

Because Ophelia has the audience of both the king and queen of Denmark, her allusion should carry with it much more weight than it is often given. It is here, then, that I see the play's attention to hospitality lean into offering us voices of resistance. When Ophelia evokes this popular folktale, we need be aware that she is answering the king himself. Claudius asks her how she is doing, and she responds that she is well, and then puts this story on the table. If this story was told to children in an effort "to deter them from such illiberal behavior to poor people," we can reasonably read this as a moment where she is trying to teach Claudius how he should be treating those who are below him in social standing. The baker's daughter's "who" is also reminiscent of the opening question of the play, "Who's there?" Not everyone, it seems, has a seat at God's table. In his position as king, he should be generous, hospitable, and kind. He is not.

Indeed, none of those in any position of power in *Hamlet* are kind. This is critical, because early in the play when Hamlet says in response to Claudius calling him his son, "A little more than kin and less than kind" (1.2.67), he gestures at the fact that Claudius, as his uncle and now his father, is his kin but he is not his kind—that is, he is not his natural father. But Hamlet also uses this wordplay to suggest that Claudius is unkindly. When we think of the way *kind* can mean both alikeness and benevolence, we can perhaps recognize why and how this play draws on the theme of hospitality. The very notion that this word expresses both alikeness and goodness simultaneously reveals that similitude ought to be valued. What, though, does this suggest about those who are unalike? Of more importance, this play clearly puts forward the idea that the bigger threat comes not from strangers, but instead from those within, as Claudius killed his own brother and plots to murder his nephew. Wickedness, like that of the baker's daughter, abounds in *Hamlet*.

If we are willing to scratch at the surface of corruption that this play holds within it, then we should look a bit more closely at the way Ophelia addresses it. Long before she delivers the lines I mention above, Ophelia is willing to resist the oppressive structures that define her existence—she is willing to voice her dissent. Often, Ophelia is imagined as a victim, as a dutiful daughter who succumbs to madness, as a young woman caught between the will of her father and the will of her lover. But the self-confidence she exhibits in her first scene tells a different story.

When Laertes offers Ophelia advice before embarking on his trip to France, he straightforwardly warns her about entertaining a relationship with Hamlet. He suggests that Hamlet "is subject to his birth" (1.3.21)—that is, as a prince, Hamlet does not necessarily have a choice in who he will marry. But this moment also works to highlight the fact that Hamlet's "birth" or birthright is imagined as superior to that of others, including Laertes and Ophelia. This notion of birthright, of course, undergirds social hierarchies and is incredibly dangerous because it suggests some individuals are born superior to others, and as such some individuals are entitled to more rights than others. In a monarchy, such as the one in Shakespeare's England, this form of government sustains the power accorded to nobility, but it stems beyond the political realm as the notion of birthright often informs the way we imagine citizenship and racial hierarchies. Indeed, the very concept of birthright works to sustain the belief in white supremacy. What, then, do we do with Laertes's suggestion that Hamlet's birthright delimits his ability to choose? More importantly, what do we do with *Hamlet*'s suggestion that birthright determines one's ability to choose?

One way to approach this, perhaps, is to take Laertes's suggestion not as a move to ask us to sympathize with those of higher social standing, but to recognize that those in higher social standing can and will take advantage of those "below" them. Laertes is, at base, warning Ophelia not to have sex with Hamlet because she is of a lower social standing. He says to her:

Then weigh what loss your honor may sustain
If with too credent ear you list his songs
Or lose your heart or your chaste treasure open
To his unmastered importunity.
Fear it, Ophelia; fear it, my dear sister[.] (1.3.33–37)

In other words, should Hamlet capitalize on his position of privilege, and should Ophelia agree to entertain his desires, she is the only one who stands to lose. This not only speaks to social hierarchies, but also to gendered hierarchies. As an unmarried young woman in an oppressive patriarchal society, Ophelia is under certain pressures to act in a certain way, and she is asked—to be certain—to set aside her own desires. We may comfortably couch these attitudes in the historical past, but we likely recognize that these attitudes persist to the present.

Laertes's advice, then, lingers thick in the air when we, for the first time, get a sense of Ophelia as a character. Her response straightforwardly addresses not only Laertes's hypocrisy but the overarching patriarchal structures that inform his thinking:

I shall the effect of this good lesson keep
As watchman to my heart. But, good my brother,
Do not, as some ungracious pastors do,
Show me the steep and thorny way to heaven,
Whiles, like a puffed and reckless libertine,

Himself the primrose path of dalliance treads
And recks not his own rede. (1.3.49–55)

While Ophelia seems focused on the fact that Laertes is not practicing what he preaches, she is deliberate in comparing his hypocrisy to that of ungracious pastors—the symbolic religious fathers who define structures of religious and moral obedience. In short, she calls out the entire system that seeks to define proper behavior for women. If, later in the play, Ophelia seems overly subservient and weak in her dealings with the will of her father and lover, it ought to remain clear that she is vividly aware of the oppressive structures that consistently render her vulnerable.

This vulnerability leads me to consider the final point in exploring the way notions of belonging and alienation often shape this play. Vulnerable bodies define *Hamlet*, as the prelude to the play involves regicide. The murder of the king not only illustrates the vulnerability of even the most powerful person in the nation, but also the political state itself. Both corporeal and political bodies are rendered vulnerable. Claudius, as murderer, ascends the throne and one cannot help but see in that fact the reality of a vulnerable nation. Beyond Claudius, though, we see Polonius, Laertes, Ophelia, Rosencrantz, Guildenstern, Gertrude, and Hamlet all rendered vulnerable. This, to my mind, is the most provocative aspect of this play when it comes to making it speak to our present moment.

When Hamlet first encounters Polonius, he is very deliberate in his desire to make Polonius feel uneasy. To this point in the play, Hamlet has already learned from the ghost that Claudius murdered the elder Hamlet. Also by this point in the play, we have learned that Ophelia related to Claudius her interactions with Hamlet, one which includes Hamlet entering her private bedroom, half-dressed and in an unstable state. In this interaction, Hamlet is nothing short of condescending to Polonius, someone he feels is below him. (This is not uncommon with Hamlet, as he also treats the gravediggers with a similar disdain.) During the interaction in question, though, Polonius ultimately feels Hamlet is nonsensical in his responses, so he says to the prince, "My lord, I will take my leave of you" (2.2.231–32). Hamlet responds, "You cannot, sir, take from me anything that I will more willingly part withal—except my life, except my life, except my life" (2.2.233–35). In that repetitious answer, Hamlet makes clear his vulnerability. He means to ridicule Polonius by suggesting that Polonius taking his leave of Hamlet is something the latter would welcome with zeal, but then Hamlet's own wordplay leads him to the sober reality that one could at any moment "take from" him his own life. It is a moment of foreshadowing, but it also underscores very vividly the vulnerability that we all face. Not one of us can say with confidence that our own life cannot be taken by another at any moment.

If we think about Hamlet's rejoinder to Polonius from a neutral lens, then we can see within his apprehensions about his own mortality something that approaches universality. However—and this is a deliberately magnified *however*—that sense of vulnerability is very, very different for some individuals. When we recognize that the Hamlet of Shakespeare's imagination is a privileged, elitist white man, then it is reasonable to suggest that his sense of his own vulnerability differs vastly from the vulnerability that Black and brown individuals face in our present-day society. To think about this play in a cross-historical manner, as we should be doing with all of Shakespeare's works, is to imagine those lines, "except my life, except my life, except my life," as carrying with them a distinctly powerful valence when it comes to issues of race and racism in our day.

To imagine a Black person delivering Hamlet's lines in that moment is to recognize how the play's attention to notions of belonging and alienation resonate in a markedly different way. From my estimation, such a move would give this play much needed cultural relevance. The very experience of a Black person being pulled over by a police office in the U.S. presents life-or-death situations, and as such we see how Hamlet could speak to this—how the lines in the play offer opportunities for important conversations. I am not alone in thinking this.

In summer 2020, The Public Theater in New York took on the much celebrated "To be or not to be" speech from *Hamlet* in an effort to make it speak to our present moment. The public lynching of George Floyd had led to widespread global protests against not only his murder but also against recursive acts of racial injustice, and as citizens of the U.S., we found ourselves in a moment. The insurrection at the U.S. Capitol was still ahead of us, but in that summer, the world seemed focused on making sure that systemic racism was not yet again swept under the proverbial rug of our nation's history of racist violence and genocide.

In their four-and-a-half-minute video entitled "#ToBeBlack," New York's Public Theater gave voice to 30 Black actors performing Hamlet's famous speech together. It is thoughtful in its design, as it puts the Black Lives Matter protests of that summer into conversation with the Civil Rights protests of the previous century and into conversation with Shakespeare. It underscores the timelessness not of Shakespeare, *Hamlet*, or this speech, but rather the timelessness of racism in our nation. It is incredibly powerful to see in the faces and voices of these actors the reality of unbelonging and alienation in this nation when, for so many of them, it is not a choice. It is an unflinching look at the exhaustion of existence.

I call this video to your attention because, even though you may be engaged in teaching *Hamlet* much further on into the 21st century, to give a sense of what The Public Theater was able to accomplish with their short film in 2020 is to understand how Shakespeare does not belong in an imagined museum but in the voices of those who can and do keep him alive in meaningful ways. (Though it's unclear for how long it will remain accessible, at this writing it can be found at https://publictheater.org /media-center/series/bns/tobeblack/.)

The truth is that I should not look at this passage, at this play, at this celebrated author in the way all those who came before me have done so—nor should our students. I, for one, do not want to walk up to his play in awe and reverence before I have read one word. Instead, I want to see how his works might make me understand my life, my world, my reality in a way I might not have considered. If Shakespeare doesn't matter to the lived experience of all our students, then he doesn't matter. When we think about the way social, gendered, and racial hierarchies define the negative experiences of so many in our society and in our classrooms, then perhaps we can find in these issues conversation worth having. It is important to look beyond the monument, to topple it if need be, and to locate therein not his voice but ours.

PART THREE

Hamlet in *Your* Classroom
With *Your* Students

The Folger Method:
You Will Never Teach Literature
the Same Way Again

Corinne Viglietta and Peggy O'Brien

Imagine a classroom where every student is so immersed in reading that they don't want to stop. A place that is buzzing with the energy of student-driven learning. Where students shout, whisper, and play with lines from Shakespeare and other authors. Where small groups discuss, with textual evidence and passion, which parts of a text are the most compelling and how to perform them effectively. Where all students bring their identities and customs, their whole selves, to fresh performances of juicy scenes. Where every student experiences firsthand that literary language is *their* language, demanding to be interpreted and reinterpreted, questioned, and yes, even resisted sometimes. Where students are doing the lion's share of the work, and the teacher, who has thoughtfully set up this zone of discovery, is observing from the side. Where joy and rigor work hand in hand. Where everyone is engaged in something that feels important and adventurous. Where every student realizes they can do hard things on their own.

This is a real place. This is *your* classroom as you try the lessons in this book. Yes, *you*.

Will it be perfect all the time? Heck no. Will it be messy, especially at first? Almost certainly. Will you have to take risks? Yes.

Does this way of teaching really work? You bet.

Don't take our word for it, though. For four decades, the Folger has been working with teachers on what has become known as the Folger Method, and here's a small sample of what teachers—mostly middle and high school teachers—have had to say:

- *"With the Folger Method, my students are reading more deeply than they ever have before. They are breaking down language and really understanding it."*

- *"I was unsure of myself and my ability to tackle Shakespeare, but this has been empowering."*

- *"Students complain when it's time to leave. I have gleefully stepped back so they can create scenes, shout words and lines, and cut speeches. They volunteer to read aloud even when reading aloud is hard for them. We dive in and focus on the words. It's working."*

37

- *"Over the course of this Folger unit, I've seen amazing things in my special education students. This one student has had an entire transformation—like, fellow teachers are asking me what happened. Before, he always had great pronunciation and sounded fluent, but he could never really understand what it was he was saying. And then all of a sudden in the middle of this play, something clicked. I think it's because he has all these strategies for understanding the words on the page now."*

- *"The Folger Method didn't just transform how I teach Shakespeare—it's changed how I teach everything."*

Great, but what *is* the Folger Method, exactly?

It is a transformative way of approaching complex texts. (And not just Shakespeare, but any complex text.) Consisting of both principles and practices, it provides a framework for everything that goes into great teaching: designing, planning, assessing, reflecting, revising, communicating, guiding, growing, listening, laughing, learning—all of it.

Behind it all is a precise, tried-and-true philosophy that we've broken down into 8 parts.

8 Foundational Principles

The more you practice this way of teaching, the more you'll see these **8 foundational principles** in action, and the clearer it all becomes. Watching your students move through the lessons in this book will give you (and them) a profound, almost visceral, understanding of these principles. They will become part of the fabric of your classroom. Teaching this way—even if it's completely new to you—will feel intuitive in no time.

1. Shakespeare's language is not a barrier but a portal. The language is what enables students to discover amazing things in the texts, the world, and themselves.

2. All students and teachers deserve the real thing—whether it's Shakespeare's original language, primary source materials, new information that expands our understanding of history, or honest conversations about tough issues that the plays present.

3. Give up Shakespeare worship. If your Shakespeare lives on a pedestal, take him down and move him to a space where he can talk to everyday people and great writers like Toni Morrison and Julia Alvarez, Frederick Douglass and Joy Harjo, F. Scott Fitzgerald and Azar Nafisi, Amy Tan and George Moses Horton, Jane Austen and Pablo Neruda, James Baldwin and Homer.

4. Throw out themes, tidy explanations, and the idea of a single right interpretation. Resist the urge to wrap up a text with a neat bow, or, as Billy Collins puts it, to tie it to a chair and "torture a confession out of it." With ambiguity comes possibility. Alongside your students, embrace the questions. How liberating!

5. The teacher is not the explainer but rather the architect. Set up the interactions through which your students and Shakespeare discover each other. This might be hard to hear (it was for Corinne at first!), but the helpful teacher is not the one who explains what the text means or who "translates" Shakespeare's words for students. The truly helpful teacher is the one who crafts opportunities for students to be successful at figuring things out for themselves. It's about getting out of the way so students can do things on their own.

6. Set students on fire with excitement about literature. When reading brings mysteries, delights, and surprises, students are motivated to read closely and cite evidence. And they gain confidence in their ability to tackle the next challenge.

7. Amplify the voice of every single student. Shakespeare has something to say to everybody, and everybody has something to say back to Shakespeare. Student voices, both literal and figurative, create the most vibrant and inclusive learning communities. The future of the humanities—and our world—depends on the insights and contributions of *all* students.

As tempting as it may be to impose our own interpretation of the text on students, or to ask students to imitate the brilliant arguments of seasoned scholars, we beg you to resist that urge. Students need to dive into a play and shape and reshape their own interpretations in order to become independent thinkers. Teaching literature is about the sparks that fly when readers of an infinite variety of perspectives engage directly and personally with the text.

8. The Folger Method is a radical engine for equity. Every student can learn this way, and every teacher can teach this way. The goal is to help all students read closely, interrogate actively, and make meaning from texts.

Now let's put these ideas into practice.

The Arc of Learning

The first step to applying these principles in class is understanding the journey, what we call **the arc of learning**, that your students will experience.

The activities in this book are not isolated, interchangeable exercises. They are a complete set of practices that work together to bring the 8 principles to life. Sequencing, scaffolding, pacing, differentiating—it's all here.

And because each of your students is unique, each journey will be unique too. If you teach AP or IB classes, this book will help each of your students navigate their own path and reach rigorous course outcomes, starting right where scholars, editors, directors, and actors start—with the words. If you teach students who have the ability and desire to dive deep—and we mean *deep*, luxuriating in the mysteries and puzzles of complex literature—the Folger Method will enable them to do just that. Alongside these students you probably also have students who need some extra support before diving deep, and these lessons are just as much for them (more on differentiation later). By its very design, this way of teaching is flexible and roomy enough to challenge and support every single learner. Use this book to meet *all* students where they are, give them space to stretch, and be amazed at what they do.

What happens over the course of a Folger unit often astonishes teachers, administrators, families, and students themselves. Remember that spirited classroom from the first paragraph? Pass by and hear students shouting lines from Romeo and Juliet's soliloquies in a cacophony. (*What in the world?*) Poke your head in and watch them mark up their scripts with notes on which words ought to be stressed or cut out entirely, which tone to use when. (*Hmmm . . . this is interesting.*) Walk into the classroom, take a seat, and observe different student performances of the same scene—and a robust whole-class discussion about the textual evidence and knowledge that led to each group's interpretive decisions. Listen to students question and teach one another. (*Whoa! Every single student just totally owned Shakespeare.*)

What at the start might appear simply as a "fun" way to meet Shakespeare's words reveals itself to be a wild and daring, deep and demanding, meaty and memorable learning experience. Behind this magic is a very deliberate design.

From day one, your students will engage directly with the language of the text(s). That's right: There's no "I do, we do, you do" teacher modeling here. Students are always doing, doing, doing. Beginning with single words and lines, your students will learn to read closely and critically and eventually tackle longer pieces of text such as speeches, scenes, text sets, and whole texts. (Real talk: Yes, scaffolding learning by increasing the length and complexity of the language means doing some prep work. It's part of being the architect. Good news: This book has already selected and chunked most of the text for you!) Like other teachers using this method, you will likely notice that pre-reading *is* reading, just in small bites. You'll also notice your students using and reusing strategies. Sometimes you'll revisit a strategy from Week One later in the unit, with a new piece of text or an added layer of complexity. For example, Choral Reading and Cutting a Scene are favorite classroom routines that teachers use multiple times not just in a Shakespeare unit but throughout the school year. Over time, as you progress through the lessons, you will observe your students doing literacy tasks that are increasingly demanding and sophisticated, and you'll all have gained a method to help you tackle any complex text.

The process of speaking lines, interrogating and editing text, negotiating meaning, deciding how language should be embodied and performed, and owning literature—and doing it all without much teacher explanation—is what matters most. Simply put, the process is more important than the product. Don't fret if the final product is not perfect (what human endeavor is "perfect," anyway?). Did the students collaborate to analyze language and create something new? Do they know what they're saying? Have they made Shakespeare's language their own? So what if a group's performance has some awkward pauses or someone mispronounces a word? If your students have been reading actively, asking and answering good questions, and reaching their own evidence-based conclusions, it's all good. The real work happens along the arc, not at the end.

9 Essential Practices

This is the moment in our live workshops when teachers typically tell us how simultaneously *excited* and *nervous* they are about trying the Folger Method.

Excited because the Principles, the Arc, the whole philosophy of turning the learning over to the students, speaks to their own deeply held conviction that all students can do much more than is often asked of them. As one high school English teacher put it, "These Principles express something I know deep down and want to act on."

Nervous because this Folger thing is really different from how most of us were taught in school. Exactly how does a teacher "act on" the 8 Foundational Principles? What happens in class? What does the teacher do and not do? What does the student do and learn? What do teachers and students have to "unlearn" or let go of in order to try this approach?

The answers to these questions lie in the nine core practices of the Folger Method—the 9 Essentials. Within the lessons that follow this chapter, you will find step-by-step instructions for these Essentials right when you need them. For now, we will provide you with a brief overview of each one.

1. Tone and Stress boosts students' confidence in speaking text aloud and explores how a text's meanings are revealed through vocal expression. Students experience firsthand how variations in tone of voice and word stress influence a listener's understanding of subtext. They see and hear that there's no single right way to interpret a text. Longtime teacher and Teaching Shakespeare Institute faculty member Mike LoMonico spent a lot of time and expertise developing this!

2. Tossing Words and Lines puts text into students' hands and mouths and gets them up on their feet reading, speaking, and analyzing the language together. Bonus: Students are able to make inferences about the text based on the words they encounter.

3. Two-line Scenes get all students up on their feet, creating and performing two-person mini-scenes. They discover how making collaborative decisions to enact text is exciting and reveals new understandings. They also realize they can encounter a text "cold" and make meaning from it all on their own—dispelling the myth that Shakespeare's language is too dense to understand.

4. Twenty-minute Plays involve the whole class in performing lines of text that becomes an express tour through the play. Early on, students learn and own the story and the language of the play and are motivated to keep reading. Folger Director of Education Peggy O'Brien originated this Essential and has perfected the art of finding the most fun-to-say lines in a play!

5. Choral Reading asks all students to read and reread a text aloud together. By changing what the "chorus" does in each rereading, this exercise gives students multiple opportunities to refine their understanding of the text. Students discover how the simple acts of speaking and rereading strengthen comprehension and analysis—all without any teacher explanation. In the chorus, there's an anonymity that's freeing, especially for English Learners and shy readers. Choral Reading is immersive, low-stakes, and really, really powerful.

6. 3D Lit enables a class or group of students to work together, figuring out (a) what is going on in a scene they have never before read with no explanation and very little help from you, and (b) how to informally act it out, making decisions as they go. This process enables them to refine their understanding as they transform the text from the page to a 3D "stage" in class. Michael Tolaydo, an actor, director, and faculty member of the Teaching Shakespeare Institute, created this groundbreaking Essential.

7. Cutting a Scene gets students close-reading with a purpose by challenging groups to eliminate half the lines from a piece of text while retaining its meaning. Since editors, scholars, directors, actors, and students have been cutting Shakespeare *forever*, yours are in good company. In fulfilling their mission as editors, students will naturally have to examine what the text says and implies, how the scene works, who's who, how language functions, and what's at stake. The fun part? Listening to your students debating which lines should stay or go and what the scene's "meaning" is anyway.

8. Promptbooks engage students in a process of text-based decision-making and collaborative annotation that reflects how they would stage a text. Many teachers and students call promptbooks "annotating with a real purpose." As with other Essentials, promptbooks are useful for students grappling with an unfamiliar text.

9. Group Scenes enable students to put all the pieces together. Students collaborate to select, cut, rehearse, memorize, and perform a scene for their classmates. Sometimes group scenes consist entirely of the original language of the text; other times they might include mashups or adaptations that incorporate home languages, pop culture, and/or the wide world of literature. Students make their own Shakespeares, demonstrating how they have used textual evidence and background knowledge not only to understand but also reinvent complex dramatic language.

A Note on Differentiation

You know better than anyone else that inside every single one of your students is a whole lot of talent and a whole lot of room to improve. Therefore, when we talk about "differentiation," we are not talking about "struggling readers" or "remediation." We are talking about the rich diversity of what everyone brings to—and takes from—the learning. And everyone—*everyone*—has a great deal to bring and take!

So, are we talking about students in your AP or IB classes? Neurodiverse students? Students with IEPs? Nontraditional students? English Learners? So-called "high-fliers"? Yes. All of the above. In other words, differentiation is about hearing, seeing, challenging, supporting, and inspiring each unique learner.

When teachers experience the Folger Method for themselves, they often point out how differentiation is woven right into the Essentials. Because this mode of teaching relies so heavily on student voice, it is inherently personalized.

Beyond this general fact, though, there are several specific ways in which the Folger Method accounts for the variety of learners in your classroom. Allow us to zoom in on just two of them.

Example #1: The Essential called "Two-line Scenes" provides opportunities for students of all reading abilities to be successful. Each student works with a partner to make a "mini-play" from just two lines of Shakespeare. If, in one pair, Student A knows just two words in their assigned line, they can base their performance on those two words, or they can collaborate with their scene partner, Student B, to work out the meaning of the rest of their line. And if Student B knows not only the literal but also the figurative meaning of both lines, they can share their understanding with Student A and work together to take on the additional challenge of expressing subtext with their voices and bodies. Differentiation is happening on two fronts here: first, through the "wiggle room" that allows each student to bring their own knowledge and creativity to the final product (sometimes called "variable outcomes" by learning experts); second, through peer collaboration. Throughout this book, you will see that students are supporting and stretching each other, and developing their own independent thinking skills, thanks to all kinds of grouping configurations.

Example #2: Since much of the Folger Method relies on selecting and chunking text for our students, there is a ready-made structure for matching students with passages that meet them where they are and stretch them to the next level. In this book you will find that a relentless focus on language is one of the best tools you have for differentiating learning. In other words, don't change the task, water anything down, or make it overly complicated—just chunk the text into appropriately challenging parts. (If you teach English Learners and multilingual students—who are used to attending very carefully to language, its sound, its sense, its nuance—all this will strike you as familiar. For more on the unique power of the Folger Method with English Learners, turn to Dr. Christina Porter's excellent essay in this book.)

7 Touchstone Questions

As you jump into this book and these lessons, try using the following "Touchstone Questions" as your guide to reflecting on your own teaching. Think of them as a kind of checklist for student-driven, language-focused learning. Like everything else in this book, they are grounded in the 8 Foundational Principles.

If you can answer "yes" to each Touchstone Question, there must be some serious sparks flying in your classroom!

1. Did I, the teacher, get out of the way and let students own their learning?

2. Is the language of the text(s) front and center?

3. Are the words of the text in ALL students' mouths?

4. Are students collaborating to develop their own interpretations?

5. Are students daring to grapple with complex language and issues in the text?

6. Has every voice been included and honored?

7. Am I always giving students the real thing, whether it's Shakespeare's language, or primary sources, or supporting tough conversations as prompted by the text?

You've Got This

The Folger Method is proof of what's possible when we as teachers step back and let students own their learning. When we teachers realize we don't need to have all the answers. When students are invited to question and grapple. When they approach language with curiosity and care. When they tackle the real thing. When everyone tries new challenges, takes big risks, and supports one another along the way. When all students realize they can do hard things on their own.

You have everything you need to make this happen. We believe in you and can't wait to hear how it goes.

Hamlet, Day-by-Day: The Five-Week Unit Plan

TEACHER-TO-TEACHER THOUGHTS AND THE GAME PLAN FOR THIS *HAMLET*

Ashley Bessicks and Stefanie Jochman

Teacher-to-Teacher Thoughts

"To be or not to be?" "To thine own self be true." The "words, words, words" of *Hamlet* are so famous that teaching them might feel impossible—either you're trudging through the mud of clichés or struggling beneath the weight of *significance*.

But what happens when we cast all of that off and look at Hamlet not as an iconic tragic hero but instead as a young man mourning a father's murder, feeling conflicted about familial loyalty? A young man who struggles to carve out his own identity, who feels uncertain about his affections and his future? Well, then Hamlet, Prince of Denmark, and Ophelia—a young woman full of just as many questions as the prince she may or may not love—start to look a lot more like the young people who sit in our classrooms—people full of poetry and vulgarity, tender anxiety and confident sarcasm, deep love and hardened mistrust, wisdom beyond their years, and arrested development.

How do we connect our students with *Hamlet*? And how do we throw off any burdensome "must dos" and "should knows" of our own experiences with Shakespeare to breathe new life and new learning (and JOY!) into a centuries-old tragedy? We think these plans are the answer. In the lessons ahead, we'll show you how to teach *Hamlet* in a way that ensures your students learn the basics through a language-focused deep dive into the play that opens up knowledge of characters, plot, and the big questions that *Hamlet* presents. Grounded in this and in their own realities, your students can come to their own interpretation of the play, as millions of people have been doing for centuries. Their own interpretation—created over these coming weeks via a series of their own active deep dives into language, character, plot, and more—is vastly preferable to SparkNotes' interpretation, or *your* English teacher's interpretation, or even your own interpretation.

The Folger Method will get us there. Our lessons begin with strategies that focus on Shakespeare's language, just like scholars, editors, actors, and directors do. These strategies enable students to **develop confidence and ease with "speaking Shakespeare"** and to recognize the events of the play. Students should **know from the first day that Shakespeare is for EVERYONE** and that there aren't any tests they must pass or levels they must achieve before they can speak Shakespeare's words or talk about what his characters have to say. And students in AP or IB or honors courses? They need to learn the same things. Considering these lines deeply working with language, and putting Shakespeare on its feet sharpens everyone's skills. And all students need this kind of sharpening.

We didn't always understand this.

Before you start *Hamlet* with your students, think about what could get in the way of their learning. For us, back then, it was the crazy idea that our kids needed to know every word of Shakespeare in order to connect to the language on the page. And there was the fear of an unmanageable classroom.

We want to encourage you to trust your students and these lessons. They put students in the driver's seat with language as their steering wheel. Moving through the Folger's arc of learning—from word to line, to speech, to scene, to play—students' exploration of *Hamlet* will always be grounded in Shakespeare's best raw material, his LANGUAGE. They will see that they—like any actor, director, or scholar—can make decisions about how to perform a word, line, speech, or scene and support their decisions with evidence from the text (as they must do any time they analyze literature, or, ideally, make most of the important decisions in their lives, right?). **These lessons invite questioning, argument, and collaboration. They ask students to compare interpretations or performance choices and ground their final decisions in the text, because entertaining multiple interpretations knocks the idea of ONE Hamlet (or ONE way of understanding Shakespeare) off its own pedestal—and cracks the play and its writer wide open.** Such a compelling way to teach! The more that students make Shakespeare and question Shakespeare and talk back to him, the more they learn and trust that the rich and complex treasure of the plays' language belongs to them. And the power to keep pushing the limits of that language does too.

These lessons lead to a culminating assessment that is a group scene performance because the performance—and all the study that leads up to it—is a formidable way for students to demonstrate their learning. **Shakespeare wrote *plays* (not books!), and those plays were performed. They are three-dimensional texts.** In putting the text on its feet and letting the words guide their performance decisions, students will have to decide which lines to keep and which to cut, how characters will present themselves—what they should wear, which props they will carry, and how they will move and speak. **All of these are conclusions that result from analysis of the text and reflections on their own lives and experiences.** In order to make these decisions, students have to read again and again, and in doing that, they strengthen their reading comprehension. The strategies students practice throughout the unit—"tossing" a word to play with its nuances, collaborating on a two-line scene to see how strings of words work with each other, reading a speech chorally to absorb its ideas and find its many internal voices, cutting a scene to get to its heart, creating promptbooks to communicate their vision for a scene, and working together to stage a three-dimensional scene from scratch . . . all of this learning is the building blocks of a culminating group performance. In fact, since our unit ramps up with actor and director Michael Tolaydo's "3D Literature," students will know that they can perform *Hamlet* from Day Two. The rest of the unit will just add more polish, a bit more flavor to the final recipe.

Along the way, we hope you'll see—as so many teachers have—that **the reading skills these strategies develop transfer to successfully learning any complex text.**

Also along the way, you will see that we introduce additional voices into this study of *Hamlet*; we'll show you how we've done that in our classrooms. Thoughts from Donna Denizé, Jocelyn Chadwick, and other resources in this book demonstrate how *Hamlet* (and Shakespeare) are *in conversation* with so many other texts. Your students deserve to hear more than Shakespeare's white, male, straight, cisgender, able, English, European, Christian voice. Invite more texts in—let those authors' voices talk back to the chatty Prince of Denmark. And make sure that your students talk back, too. Their "words, words, words" matter—and these plans will amplify their voices.

FROM ASHLEY BESSICKS

In my first year, I taught *Romeo and Juliet* to a class of ninth-grade students. I started the unit sharing a few key facts about Shakespeare's life. Then we spent nine weeks trudging through the reading and my interpretation of the play. I even gave students a script that interpreted the lines in modern English. I told them to read most of the play for homework. And in class we found examples of iambic pentameter and learned a pretty impressive list of archaic words. And every day, we had a quiz on them.

We all hated this unit.

I learned early on that this approach to teaching texts, including this play, doesn't work for my kids or me. When I decided to try something that I was admittingly scared to do—give my kids a scene to perform—it was the first time I had gotten out of the way of their learning. Every year since then, my kids perform. And we didn't have a space for it either. My kids performed in hallways and stairwells, and have disrupted our school library. Costumes? Whatever we found around our homes and school made fantastic props and attire. I think the theme here is, don't sweat the small stuff. Just let your students go!

FROM STEFANIE JOCHMAN

Like Ashley, I trudged through my first few years of teaching Shakespeare. When I taught *Macbeth* to juniors, we read scenes at night and then I explained what they meant the next day. Or we would watch the movie and then talk about what happened. I encouraged students to purchase copies of "translated" Shakespeare because it would make the experience "easier," and our final assessments were students' creation of an annotated study guide for the play—lists of symbols and scene summaries, and short theme and character analyses that I thought would serve students because it would make sure they had all of their Shakespeare bases covered. I was so afraid that they wouldn't know what everyone else was "supposed to know" about the play.

We all hated this unit.

I may not have realized it then, but these choices made students feel that Shakespeare was a mysterious writer who spoke in code. We've both been there as teachers, and along that path, students begin to think that Shakespeare isn't something they can do.

Cut to a year when I taught ninth graders and set them loose in the auditorium with scenes from *Romeo and Juliet*. And when the auditorium wasn't free, we found vacant hallways for practice, and when the hallways were busy, I moved the desks in my classroom around and found a corner for each group to rehearse. Whether we had lots of space or a little, we were having fun, I was getting out of the way, and students were learning—with very little input or explanation from me.

Now, my students study *Hamlet*, and they ride around on wheeled desk chairs as King Hamlet's ghost, collectively shout and whisper questions across the room to parse Hamlet's soliloquies, and find all sorts of goofy ways to confuse poor Rosencrantz and Guildenstern in their search for Polonius's body. The work is loud and messy and weird and wonderful.

We all love this unit.

The Game Plan for This *Hamlet*

The overview chart below demonstrates how the five weeks of lessons shared in this book lead to the final project: a student-created scene performance and written defense of the choices evident in the scene performed. The lessons explore Acts 1–3, with students taking over to perform from a menu of scenes in Acts 4 and 5. These lessons don't cover everything—we may have even skipped your favorite speeches or scenes!—but this unit was designed with students' active analyses, connections, and discoveries in mind. Students should consider their own existence while they spend time with this existentialist prince.

These lessons can be completed without assigning much homework in between and could be used in isolation from one another (most of the time). As we will say often during the next pages, you know your students. Scenes studied in class one day could be read the night before; scenes skipped by these lessons could become fun class warm-ups as pantomimes or mini-versions of a 20-Minute Play. Or maybe students will perform those missing scenes for their final projects. These lessons also offer opportunities to connect with members of your World Language department and other multilingual speakers in your school community. Invite them to be guest readers of "To Be or Not to Be" in multiple languages.

The procedure for each lesson is called **"What Students Hear (From You) and (Then What They'll) Do."** In that section of each lesson, we've written instructions for what you will say (thus, what students hear) and what you will see students do as the lesson proceeds. We have no desire to script you, but figure that this is probably the most expedient way to get across what you and your students will do in class. It's as close as we can get to inviting you into our classrooms to watch and listen as a lesson unfolds. In some places, we share additional "teacher thoughts" that should factor into the work in a **TEACHER NOTE**. The lessons close with **"Here's What Just Happened in Class,"** so you can get a sense of what students learned and what skills they practiced over the course of the lesson.

DAY-BY-DAY

Week/Act	Questions Guiding Exploration of the Play	Lessons	Connections to Steps of the Final Project
1 Act 1	What is this play? How do I read it?	**1.** Speak Shakespeare by tossing juicy *Hamlet* lines and making two-line scenes **2.** Put 1.1 on its feet with 3D Lit (Day 2) **3.** Put 1.1 on its feet with 3D Lit (Day 3) **4.** Perform a Twenty-Minute *Hamlet* **5.** A Little Context on Studying Willie Shakes These Days	**Dive Deep:** Students determine what's going on in the play or scene
2 Act 1	Who are these characters? How do I connect with them?	**6.** Meet Hamlet's Family (two-line scenes) **7.** Meet Hamlet's Family (3D Lit) **8.** Hamlet's First Soliloquy (choral reading) **9.** Meet Ophelia's Family (tossing lines) **10.** Explore relationships between ourselves and society with Ophelia and Janie Crawford from *Their Eyes Were Watching God*	**Dive Deep:** Students determine: Who are the characters? What are they saying? What do they want? What are their relationships with one another? Why should someone care about these people and their scenes today?

3 Acts 2 & 3	What is everyone feeling? How do I know? When have I felt that way?	**11.** Write Ophelia's Soliloquy **12.** Find the voices in Hamlet's 2.2 soliloquy (choral reading) **13.** Challenge Hamlet (and Shakespeare) with the words of Frederick Douglass **14.** Make and defend choices about textual variants with Hamlet's 3.1 soliloquy **15.** Make and defend choices about interpretation in 3.1	**Consider the End Goal** Students defend their choices when making decisions about interpretation and performance
4 Act 3	How can I tell this story?	**16.** Put actions to Shakespeare's words with dumb-shows **17.** Examine facsimiles of rare prompt-books **18.** Explore Claudius's "Double Business" with promptbooks **19.** Analyze Hamlet by cutting and placing soliloquies **20.** Practice 3D Lit on your own with parts of 3.4 in relay **21.** Students perform the 3.4 relay	**Be Directors!** Students practice cutting, promptbooking, and adding to a scene
5 Acts 4 & 5	How will WE tell the rest of this story together? How does the text guide our decisions?	**22.** Introduce the Final Project **23.** Cut the scene and add outside texts and promptbook **24.** Rehearse the scene and write the rationale **25.** Perform!	**Using Text as Evidence, Analysis, Rehearse, Perform, and Write Your Defense**

WEEK ONE: LESSON 1

Having Fun with *Hamlet*:
Tossing Lines and Two-Line Scenes

Here's What We're Doing Today and Why

In this lesson (and the rest of the lessons this week), students will get to know *Hamlet*'s language, plot, and characters with the help of Folger Essentials. We'll share simple descriptions of what students will do. If you haven't already, refer to the Folger Method chapter for additional information about the what, how, and why of the Folger Method and these essential classroom practices.

Today, students will toss lines and create two-line scenes. Tossing words and lines allows students to get familiar with the language and engages them with opportunities to read, speak, and analyze the text together. Today's lesson is about students taking the lead, speaking Shakespeare's words, and working together to make discoveries about themselves and *Hamlet*.

What Will I Need?

- Two-line scene cards – **RESOURCE #1.1** at the end of this lesson

- Some beanbags or anything soft that can be thrown safely

How Should I Prepare?

- Print and cut out the *Hamlet* line cards.

Agenda (~ 45-minute class period)

- ❏ Tossing Lines: 10 minutes

- ❏ Two-line Scenes: 20 minutes

- ❏ Reflection Round: 15 minutes

Here's What Students Hear (From You) and (Then What They'll) Do

Part One: Tossing Lines

1. Choose a line from the stack of lines.

2. Move around the room and read your line aloud over and over. As you move, play with the tone and stress of different words in the line. Change your volume each time you read.

3. Make a circle of five or six people. Each circle has one beanbag or soft toy.

4. "Toss lines" within each circle by tossing a beanbag to one another and saying your line in different ways each time you catch the beanbag. Make sure everyone in the circle speaks before anyone gets the beanbag twice. Toss lines as many times as you can before I say "Stop."

5. Make a big circle with the whole class.

6. Without the beanbag, share lines person-to-person around the circle. Then repeat by going around the circle a second time in the opposite direction.

7. Discuss in the circle:

   a. What kind of world do you think we're about to enter as we begin *Hamlet*?

   b. What makes you say this?

   c. What else do you notice about the words or lines you just shared?

Part Two: Two-Line Scenes

1. Move around the room saying your line again.

2. Find a partner.

3. You have five minutes to create and rehearse a scene that uses only your two lines.

4. Form a big circle again; it's time to perform your scene!

5. When it's your turn, step forward with your partner and perform your scene after your class counts you down. Together the class chants "3 . . . 2 . . . 1 . . . Action!," then you and your partner perform your two-line scene.

6. When you finish your scene, take a bow while the class applauds wildly!

Part Three: Reflection Rounds

[**TEACHER NOTE:** To conclude today's lesson, we'll do a "round" that includes all voices and that helps students reflect on what they've just experienced. We learned about these from Teaching Shakespeare Institute faculty member Michael Tolaydo. When he starts rounds, he puts to use a range of verbs that include "observed," "discovered," "noticed," "resented," "learned," "saw," "wonder," and more. We tend to use fewer verbs, yet we've experienced firsthand how useful these rounds are to students—and to us, too—so you'll find them popping up frequently in this unit.]

Stay in your big circle. Respond to the following sentence beginnings with one word or a short sentence. We'll go around the circle so everyone can answer.

   a. I observed . . .

   b. I learned . . .

   c. I wondered . . .

   d. *If responses stay focused on the language and activities, teachers should add:* What did you learn about yourself? Students respond in one sentence.

Here's What Just Happened in Class

- Shakespeare's words were in students' mouths.

- Students collaborated with one another and got familiar with key words and juicy lines from *Hamlet*.

- Students' voices were amplified, and they made decisions about how to interpret the text.

- You got out of the way and allowed students to do all of this on their own.

Hamlet Line Cards

Who's there?	Stay! Speak! Speak! I charge thee, speak!
How is it that the clouds still hang on you?	I shall in all my best obey you, madam.
Give me your pardon, sir. I have done you wrong	O heat, dry up my brains!
O, from this time forth My thoughts be bloody or be nothing worth!	The devil take thy soul!
O, speak to me no more!	Get thee to a nunnery.
O, I am slain!	O day and night, but this is wondrous strange.
Do not look upon me.	Alack, what noise is this?
I will fight with him . . . until my eyelids will no longer wag!	I prithee take thy fingers from my throat
Though this be madness, yet there is method in 't.	You will lose, my lord.
These are but wild and whirling words	Tell my story.
You speak like a green girl	I do not know, my lord, what I should think.
He waxes desperate with imagination.	Who calls me "villain"?

I am pigeon-livered	O, what a noble mind is here o'erthrown!
Do you think I am easier to be played on than a pipe?	I will speak daggers to her
Bow, stubborn knees	Good my lord, be quiet
Why, what a king is this!	I'll be your foil.
O, my lord, my lord, I have been so affrighted!	Man delights not me
Take you me for a sponge, my lord?	O, what a noble mind is here o'erthrown!
You are a fishmonger.	What a piece of work is a man?

"Who's There?": Putting *Hamlet* 1.1 on Its Feet

Here's What We're Doing and Why

Across these two class periods, students will closely read and perform Act 1, Scene 1 of *Hamlet* using the Folger Essential 3D Lit. This will show students that they have the power to read and understand Shakespeare with very little help from you. The text that students will use is the 1.1 scene that has been cut to focus on action and dialogue that doubles as stage directions. Starting a Shakespeare unit by asking students to stage a scene might seem like dumping a beginning swimmer into the deep end of the pool, but you'll be surprised how quickly students learn to "float," and how the problem-solving and critical thinking students practice in this activity prepare them for close-reading of other scenes. At times, it's going to feel like organized chaos in your classroom, and that's okay. The point is for students to use the text to lead the decisions they make about the scene.

With these lessons, they are plunging headfirst into the work they will do at the end of a unit: working together to understand many aspects of a scene and then put it on its feet.

What Will I Need?

- Copies of *Hamlet* Act 1, Scene 1 (cut and without stage directions) – **RESOURCE #1.2**

How Should I Prepare?

- Arrange your classroom so that all students can be seen (circle, semicircle); move desks and tables out of the way if possible

Agenda (~ TWO 45-minute class periods)

- ❏ Read and Own the Scene: 45 minutes
- ❏ Put the Scene on Its Feet: 45 minutes

Here's What Students Hear (From You) and (Then What They'll) Do

Lesson 2: Read and Own the Scene

1. Everyone, sit in a circle, each with a copy of the text and a pencil.

2. Everyone, read the scene aloud, together in one voice. Read quickly and loudly; try to stay on pace with the group.

3. Share your level of understanding on a scale of 1–10.

4. Read the text again, this time sequentially, person-by-person, and end punctuation to end punctuation. In general, when we read like this, readers change at a period, a semicolon, a colon, a question mark, an exclamation point. Readers do not change at a comma.

5. Think a bit about these questions:

   a. "Who are these people?"

   b. "How do you know from the text?"

   c. "What is going on here?"

   d. "How do you know that from the text?"

   e. "Where are they?"

   f. "How do you know that from the text?"

6. Let's read aloud again, sequentially, person-by-person, and this time change readers at the end of each character's speech.

7. How about these questions?

   a. "What else do you notice about these people?"

   b. "How do you know that from the text?"

   c. "How do they feel about each other?"

   d. "And how do you know that from the text?"

8. Read one more time, character by character, this time marking words or ideas you don't fully understand.

9. After this reading, let's discuss your notations and make decisions together about what the unfamiliar words and phrases mean.

10. Rate your level of understanding again on a scale of 1–10 and then respond to the following questions:

    a. What do you understand now that you didn't understand before?

    b. What contributed to that understanding?

Lesson 3: Use Yesterday's Discoveries to Put the Scene on Its Feet

[TEACHER NOTE: For this next portion of the lesson, a few students will be actors and the rest of the class will become directors. Our role as teachers is to facilitate the directors' work. Get out of the way as much as you can. This is not at all about a product; rather, it engages all students in the process of learning about a scene and some of the many possible variations in this scene and all of Shakespeare. **The teacher should not direct.** This is the work of student directors because it continues to engage them in the scene and in the work.]

Also, as you move through the next steps, remember that any time the directors make suggestions or decisions, they must be prompted to support their decisions with evidence from the text.

1. One or two students will serve as stage managers who record the directors' promptbook, a record of stage directions and other decisions for the scene.

2. Create a space to stage the scene.

3. Cast the parts.

[**TEACHER NOTE:** First, whether or not to cast an actor as King Hamlet's ghost should be the choice of the class—so much good discussion happens around this choice! You will cast the other parts because your sensibilities about your students are the best.]

4. Bring your actors to the stage. All the students who are not acting are directors. No one sits out.

5. Directors make decisions about the set and "build" the set with objects found in the classroom.

   a. Are there any necessary props, furniture, or features?

   b. Where are the entrances and exits?

6. Directors place the actors in their positions for the start of the scene.

7. Actors begin running the first few lines of the scene. (*"Who's there?" to the entrance of Horatio and Marcellus is a good first place to pause.*)

8. Directors share what they noticed, what needs to change, and what might be missing.

   a. [**TEACHER NOTE:** Some details our classes often need to review:
      - What time is it? What is it like outside? How do we know, and how can we perform that?
      - Who is starting a shift? Who is finishing one? How do we know, and how can we perform that?
      - What's Horatio's attitude toward the ghost? How do we know? How can the actor perform that?]

   b. Check on the set—do any adjustments need to be made?

9. Run the first part of the scene again and keep going. Throughout, directors can pause the scene when they see a change that needs to be made, always supporting their changes with evidence from the text.

10 Repeat this "run the scene/pause for redirection/rerun the lines" process until the scene closes or your end-of-class bell nears.

11. To conclude, perform some rounds:

   a. I observed . . .

   b. I learned . . .

   c. I discovered . . .

   d. *If responses stay focused on the language and activities, teachers should add:* What did you learn about yourself?

Here's What Just Happened in Class

- Students discovered the plot, setting, characters, and conflict in 1.1:
    - It's a cold night in Denmark.
    - The ghost of the late King of Denmark has been haunting the castle.
    - The ghost appears to Barnardo, Marcellus, and Horatio (a friend to Prince Hamlet).
    - The men wonder what the ghost wants and will ask Hamlet to help them figure that out.
- Students used Shakespeare's text to make decisions about their scenes.
- Students questioned an unfamiliar scene and directed themselves on how to stage it for an audience.
- Students deepened their understanding of 1.1 by taking on the roles of actors, directors, and audience.
- Students did all of this with very little direction from you.

RESOURCE #1.2

Hamlet 1.1, Edited

BARNARDO	Who's there?
FRANCISCO	Nay, answer me. Stand and unfold yourself.
BARNARDO	Long live the King!
FRANCISCO	Barnardo. You come most carefully upon your hour.
BARNARDO	'Tis now struck twelve. Get thee to bed, Francisco.
FRANCISCO	For this relief much thanks. 'Tis bitter cold, And I am sick at heart.
BARNARDO	Have you had quiet guard?
FRANCISCO	Not a mouse stirring.
BARNARDO	Well, good night. If you do meet Horatio and Marcellus, The rivals of my watch, bid them make haste.
FRANCISCO	I think I hear them.—Stand ho! Who is there?
HORATIO	Friends to this ground.
MARCELLUS	And liegemen to the Dane.
FRANCISCO	Give you good night.
MARCELLUS	O farewell, honest soldier. Who hath relieved you?
FRANCISCO	Barnardo hath my place. Give you good night.
MARCELLUS	Holla, Barnardo.
BARNARDO	Say, what, is Horatio there?
HORATIO	A piece of him.
BARNARDO	Welcome, Horatio.—Welcome, good Marcellus.
HORATIO	What, has this thing appeared again tonight?
BARNARDO	I have seen nothing.

MARCELLUS   Horatio says 'tis but our fantasy
    And will not let belief take hold of him
    Touching this dreaded sight twice seen of us.
    Therefore I have entreated him along
    With us to watch the minutes of this night,
    That, if again this apparition come,
    He may approve our eyes and speak to it.

HORATIO   Tush, tush, 'twill not appear.

BARNARDO   Sit down awhile,
    And let us once again assail your ears,
    That are so fortified against our story,
    What we have two nights seen.

HORATIO   Well, sit we down,
    And let us hear Barnardo speak of this.

BARNARDO   Last night of all,
    When yond same star that's westward from the pole
    Had made his course t' illume that part of heaven
    Where now it burns, Marcellus and myself,
    The bell then beating one

MARCELLUS   Peace, break thee off! Look where it comes again.

BARNARDO   In the same figure like the King that's dead.
    Looks he not like the King? Mark it, Horatio.

HORATIO   Most like. It harrows me with fear and wonder.

BARNARDO   It would be spoke to.

MARCELLUS   Thou art a scholar. Speak to it, Horatio.

HORATIO   What art thou that usurp'st this time of night,
    Together with that fair and warlike form
    In which the majesty of buried Denmark
    Did sometimes march? By heaven, I charge thee speak.

MARCELLUS   It is offended.

BARNARDO   See, it stalks away.

HORATIO   Stay! speak! speak! I charge thee, speak!

MARCELLUS   'Tis gone and will not answer.

"The Play's the Thing": *Hamlet* in 20 Minutes

Here's What We're Doing and Why

Students will perform a twenty-minute version of *Hamlet*. Twenty-Minute Plays are an efficient and lively means to orient students to any text and are another on-ramp for them to tangle with the language and physicality of a complex text together. They build off the previous three Essentials, which delved into language with a laser focus on lines, and place students' interpretation of lines in the context of a longer text. As a prereading activity, Twenty-Minute Plays pique student interest by giving them just enough of the plot, characters, and conflict to leave them wanting more. And don't worry about spoilers! Many in Shakespeare's audience knew the whole story of his plays before they ever got to the theater.

Today's lesson will give students ownership of some of *Hamlet*'s most famous (and infamous) lines. You can repeat this activity later in the unit as a way to review (or fast-forward through) the action in various acts or scenes. In the future, put students in charge of selecting lines and writing scripts. In this lesson, students are making meaning of the language and action. They are using evidence from the text to support their performance choices. Students will demonstrate this by pairing their words with actions.

What Will I Need?

- Twenty-Minute *Hamlet* Narrative (for the teacher) – **RESOURCE #1.4A**
- Twenty-Minute *Hamlet* Lines cut into strips – **RESOURCE #1.4B**
- Copies of *Hamlet* play map, p. 26 in this book

How Should I Prepare?

- Organize your class into groups of 2–4 students

Agenda (~ 45-minute class period)

- ❏ Initial instructions: 5 minutes
- ❏ Practice/prep time: 10 minutes
- ❏ Performance: 20 minutes
- ❏ Reflection Round: 5 minutes
- ❏ Play-map extension: 5 minutes if there is time

Here's What Students Hear (From You) and (Then What They'll) Do:

Part One: Twenty-Minute Play

1. Form small groups and receive your lines. Each group will perform more than one line.

2. Groups, you take time to practice dramatic enactments of each of their lines, making sure that for each enactment:

   • All group members are involved in each enactment

   • All group members read each line

   • All enactments involve some kind of movement before, during, or after each line

3. Groups perform lines as the teacher reads the narration, calling out numbers as they appear in the script to cue each group.

4. Wild applause at this wonderful *Hamlet*!

Part Two: Form a circle for some reflection rounds.

1. Go around the circle to share your responses to the following prompts:

   a. I noticed . . .

   b. I discovered . . .

   c. I learned . . .

   d. *If responses stay focused on the language and activities, teachers should add:* What did you learn about yourself?

Part Three: Play-Map Extension (if there's time)

1. Receive your personal copies of play map or look at a projected image of the map on the whiteboard.

2. Decide which lines that your group performed pair with some of the images on the play map.

3. Write lines above those images on your copy of the map.

4. In a class discussion, share the lines and images you paired and why you paired them.

5. Store your map somewhere where you won't lose it! We'll return to our maps as we move through the play.

Here's What Just Happened in Class

• Students learned the basics of the plot, characters, and action of *Hamlet*.

• Students collaborated with their peers to own the language and enact the plot.

• Students made connections between lines, plot, and characters.

• Students personalized a play map with language and pictures that will be a reference for future lessons.

Twenty-Minute *Hamlet* Narrative

Once upon a time at Elsinore Castle, there was a lot happening. Let's start at the very beginning, the very first line of the play. [1. WHO'S THERE?] We find that it's very quiet at Elsinore Castle. [2. NOT A MOUSE STIRRING.] Things are not good. [3. SOMETHING IS ROTTEN IN THE STATE OF DENMARK.] It's eerie, things aren't quite right. There are problems and mysteries afloat. Someone has seen a ghost, and we also hear about a [4. MURDER!].

Soon into this play, you meet the main characters. Probably the most important one. [5. IT IS I! HAMLET THE DANE!] Then you meet his mother—Gertrude—as well as the evil stepfather Claudius, Polonius, Laertes, and other members of the court. We learn that Laertes is going abroad, and we hear him get some advice from his old man, Polonius. [6. NEITHER A BORROWER NOR A LENDER BE.] At Claudius's invitation, two school friends of Hamlet's join the court. [7. THANKS, ROSENCRANTZ AND GENTLE GUILDENSTERN. THANKS, GUILDENSTERN AND GENTLE ROSENCRANTZ.] We also meet Ophelia, Hamlet's love interest, to whom Hamlet says: [8. I DID LOVE YOU — ONCE].

Players come to the castle—people watched plays instead of getting online or playing video games—and Hamlet welcomes them. [9. THEN CAME EACH ACTOR ON HIS ASS.] They put on a little play at court, which Hamlet uses to try and nail Claudius for the murder of Hamlet's father. During the play, Gertrude says: [10. THE LADY DOTH PROTEST TOO MUCH METHINKS]. And Claudius says: [11. GIVE ME SOME LIGHT! AWAY!]. After the play, Hamlet goes to his mother's closet, which is what Shakespeare calls a bedroom. He sees some movement behind the arras, which is what Shakespeare calls a curtain. Hamlet says: [12. HOW NOW, A RAT!]. Hamlet kills Polonius. And then he says: [13. I'LL LUG THE GUTS INTO THE NEIGHBOR ROOM]. And still, he has some advice for his mother. [14. GOOD NIGHT, BUT GO NOT TO MINE UNCLE'S BED.]

In the meantime: Ophelia begins to act strangely, goes mad, and drowns. [15. SWEETS TO THE SWEET! FAREWELL!] And Laertes is back, he's furious, and Claudius uses Laertes's fury to get rid of Hamlet. He arranges for a duel. Look for a poison sword and a poison cup somewhere here. [16. A HIT! A VERY PALPABLE HIT!] Gertrude drinks the wrong cup, and she dies. [17. LOOK TO THE QUEEN! HO!] Hamlet stabs Laertes, and as he dies, he identifies the real culprit. [18. THE KING . . . THE KING'S TO BLAME!] And Horatio winds up the action. [19. GOOD NIGHT, SWEET PRINCE, AND FLIGHTS OF ANGELS SING THEE TO THY REST.] And that's *Hamlet!*

RESOURCE #1.4B

Twenty-Minute *Hamlet* Lines

1. WHO'S THERE?

2. NOT A MOUSE STIRRING.

3. SOMETHING IS ROTTEN IN THE STATE OF DENMARK.

4. MURDER!

5. IT IS I! HAMLET THE DANE!

6. NEITHER A BORROWER NOR A LENDER BE.

7. THANKS, ROSENCRANTZ AND GENTLE GUILDENSTERN. THANKS, GUILDENSTERN AND GENTLE ROSENCRANTZ.

8. I DID LOVE YOU—ONCE.

9. THEN CAME EACH ACTOR ON HIS ASS.

10. THE LADY DOTH PROTEST TOO MUCH METHINKS.

11. GIVE ME SOME LIGHT! AWAY!

12. HOW NOW, A RAT!

13. I'LL LUG THE GUTS INTO THE NEIGHBOR ROOM.

14. GOOD NIGHT, BUT GO NOT TO MINE UNCLE'S BED.

15. SWEETS TO THE SWEET! FAREWELL!

16. A HIT! A VERY PALPABLE HIT!

17. LOOK TO THE QUEEN! HO!

18. THE KING . . . THE KING'S TO BLAME!

19. GOOD NIGHT, SWEET PRINCE, AND FLIGHTS OF ANGELS SING THEE TO THY REST.

WEEK ONE: LESSON 5

Shakespeare in Context

Here's What We're Doing and Why

Today we'll take a minute to allow students to discover that the universe of Shakespeare is bigger, more diverse, and more interesting than your students may realize. This lesson is all about giving everyone a glimpse into some of the most expansive, exciting, and surprising aspects of studying Shakespeare, his words, and his world. It zooms out beyond *Hamlet* for a moment.

By the end of this lesson, students will have examined their own ideas about Shakespeare's world. They will have enlarged their sense of history by studying 5 primary source documents spanning the 1600s to the 1900s. They will have reflected on the wide world of Shakespeare and their place in it.

What Will I Need?

- Portrait of Abd el-Ouahed ben Messaoud ben Mohammed Anoun, Moroccan ambassador to Queen Elizabeth I, ca. 1600 – **RESOURCE #1.5A**

- John Smith's Map of Virginia and the Chesapeake, a 1631 copy of the 1612 original – **RESOURCE #1.5B**

- Portraits by Wenceslaus Hollar, 1645 – **RESOURCE #1.5C**

- Ira Aldridge's First Appearance at Covent Garden as Othello, 1833 – **RESOURCE #1.5D**

- *Romeo y Julieta*, "Prologo," Pablo Neruda, written in 1964, published in 2001 – **RESOURCE #1.5E**

- 6 Mind-blowing Facts about Shakespeare and History – **RESOURCE #1.5F**

- Large paper, markers, or something similar for the gallery walk we're calling "Document Speed Dating"

How Should I Prepare?

- Set up your classroom for "Document Speed Dating": Post the 5 documents at various stations around the room, and make sure that (1) the images are big and clear enough for everyone to see details and (2) there's enough space around each document for students to respond in writing. You can use whiteboards, butcher paper, or Post-it Notes—just make sure there's room for everyone to "talk back" to each image.

- Organize your students into five groups, each one starting at a different station.

Agenda (~ 45-minute class period)

❑ Prior-Knowledge Freewrite: 7 minutes

❑ Speed Dating Instructions: 3 minutes

❑ Speed Dating Exercise: 21 minutes

❑ The List: 6 minutes

❑ Reflection Round: 8 minutes

Here's What Students Hear (From You) and (Then What They'll) Do

Part One: Prior-Knowledge Freewrite

1. **Write:** Jot down your thoughts on any of the following questions. When you imagine the world of Shakespeare, what do you see? What images come to mind? Who are the people? What do they look and sound like? What are the places and objects? What's the vibe?

2. **Talk:** Turn to a classmate and discuss what each of you wrote.

3. **Share:** As a class, we'll share the images and ideas that arose in the paired conversations.

[**TEACHER NOTE:** Record student responses on the board in a broad way—no need to be exhaustive here. The point is to capture things like "people in ruffs and crowns" or "outdoor theaters" or "white Europeans" or "candlelight and quills" or "street fighting" or "plague" or "boring" or "lively" or "smelly clothes" or "harp music"—whatever comes to your students' minds. Welcome all responses without editorializing.]

Part Two: Document Speed Dating

1. Now you are going to meet actual historical documents from the world of Shakespeare. Your job is to look very closely at what you see and write down your observations right alongside the document. Keeping in mind your earlier impressions of Shakespeare's world, what in each image jumps out at you? What do you wonder about?

[**TEACHER NOTE:** You can keep the "What in the image jumps out at you?" prompt posted for students to see throughout this exercise.]

2. Get into your groups and begin at your assigned station. Each group should be at a different station.

3. You will have roughly 3 minutes at each station. As a group, move to the next station when you hear "Next!" Continue until every group has studied and written observations about all 5 documents.

4. Now that everyone has gone on a "speed date" with each document, return to your seat and find a partner. With this partner, discuss the main things that jumped out at you in these documents. Did anything surprise you? Did you learn anything new about the world of Shakespeare? We'll share more as a whole class in a few moments.

Part Three: The List

1. Let's look at the list of "6 Mind-blowing Facts about Shakespeare and History." (**RESOURCE #1.5F**)

[**TEACHER NOTE:** Call for 6 volunteers to read each fact aloud. Save discussion for the reflection round below.]

Part Four: Reflection Rounds

1. Now it's time for each of you to share your reflections on today's learning. We'll do 2 rounds. Remember, just one sentence and not more at this point. We want to hear from EVERY voice!

2. First, finish the sentence, "Something that changed my original mental picture of Shakespeare's world was . . ."

3. Second, finish the sentence, "I am still wondering . . ."

[**TEACHER NOTE:** As closure, ask students to summarize the main ways that these primary source documents have enlarged or transformed their collective understanding of the universe of Shakespeare.]

Here's What Just Happened in Class

- Students have identified and interrogated their prior knowledge—and assumptions—of Shakespeare's world.

- Students have examined five different primary source documents spanning four centuries in order to enlarge their understanding of Shakespeare and history. They have seen for themselves that Shakespeare's Britain was multicultural and very much connected to the Americas.

- Students know important and surprising facts about the wide world of Shakespeare.

RESOURCE #1.5A

Abd el-Ouahed ben Messaoud ben Mohammed Anoun,
Ambassador from Morocco to the court of Queen Elizabeth I,
beginning in 1600.

RESOURCE #1.5B

John Smith's Map of Virginia, the original published first in 1612, then included in the
first edition of his book that was published in 1624. His book was popular—
this image map is copied from the second edition of his book, published in 1631.

RESOURCE #1.5C

Portraits by Wenceslaus Hollar, made in and around 1645

RESOURCE #1.5D

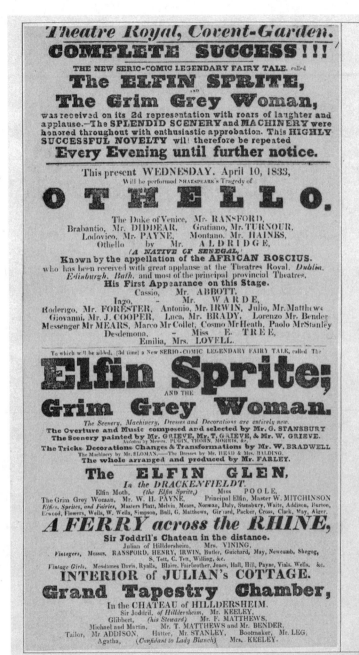

Ira Aldridge's first appearance at Covent Garden as Othello

RESOURCE #1.5E

PRÓLOGO

ENTRA EL CORO

CORO
 En la bella Verona esto sucede:
 dos casas ambas en nobleza iguales
 con odio antiguo hacen discordia nueva.
 La sangre tiñe sus civiles manos.

Dos horas durará en nuestro escenario esta historia: escuchadla con paciencia, suplirá nuestro esfuerzo lo que falte.

Romeo y Iulieta, Pablo Neruda,
written 1964, published 2001

6 Mind-blowing Facts about Shakespeare and History

1. There were many people of different ethnicities and religions in Shakespeare's Britain. An important facet of this history: Africans participated in life at many social levels. Many were baptized—Protestant parishes retain the records. Black citizens included merchants, silk weavers, seamstresses, shoemakers, a circumnavigator who sailed with Sir Francis Drake, and a royal musician.

2. During her coronation festivities in 1600, Queen Elizabeth I entertained a large delegation of Muslim African officials, including Moroccan Ambassador Abd el-Ouahed ben Messaoud ben Mohammed Anoun. He returned to court often and served as her advisor. Some think that Shakespeare might have seen him and other African diplomats at court and drawn inspiration from them.

3. William Shakespeare was writing plays as English settlers colonized Jamestown, Virginia, in 1607. It's generally thought that he based his play *The Tempest* on accounts of a well-known shipwreck that occurred off the coast of Bermuda. The ship was called *Sea Venture* and it was on its way to Jamestown.

4. Ira Aldridge was the first African American actor to play the role of Othello at a professional theater: the Theatre Royal, Covent Garden, London, in 1833. Born in New York City, Aldridge performed Shakespeare all over Europe because as a Black man, he could not have done so in America. He was perhaps the first American star of the international Shakespeare stage. More than 100 years later, in 1943, Paul Robeson was the first African American actor to play Othello in the United States—on Broadway.

5. It was not until 1660 that the first woman actor performed Shakespeare onstage. Until then, men and boys had played all the parts. At this point, though, women took on not just female characters, but also male characters.

6. Shakespeare's works have been adapted and performed around the globe for centuries, and they have been translated into over 100 languages.

Understanding Status in *Hamlet,* Literature, and Life

Here's What We're Doing and Why

In these two sequential lessons, students will first explore the idea of "status"—what it is, how it changes in literary characters, in families, and in life, and how actors can portray it onstage. In the next lesson, as a class, they will dive into what is sometimes called "Hamlet's family scene" (1.2.66–130). Then, students will consider options and make decisions about the status, personality, and conflict of each character.

What Will I Need?

- Numbered slips for the status game

How Should I Prepare?

- To prepare for the status game, create a set of numbered slips—numbered 1 to 10. There should be enough slips for every student in the class. They should all be numbered 1 to 10, so there will be multiples of each number.

- Read through this lesson and review the line cards and scene excerpt; if at this point your students need less text, feel free to shorten the scene and remove some of the line cards before class begins.

Agenda (~ 45-minute period)

- ❑ Setup: 5 minutes
- ❑ Take One: 10 minutes
- ❑ Take Two Taking the Chair: 15 minutes
- ❑ Reflection Rounds: 15 minutes

Here's What Students Hear (From You) and (Then What They'll) Do

Each of you will choose a numbered slip from a hat (or something). Keep your status number a secret. The highest number=highest status; the lowest number=lowest status.

1. **Take One:** There is a special concert (name the group) that is planned in this neighborhood, tickets are hard to get, and the line to buy tickets starts in this classroom! People with the highest status will be at the head of the line, first able to buy tickets. The people with the lowest status at the back. Keeping your number a secret, line up according to where you think you belong.

2. Now that the line has formed, let's have everyone call out their numbers, starting with the head of the line.

3. After all numbers are called, discuss:

- "What is status?"
- "How did you get a sense of where to line up?"
- "Other observations?"

4. Let's collect your numbers, we'll redistribute, and you'll take another number. Keep this number a secret too.

5. Take Two: Form a circle with a chair in the center.

6. Two at a time, students will enter the center of the circle. The goal of each of you is to sit in the chair. Keeping your status number in mind, put both your words and your body movement to work so that you "get" to sit in the chair as you deserve! Remember to keep your number a secret.

7. After a couple of minutes, another pair rotates into the center. This process repeats until all pairs have stood in the center and negotiated for the chair.

8. Discuss:

- Who had the highest status?
- How did you know?
- Who had the lowest status?
- How did you know?
- Who maneuvered the best?

9. To conclude the status focus, do rounds:

- I discovered . . .
- I learned . . .
- I thought . . .
- *If responses stay focused on the language and activities, teachers should add:* What did you learn about yourself?

Hamlet 1.2.66–130: His Family Through Lenses of Status, Personality, and Conflict

Here's What We're Doing and Why

As a class, students will read an excerpt from *Hamlet* 1.2.66–130, sometimes called "Hamlet's family scene." Then, students will consider options and make supported observations about the status, personality, and conflict of each character. This lesson supports students' close-reading of dialogue, and it also introduces some of the central conflicts of *Hamlet*, which we will revisit when we explore Hamlet's first soliloquy in the next lesson.

We find that this family scene is one that all students can relate to. Engage those personal connections and ask students to think about how their own experiences might inform their view of Hamlet, Claudius, and Gertrude. When students explore dialogue and conflict today, they are diving deep into analysis of characters and plot, and developing their critical thinking and analytical skills. This will serve them through the rest of this play and through many other complex texts as well.

What Will I Need?

- Copies of *Hamlet* 1.2.66–130 – **RESOURCE #2.2**

Agenda (~ 45-minute period)

❑ Dive in. Work through actively reading this scene, using the steps outlined in 3D Lit, the steps we used in our dive into Act 1, Scene 1 in last week: 30 minutes

❑ Reflection (either written individually or discussed generally): 15 minutes

Here's What Students Hear (From You) and (Then What They'll) Do

Part One: Dive In (and continuing right along from our Status lesson yesterday)

1. Sit in a circle with copies of the script.

2. Read the scene following the steps of 3D Lit. (see Week One, Lessons 2+3 for a review of those steps)

3. Hold up fingers to show your level of understanding. (1 = I'm lost, 3 = I've got this!)

4. Read the scene differently, and a couple of more times.

5. Hold up fingers to show your level of understanding. If, on a scale of 1–3, most are at a 2, move on to the questions below. If most students are still at a 1, reread the scene and check for understanding again.

    a. What's happening here? How do you know?

    b. How do these characters seem to feel about each other? How do you know?

    c. What status numbers would you assign to the characters in this scene? Why?

    d. Can you sense any conflict? If so, what is the conflict? What's causing it?

Part Two: Reflection (either written individually or discussed generally)

1. Reflect on what we just read and talked about:

    a. How would you respond to Claudius's and Gertrude's lines if you were Hamlet?

    b. Have you had moments of conflict like this with your family or other authority figures in your life? What were the consequences of moments like this?

    c. Other observations on this scene and what's going on here?

Here's What Just Happened in These Last Two Classes

- Students demonstrated specific status, connected to their own knowledge of status, and applied that to how status shapes character and conflict in the play.

- Students learned that Hamlet's, Gertrude's, and Claudius's actions in the play are influenced by their status and how they see themselves.

- Students supported their inferences about characters and conflicts with evidence from the text.

- Students made a personal connection with Hamlet and thought about the role of status in their own lives and the world around them.

RESOURCE #2.2: *HAMLET* 1.2.66–132

The Royal "Family" in Conversation

KING

But now, my cousin Hamlet and my son—

HAMLET, *aside*

A little more than kin and less than kind.

KING

How is it that the clouds still hang on you?

HAMLET

Not so, my lord; I am too much in the sun.

QUEEN

Good Hamlet, cast thy nighted color off,   70
And let thine eye look like a friend on Denmark.
Do not forever with thy vailèd lids
Seek for thy noble father in the dust.
Thou know'st 'tis common; all that lives must die,
Passing through nature to eternity.   75

HAMLET

Ay, madam, it is common.

QUEEN

If it be,
Why seems it so particular with thee?

HAMLET

"Seems," madam? Nay, it is. I know not "seems."
'Tis not alone my inky cloak, good mother,   80
Nor customary suits of solemn black,
Nor windy suspiration of forced breath,
No, nor the fruitful river in the eye,
Nor the dejected havior of the visage,
Together with all forms, moods, shapes of grief,   85
That can denote me truly. These indeed "seem,"
For they are actions that a man might play;
But I have that within which passes show,
These but the trappings and the suits of woe.

KING

    'Tis sweet and commendable in your nature, Hamlet,   90
    To give these mourning duties to your father.
    But you must know your father lost a father,
    That father lost, lost his, and the survivor bound
    In filial obligation for some term   95
    To do obsequious sorrow. But to persever
    In obstinate condolement is a course
    Of impious stubbornness. 'Tis unmanly grief.
    It shows a will most incorrect to heaven,
    A heart unfortified, a mind impatient,   100
    An understanding simple and unschooled.
    For what we know must be and is as common
    As any the most vulgar thing to sense,
    Why should we in our peevish opposition
    Take it to heart? Fie, 'tis a fault to heaven,   105
    A fault against the dead, a fault to nature,
    To reason most absurd, whose common theme
    Is death of fathers, and who still hath cried,
    From the first corse till he that died today,
    "This must be so." We pray you, throw to earth   110
    This unprevailing woe and think of us
    As of a father; for let the world take note,
    You are the most immediate to our throne,
    And with no less nobility of love
    Than that which dearest father bears his son   115
    Do I impart toward you. For your intent
    In going back to school in Wittenberg,
    It is most retrograde to our desire,
    And we beseech you, bend you to remain
    Here in the cheer and comfort of our eye,   120
    Our chiefest courtier, cousin, and our son.

QUEEN

    Let not thy mother lose her prayers, Hamlet.
    I pray thee, stay with us. Go not to Wittenberg.

HAMLET

    I shall in all my best obey you, madam.

KING

    Why, 'tis a loving and a fair reply.   125
    Be as ourself in Denmark.—Madam, come.
    This gentle and unforced accord of Hamlet

Sits smiling to my heart, in grace whereof
No jocund health that Denmark drinks today
But the great cannon to the clouds shall tell,   130
And the King's rouse the heaven shall bruit again,
Respeaking earthly thunder. Come away.

"Heaven and Earth, Must I Remember?": Close-Reading Hamlet's First Soliloquy

Here's What We're Doing and Why

Students will close-read Hamlet's first soliloquy—the "too, too sullied flesh" one—using the Choral Reading Essential. (Feel free to review more on choral reading in the Folger Method chapter.) This lesson supports students' active reading, speaking, and listening—and the soliloquy makes clear Shakespeare's use of language and literary devices to develop Hamlet's character. It's a different way to take a deep dive into a text, providing them with strategies for reading and interpreting Shakespeare's texts as well as opportunities to see how volume, tone, or even physical distance between characters can shape an audience's experience of a scene.

Our students sometimes struggle when first reading verse; they treat one line as a whole idea, when the complete thought may run for more than one line of verse. Choral Reading can be a useful exercise for helping students to "hear" complete thoughts in Shakespeare's verse. Since our focus today is on understanding Hamlet and his response to the events of 1.2, we've already divided the script for you. If you would like to create your own script or create an activity where students divide the script for themselves, the free, online Folger Shakespeare is your friend forever (folger.edu/shakespeares-works). It makes cutting and pasting the text of any play easy and convenient.

What Will I Need?

- Class set of the soliloquy divided into two parts for choral reading – **RESOURCE #2.3**

- Paper or some device for written reflection

How Should I Prepare?

- Arrange the room so that you have space to create two parallel lines of students in the center or at the front of the room.

Agenda (~ 45-minute period)

- ❑ Quick Review: 5–10 minutes
- ❑ Choral Reading: 15–20 minutes
- ❑ Reflection/Discussion: 10–15 minutes

Here's What Students Hear (From You) and (Then What They'll) Do

Quick Review

1. Where are we in the plot? Return to your memory of your Twenty-Minute *Hamlet* or your play map and let's remind ourselves if we need to.

2. Revisit the speech we last worked on (1.2.66–130): What did Gertrude and Claudius say to Hamlet during the scene we read together? How did you think he felt?

Part One: Choral Reading

Here, we follow the steps for Choral Reading, a Folger Essential.

1. Read the script of the speech as loud and fast while still staying together with the rest of the class.

2. Read the speech again, loud and fast. Think about how you feel when you argue with your family. Read it that way.

3. By a show of fingers (1=I'm lost, 3=I've got this!), indicate your understanding of the speech.

4. Now, read person-to-person, speaker-to-speaker.

5. By a show of fingers, indicate your understanding.

6. What do you notice about this speech? What do you hear?

7. Next, I'll ask two volunteers (Reader 1 and Reader 2) to read the speech by alternating lines.

8. After listening to our volunteers read, what do you think Hamlet is thinking about or feeling? How do you know?

9. Next, form two lines that face each other.

10. Take turns reading the passage chorally, alternating sides, speaking the passage back and forth.

11. After this reading, check again for understanding using the finger system. If more students are holding up two fingers, ask: **"What more did you notice about the speech in this reading?"** Remind students to point out words or lines in the speech that help them to develop their answers.

12. Read the speech again; this time try assigning a volume to side 1 and side 2 (side 1 will always shout; side 2 will always whisper). After this reading, check in again: What new understanding do students have of the speech? Did they think the dynamics were appropriate for what their side read? Why or why not?

13. If another reading is needed to boost comprehension of what's being said, try one of these variations:

    a. Start soft; each side gets increasingly louder

    b. Start loud; each side gets increasingly softer

    c. Each group takes one small step toward the center each time they read

    d. Groups begin facing each other and take one step away each time they read

Follow this reading with a few more questions: What new understanding do you have of the speech? What words or phrases are still unclear? What was the effect of the new reading variation?

Part Two: Questions

1. Discuss:

    a. How does Hamlet seem to feel about his mother? How do you know?

    b. How does Hamlet feel about Claudius, his uncle and new stepfather? How do you know?

    c. How does Hamlet seem to feel about his late father, the king? How do you know?

    d. How does Hamlet feel about himself? How do you know?

    e. How would you describe Hamlet's personality, based on this speech? What does he seem to value in others? What does he seem to expect or demand of himself?

Part Three: Written Reflection

    a. How would you summarize this speech in one sentence?

    b. What do you think Hamlet will do or say next? What leads you to that prediction?

    c. If you were Hamlet, what would you do next?

Here's What Just Happened in Class

- Students made sense of a complex speech without your help:
  - Hamlet is upset by his mother and Claudius's quick marriage following his father's death and funeral.
  - Hamlet may also be disgusted or frustrated with himself and want to die.
  - Hamlet misses his father.
- Students explored multiple interpretations of words, lines, and meanings of Hamlet's soliloquy.
- Students predicted what Hamlet's next action could be.
- Students made a personal connection with Hamlet.

RESOURCE #2.3

Hamlet 1.2.133–164
Hamlet's First Soliloquy

SIDE 1:	O, that this too, too sullied flesh would melt, Thaw, and resolve itself into a dew,
SIDE 2:	Or that the Everlasting had not fixed His canon 'gainst self-slaughter!
SIDE 1:	O God, God, How weary, stale, flat, and unprofitable Seem to me all the uses of this world!
SIDE 2:	Fie on 't, ah fie!
SIDE 1:	'Tis an unweeded garden That grows to seed.
SIDE 2:	Things rank and gross in nature Possess it merely.
SIDE 1:	That it should come to this:
SIDE 2:	But two months dead—nay, not so much, not two.
SIDE 1:	So excellent a king, that was to this Hyperion to a satyr;
SIDE 2:	so loving to my mother That he might not beteem the winds of heaven Visit her face too roughly.
SIDE 1:	Heaven and Earth, Must I remember?
SIDE 2:	Why, she would hang on him As if increase of appetite had grown By what it fed on.
SIDE 1:	And yet, within a month
SIDE 2:	(Let me not think on 't; frailty, thy name is woman!),
SIDE 1:	A little month, or ere those shoes were old With which she followed my poor father's body,
SIDE 2:	Like Niobe, all tears—
SIDE 1:	why she, even she
SIDE 2:	(O God, a beast that wants discourse of reason Would have mourned longer!)
SIDE 1:	married with my uncle, My father's brother,

SIDE 2:   but no more like my father Than I to Hercules.

SIDE 1:   Within a month, Ere yet the salt of most unrighteous tears Had left the flushing in her gallèd eyes, She married.

SIDE 2:   O, most wicked speed, to post With such dexterity to incestuous sheets!

SIDE 1:   It is not, nor it cannot come to good.

SIDE 2:   But break, my heart, for I must hold my tongue.

"I do not know, my lord, what I should think": Meet Ophelia and Her Family in *Hamlet* 1.3.1–145

Here's What We're Doing and Why

This lesson uses the Tossing Lines Essential to help students develop understanding of characters, particularly Ophelia and her family. In 1.3, Laertes and Polonius give Ophelia advice about Hamlet. Students will closely read passages from the scene and make decisions about what the language tells us about Polonius's and Laertes's opinions of Ophelia and Hamlet. The key question: What does the study of this dialogue tell us about the characters' relationships and their values?

Because of limited time, students will not read the full scene in class but will have a chance to examine key lines to understand characters' relationships. If you decide to assign the reading for homework, do so after this lesson, since after this class, students will be more familiar with it.

What Will I Need?

- A set of line cards for each student from *Hamlet* 1.3.1–145 – **RESOURCE #2.4**

- Dictionaries or glossaries

How Should I Prepare?

- Cut **RESOURCE #2.4** into cards.

- Arrange the classroom so that students can stand and sit in circles (move desks if possible)

- Assign groups for students (three students in each group)

Agenda (~ 45-minute period)

❑ **Warm-up:** 10 minutes

❑ **Tossing Lines:** 20 minutes

❑ **Reflection:** 10 minutes

Here's What Students Hear (From You) and (Then What They'll) Do

Part One: Warm-up

1. What is the best advice you have gotten? Who did you get it from? What did/do you think of that advice?

2. The lines we're about to read will help us get to know Ophelia's family. In this scene, Laertes and Polonius give Ophelia advice about Hamlet.

Part Two: Tossing Lines

1. Count off to form groups of three; within each group of three, count off to three again. Distribute the line-toss cards to students based on their number (#1 = Laertes, #2 = Polonius, #3 = Ophelia). Each student should get one random card for their character.

2. Group together by number/character. Take a couple of minutes to say lines independently a few times. Toss lines in the group.

[**TEACHER NOTE:** The Ophelia group has fewer lines; students may share and/or repeat.]

3. Discuss as a class:

    a. What do you notice?

    b. What do you wonder?

    c. What patterns do you see or hear in your character's speech?

4. Form new groups of three students each. This time, each group should have an Ophelia, Polonius, and Laertes (1, 2, and 3).

5. Toss lines again in this new group.

6. Discuss as a class:

    a. What do you observe?

    b. What do you wonder? (and feel free to use any of those great Reflection verbs!)

    c. What do these lines suggest about how the characters relate to each other? How do you know?

    d. What do Polonius and Laertes seem to expect of Ophelia? How do you know?

    e. What does Ophelia seem to expect of herself? Of her family? How do you know?

    f. How does Ophelia seem to feel about her father's and brother's words? How do you know?

    g. Does anything about Ophelia's family dynamic feel familiar? Explain.

A future lesson will ask you to consider writing a soliloquy for Ophelia—what she might have said in a soliloquy following this scene, just as Hamlet delivered a soliloquy after the scene with his family. In your notebooks or on a shared document, make a list of some things that Ophelia might say in her speech.

7. Close with some rounds:

    a. I felt . . .

    b. I resented . . .

   c. I'm thinking about . . .

   d. *If responses stay focused on the language and activities, teachers should add:* What did you learn about yourself?

Here's What Just Happened in Class

- Students made a personal connection with the whole scene, with Ophelia, and maybe with Laertes.

- Students used textual evidence to make inferences about characters and conflicts:
    - Polonius and Laertes tell Ophelia not to see Hamlet again.
    - Polonius expects Ophelia to obey.
    - Ophelia accuses Laertes of being a hypocrite "show me the steep and thorny way to heaven, whiles . . . himself the primrose path of dalliance treads and recks not his own rede." (1.3.52–54)
    - While Ophelia is conflicted (1.3.114), she ultimately says that she will "obey." (1.3.145)

RESOURCE #2.4

Line Cards: Ophelia's Family

Laertes and Polonius	Ophelia
Do not sleep, But let me hear from you. *Laertes 1.3.3–4* *1*	I shall the effect of this good lesson keep As watchman to my heart. *Ophelia 1.3.49–50* *3*
For Hamlet, and the trifling of his favor, Hold it a fashion and a toy in blood. *Laertes 1.3.6–7* *1*	Do not, as some ungracious pastors do, Show me the steep and thorny way to heaven, Whiles, like a puffed and reckless libertine, Himself the primrose path of dalliance treads And recks not his own rede. *Ophelia 1.3.51–55* *3*
Perhaps he loves you now, and now no soil nor cautel doth besmirch the virtue of his will. *Laertes 1.3.17–19* *1*	'Tis in my memory locked, And you yourself shall keep the key of it. *Ophelia 1.3.92–93* *3*
He may not, as unvalued persons do, Carve for himself, for on his choice depends The safety and the health of this whole state. *Laertes 1.3.22–24* *1*	He hath, my lord, of late made many tenders Of his affection to me. *Ophelia 1.3.108–109* *3*
Weigh what loss your honor may sustain If with too credent ear you list his songs Or lose your heart or your chaste treasure open To his unmastered importunity. *Laertes 1.3.33–35* *1*	I do not know, my lord, what I should think. *Ophelia 1.3.114* *3*

The chariest maid is prodigal enough If she unmask her beauty to the moon. *Laertes 1.3.40–41* *1*	My lord, he hath importuned me with love In honorable fashion *Ophelia 1.3.119–120* *3*
The canker galls the infants of the spring Too oft before their buttons be disclosed, *Laertes 1.3.43–44* *1*	I shall obey, my lord. *Ophelia 1.3.145* *3*
Best safety lies in fear. *Laertes 1.3.47* *1*	
Ophelia [. . .] remember well What I have said to you. *Laertes 1.3.90–91* *1*	
You do not understand yourself so clearly As it behooves my daughter and your honor. *Polonius 1.3.105–106* *2*	
You speak like a green girl. *Polonius 1.3.110* *2*	
Do you believe his "tenders," as you call them? *Polonius 1.3.112* *2*	
I will teach you. *Polonius 1.3.114* *2*	

Tender yourself more dearly, Or [. . .] you'll tender me a fool. *Polonius 1.3.116–118* 2	
From this time Be something scanter of your maiden presence. *Polonius 1.3.129–130* 2	
Set your entreatments at a higher rate Than a command to parle. *Polonius 1.3.131–132* 2	
Do not believe his vows, for they are brokers, Not of that dye which their investments show, But mere implorators of unholy suits. *Polonius 1.3.136–138* 2	
I would not, in plain terms, from this time forth Have you so slander any moment leisure As to give words or talk with the Lord Hamlet. *Polonius 1.3.141–143* 2	
Look to 't, I charge you. *Polonius 1.3.144* 2	

WEEK TWO: LESSON 5

"Then They Act and Do Things Accordingly": Shakespeare and Zora Neale Hurston Meet, and Ophelia and Janie Do, Too.

Here's What We're Doing and Why

Their Eyes Were Watching God, Zora Neale Hurston's extraordinary novel, was published in 1937. *Hamlet* was first published in 1603. In this lesson, students will work across four centuries, diving into an excerpt from *Their Eyes Were Watching God* to discover Janie. Like Ophelia, Janie Crawford hears a lot of advice from her family and community about how she ought to behave. Students will explore selected passages in *Eyes* by cutting them (Cutting a Scene or a Text, a popular Essential). This prompts careful reading and decisions about the heart of a passage supported by evidence from the text. Today, students will think about how Janie reflects or rejects the values and expectations of her society, and they'll discuss how Janie's identity, Ophelia's identity, and their own are shaped by those values and expectations.

Their Eyes Were Watching God is set in Eatonville, Florida, the first self-governing city incorporated by African Americans in 1887. The novel provides a window into rural southern culture and the influences that were found in that culture.

[TEACHER NOTE: Please take note of the pejorative language that appears in this passage. We have purposely not removed it, but we have constructed this lesson so that neither teacher nor students will be reading this language aloud. The N-word is an obscenity that has been and still is a hurtful insult to African Americans and darker-skinned persons of other racial and ethnic groups when used by those who are not African American or darker-skinned people. Using the N-word in this way is often part of a racially motivated attack, whether verbal or physical. Sometimes members of the African American community and darker-skinned persons use the word among themselves, to resist the hurt that this word brought to their ancestors and brings to them now. We want to completely avoid the spoken N-word, though, because its original intent was to cause profound injury to Black and brown people.

We feel that we cannot ignore or skirt conversation about this language because doing so allows the hate and prejudice of that language to fester and perpetuate. You know your students. Students' feelings and reactions to words depend on many factors, including demographics. Please take the time to handle conversations and questions that may come up with care.]

What Will I Need?

- Bring line cards on *Hamlet* 1.3 from previous lesson – **RESOURCE #2.4**
- Print copies of excerpts from *Their Eyes Were Watching God* – **RESOURCE #2.5**

How Should I Prepare?

- Read up on Cutting a Scene in the Folger Method chapter.

Agenda (~ 45-minute period)

- ❏ Introduction: 5 minutes
- ❏ Cutting *Eyes*: 15 minutes
- ❏ Ophelia and Janie: 15 minutes
- ❏ Write a Reflection: 10 minutes

Here's What Students Hear (From You) and (Then What They'll) Do

Part One: Introduction

1. Influences are all around us! What influences do you absorb? Which ones do you reject?

2. What is one's sense of identity influenced by? Sense of purpose? Potential? Parents and peers? Life experiences? Gender? Race? Status (or perceived status)? Values?

3. By a show of hands, how many of your responses connect to this idea of identity? Turn and talk to a neighbor to explain how.

Part Two: Dig In—Janie

1. Half of you will work with the excerpt from Chapter 1 and the other half the excerpt from Chapter 2 of *Their Eyes Were Watching God*.

2. You will sit in groups of 3–4 with their texts and have 10 minutes to read it to yourselves.

3. Then students will cut their passage in half to expose what they see as the heart of the passage.

4. After 20 minutes, groups will explain their process and their editing choices. (They will disagree, and this is evidence that they are grappling with meaning.)

5. Then each student will select what they think is the most essential line and word of the passage.

6. Each student shares their essential line and word.

Part Three: Janie and Ophelia

10. Pass out the line cards from *Hamlet* 1.3—one to each student. Ask groups to incorporate their understanding of Ophelia into their thinking about Janie.

    a. Initial observations?

    b. What do people say to and about Ophelia?

    c. What does Ophelia absorb?

    d. What does Ophelia reject?

    e. What do people say to and about Janie?

    f. What does Janie absorb?

    g. What does Janie reject?

    h. Differences? Similarities?

Part Four: Write a Reflection

11. Think about what we know about what influences identity and also the characters we've studied. What elements of identity do Ophelia and Janie push against or perpetuate? Use lines from *Hamlet* and *Their Eyes Were Watching God* as evidence.

[**TEACHER NOTE:** If students need additional prompting, consider providing the following contributing facets of Ophelia's and Janie's identities:

- Gender
- Family
- Race
- Status (or perceived status)
- Values]

Here's What Just Happened in Class

- Students brought together two different characters from two very different authors to illuminate elements of identity—both in literary analysis and in their own lives.

- Students collaborated with peers to critically read and edit a text, and justified their editing choices.

- Students discovered that there is no single right interpretation of a text.

- Students used textual evidence to make inferences about characters and conflicts, and to reflect on their own. For Janie:

    – Eatonville's community expects Janie to wear dresses and keep her hair up.

    – Janie's nanny expects her to be married.

    – Janie rejects the expectations others have of her: "She merely hunched over and pouted at the floor."

RESOURCE #2.4

Excerpts from *Their Eyes Were Watching God*

From *Their Eyes Were Watching God*, Chapter 1, pp. 1–2:

Ships at a distance have every man's wish on board. For some they come in with the tide. For others they sail forever on the horizon, never out of sight, never landing until the Watcher turns his eyes away in resignation, his dreams mocked to death by Time. That is the life of men.

Now, women forget all those things they don't want to remember, and remember everything they don't want to forget. The dream is the truth. Then they act and do things accordingly.

So the beginning of this was a woman and she had come back from burying the dead. Not the dead of sick and ailing with friends at the pillow and the feet. She had come back from the sodden and the bloated; the sudden dead, their eyes flung wide open in judgment.

The people all saw her come because it was sundown. The sun was gone, but he had left his footprints in the sky. It was the time for sitting on porches beside the road. It was the time to hear things and talk. These sitters had been tongueless, earless, eyeless conveniences all day long. Mules and other brutes had occupied their skins. But now, the sun and the bossman were gone, so the skins felt powerful and human. They became lords of sounds and lesser things. They passed notions through their mouths. They sat in judgment.

Seeing the woman as she was made them remember the envy they had stored up from other times. So they chewed up the back parts of their minds and swallowed with relish. They made burning statements with questions, and killing tools out of laughs. It was mass cruelty. A mood come alive. Words walking without masters; walking altogether like harmony in a song.

"What she doin' coming back here in dem overhalls? Can't she find no dress to put on?—Where's dat blue satin dress she left here in?—Where all dat money her husband took and died and left her?—What dat ole forty year ole 'oman doin' wid her hair swingin' down her back lak some young gal?—Where she left dat young lad of a boy she went off here wid?—Thought she was going to marry?—Where he left her?—What he done wid all her money?—Betcha he off wid some gal so young she ain't even got no hairs—why she don't stay in her class?—"

From *Their Eyes Were Watching God*, Chapter 2, pp. 12–13:

Nanny's head and face looked like the standing roots of some old tree that had been torn away by storm. Foundation of ancient power that no longer mattered. The cooling palma christi leaves that Janie had bound about her grandma's head with a white rag had wilted down and become part and parcel of the woman. Her eyes didn't bore and pierce. They diffused and melted Janie, the room and the world into one comprehension.

"Janie, youse uh 'oman, now, so—"

"Naw, Nanny, naw, Ah ain't no real 'oman yet."

The thought was too new and heavy for Janie. She fought it away.

Nanny closed her eyes and nodded a slow, weary affirmation many times before she gave it voice.

"Yeah, Janie, youse got yo' womanhood on yuh. So Ah mout ez well tell yuh whut Ah been savin' up for uh spell. Ah wants to see you married right away."

"Me, married? Naw, Nanny, no ma'am! Whut Ah know 'bout uh husband?"

"Whut Ah seen just now is plenty for me, honey, Ah don't want no trashy nigger, no breath-and-britches, lak Johnny Taylor usin' yo' body to wipe his foots on."

Nanny's words made Janie's kiss across the gatepost seem like a manure pile after a rain.

"Look at me, Janie. Don't set dere wid yo' head hung down. Look at yo' ole grandma!"

Her voice began snagging on the prongs of her feelings. "Ah don't want to be talkin' to you lak dis. Fact is Ah done been on mah knees to mah Maker many's de time askin' please—for Him not to make de burden too heavy for me to bear."

"Nanny, Ah just—Ah didn't mean nothin' bad."

"Dat's what makes me skeered. You don't mean no harm. You don't even know where harm is at. Ah'm ole now. Ah can't be always guidin' yo' feet from harm and danger. Ah wants to see you married right away."

"Who Ah'm goin' tuh marry off-hand lak dat? Ah don't know nobody."

"De Lawd will provide. He know Ah done bore de burden in de heat uh de day. Somebody done spoke to me 'bout you long time ago. Ah ain't said nothin' 'cause dat wasn't de way Ah placed you. Ah wanted yuh to school out and pick from a higher bush and a sweeter berry. But dat ain't yo' idea, Ah see."

"Nanny, who—who dat been askin' you for me?"

"Brother Logan Killicks. He's a good man, too."

"Naw, Nanny, no ma'am! Is dat whut he been hangin' round here for? He look like some ole skullhead in de grave yard."

The older woman sat bolt upright and put her feet to the floor, and thrust back the leaves from her face.

"So you don't want to marry off decent like, do yuh? You just wants to hug and kiss and feel around with first one man and then another, huh? You wants to make me suck de same sorrow yo' mama did, eh? Mah ole head ain't gray enough. Mah back ain't bowed enough to suit yuh!"

The vision of Logan Killicks was desecrating the pear tree, but Janie didn't know how to tell Nanny that. She merely hunched over and pouted at the floor.

"You yourself shall keep the key of it": Speaking for Ophelia

Here's What We're Doing and Why

Today, students will explore the characters in both *Hamlet* and *Their Eyes Were Watching God* with respect to their relationships to both their families and their societies. Students will also explore elements of identity and expectations in their own lives.

After analyzing and reflecting on what they've observed, students will write a soliloquy about how they—the lead characters in their own lives—feel about the expectations they face. If students are uncomfortable writing or speaking about themselves, they can write a soliloquy for Ophelia; this soliloquy will demonstrate their understanding of her character after the deep dive of the last two days.

The soliloquies students write today are all about making decisions. As they head toward their final scene work in a couple of weeks, students will have to think deeply about who characters are, what they want, and why someone today should care about the play and characters. Today's thinking will help them continue to develop those skills.

What Will I Need?

- Copies of Hamlet's first soliloquy – **RESOURCE #3.1A**

- Copies of Ophelia's family line set – **RESOURCE #3.1B**

- Copies of *Their Eyes Were Watching God* excerpts – **RESOURCE #2.5** (from our last session)

How Should I Prepare?

- Make copies of the resources above for students

- Assign student pairs

Agenda (~ 45-minute period)

- ❏ Freewrite on identity and conflict: 5 minutes

- ❏ Revisit and reflect on passages from *Hamlet* and *Their Eyes Were Watching God*: 30 minutes

- ❏ Closing: 10 minutes

Here's What Students Hear (From You) and (Then What They'll) Do

Introduction

1. Freewrite: Reflect on and write about factors that contribute to your identity: gender, ethnicity, family, society. What internal conflicts do you feel about any of these factors? (5 minutes)

Revisit and Reflect with Your Partner

1. Get together your copies of Hamlet's 1.2 soliloquy, the excerpt of 1.3, and the passages from *Their Eyes Were Watching God*.

2. Take 5–10 minutes to review your reading and identify the internal conflicts you see or hear in the characters, and the lines that reveal those conflicts.

3. Turn and talk: Discuss with your partner the conflicts you noticed and lines you highlighted.

4. Time to write: You've identified the internal conflicts that are evident in all three of these passages. Write a soliloquy that reflects your internal conflict about identity, or, if it's more comfortable for you, write a soliloquy that Ophelia would deliver after the scene with her family in 1.3. What would you or she say in a moment like this?

5. Invite students to share their soliloquies.

6. Close again with some rounds.

    a. I learned . . .

    b. I appreciated . . .

    c. I resented . . .

    d. I wondered . . .

    e. Something I learned about myself is . . .

Here's What Just Happened in Class

- Students thoughtfully compared characters from two very different works.

- Students wrote about themselves or wrote from a character's perspective.

- Students made Shakespeare their own by relating thoughts and feelings expressed in the play to what they have experienced personally.

- As Shakespeare's characters do, students worked through internal conflict through a soliloquy.

RESOURCE #3.1A

Hamlet's 1.2 Soliloquy

HAMLET

O, that this too, too sullied flesh would melt,
Thaw, and resolve itself into a dew,
Or that the Everlasting had not fixed   135
His canon 'gainst self-slaughter! O God, God,
How weary, stale, flat, and unprofitable
Seem to me all the uses of this world!
Fie on 't, ah fie! 'Tis an unweeded garden
That grows to seed. Things rank and gross in nature   140
Possess it merely. That it should come to this:
But two months dead—nay, not so much, not two.
So excellent a king, that was to this
Hyperion to a satyr; so loving to my mother
That he might not beteem the winds of heaven   145
Visit her face too roughly. Heaven and Earth,
Must I remember? Why, she would hang on him
As if increase of appetite had grown
By what it fed on. And yet, within a month
(Let me not think on 't; frailty, thy name is woman!),   150
A little month, or ere those shoes were old
With which she followed my poor father's body,
Like Niobe, all tears—why she, even she
(O God, a beast that wants discourse of reason
Would have mourned longer!), married with my   155
    uncle,
My father's brother, but no more like my father
Than I to Hercules. Within a month,
Ere yet the salt of most unrighteous tears
Had left the flushing in her gallèd eyes,   160
She married. O, most wicked speed, to post
With such dexterity to incestuous sheets!
It is not, nor it cannot come to good.
But break, my heart, for I must hold my tongue.

RESOURCE #3.1B

Ophelia's Family

Laertes	Ophelia	Polonius
Do not sleep, But let me hear from you. *Laertes 1.3.3–4*	I shall the effect of this good lesson keep As watchman to my heart. *Ophelia 1.3.49–50*	You do not understand yourself so clearly As it behooves my daughter and your honor. *Polonius 1.3.105–106*
For Hamlet, and the trifling of his favor, Hold it a fashion and a toy in blood. *Laertes 1.3.6–7*	Do not, as some ungracious pastors do, Show me the steep and thorny way to heaven, Whiles, like a puffed and reckless libertine, Himself the primrose path of dalliance treads And recks not his own rede. *Ophelia 1.3.51–55*	You speak like a green girl. *Polonius 1.3.110*
Perhaps he loves you now, and now no soil nor cautel doth besmirch the virtue of his will. *Laertes 1.3.17–19*	'Tis in my memory locked, And you yourself shall keep the key of it. *Ophelia 1.3.92–93*	Do you believe his "tenders," as you call them? *Polonius 1.3.112*
He may not, as unvalued persons do, Carve for himself, for on his choice depends The safety and the health of this whole state. *Laertes 1.3.22–24*	He hath, my lord, of late made many tenders Of his affection to me. *Ophelia 1.3.108–109*	I will teach you. *Polonius 1.3.114*
Weigh what loss your honor may sustain If with too credent ear you list his songs Or lose your heart or your chaste treasure open To his unmastered importunity. *Laertes 1.3.33–35*	I do not know, my lord, what I should think. *Ophelia 1.3.114*	Tender yourself more dearly, Or [. . .] you'll tender me a fool. *Polonius 1.3.116–118*
The chariest maid is prodigal enough If she unmask her beauty to the moon. *Laertes 1.3.40–41*	My lord, he hath importuned me with love In honorable fashion. *Ophelia 1.3.119–120*	From this time Be something scanter of your maiden presence. *Polonius 1.3.129–130*
The canker galls the infants of the spring Too oft before their buttons be disclosed. *Laertes 1.3.43–44*	I shall obey, my lord. *Ophelia 1.3.145*	Set your entreatments at a higher rate Than a command to parle. *Polonius 1.3.131–132*

Best safety lies in fear. *Laertes 1.3.47*		Do not believe his vows, for they are brokers, Not of that dye which their investments show, But mere implorators of unholy suits. *Polonius 1.3.136–138*
Ophelia [. . .] remember well What I have said to you. *Laertes 1.3.90–91*		I would not, in plain terms, from this time forth Have you so slander any moment leisure As to give words or talk with the Lord Hamlet. *Polonius 1.3.141–143*
		Look to 't, I charge you. *Polonius 1.3.144*

WEEK THREE: LESSON 2

"Am I a Coward?":
Hamlet's 2.2 Soliloquy

Here's What We're Doing and Why

In this lesson, students will perform a choral reading of Hamlet's 2.2 soliloquy and then work together to find the battling voices in the speech. Students have learned through choral reading before, and this Essential is particularly useful in this lesson. They will notice for themselves how Hamlet evolves in the play and how Shakespeare uses language to illustrate the complexities and conflicts in his character.

At the end of the soliloquy, Hamlet decides to get to Claudius's conscience by putting on a play—a real epiphany moment for him. Some of this language should be a lightning rod for conversation in the classroom. At the beginning of the speech, Hamlet says, "Oh what a rogue and peasant slave am I," but is that an apt comparison for him to make? Can this Prince of Denmark honestly compare his situation to that of an enslaved person? (Frederick Douglass has more to say about this in the next lesson.)

Finding the two voices in Hamlet's soliloquy today will help students to hear the conversation he is having with himself. It will also help them put Hamlet in conversation with Frederick Douglass, the writer at the center of tomorrow's lesson. The excerpt from *The Narrative of the Life of Frederick Douglass*, in which Douglass describes life in slavery and the moment when he had his own epiphany and recognized "the pathway from slavery to freedom," ought to lead students to "talk back" to Shakespeare.

In addition, this lesson, like many of the others, asks students to defend the interpretive choices they make when working with Shakespeare's text. This connects to the final project step where students will use Shakespeare's language to make decisions about the big idea of their scenes and then cut and direct the text to amplify that idea.

What Will I Need?

- Copies of Hamlet's 2.2 speech, one per student – **RESOURCE #3.2**

How Should I Prepare?

- Arrange your classroom to accommodate choral reading and performance
- Organize the class into groups of 4–6 students

Agenda (~ 45-minute period)

❑ Review and introduction: 5 minutes

❑ Choral Reading: 15 minutes

❑ Finding the Argument: 25 minutes

Here's What Students Hear (From You) and (Then What They'll) Do

Review and Introduction

1. It's early in a new week, and we've spent a while with Ophelia and her family, so let's review what we've learned about the events and characters in *Hamlet* so far. Return to your memory of your Twenty-Minute *Hamlet* or the play map if you need to.

   a. Who is Hamlet? How would you describe him and why? What has he done so far?

   b. Who is Gertrude? How would you describe her and why? What has she done so far?

   c. Who is Claudius? How would you describe him and why? What has he done so far?

2. Have you ever been influenced to change your behavior after hearing someone else's story or watching a powerful film or television show? Share some examples of the changes you made with the class.

Part One: Choral Reading

1. Hamlet, like you, knows the power of a good story. Here's some important context in the development of this story:

   a. We have learned that the ghost that has been haunting the castle in the very first scene we studied and performed has returned and told Hamlet that Claudius poisoned King Hamlet.

   b. The ghost (of the dead King Hamlet) makes Hamlet vow to avenge his father's death.

   c. In the next act, traveling players arrive at Elsinore castle, and Hamlet watches an actor perform a monologue about a Greek hero's revenge. In the monologue, the hero kills the man who killed his father, but then he must witness the grief of Hecuba, the now-dead enemy's wife. The actor cries for Hecuba as he describes her sorrow. When the actors and Hamlet's friends leave the room, Hamlet is left alone to reflect on what he saw. The speech we'll read today is Hamlet's reflection on the performance.

2. Hand out copies of the Choral Reading script.

3. Form a circle as a class.

4. For the first round of Choral Reading, read the speech in unison.

5. Read the speech—in unison, but this time louder and faster—again.

6. Show your understanding using the 1–3 finger scale from previous lessons.

7. Now, read the speech one by one around the circle, changing speakers at end punctuation marks.

8. Show your understanding using the 1–3 finger scale.

9. Discuss:

   a. What do you think Hamlet is thinking about or feeling? How do you know? Point to lines in the speech that support your thinking.

10. Now, two volunteers will read the speech, alternating at each end punctuation mark.

11. Discuss:

   a. What more did you notice about the speech after this reading? Point to lines that support your thinking.

   b. How does Hamlet feel about himself? Point to lines that support your thinking.

   c. How does he feel about Claudius? Point to lines that support your thinking.

   d. What has he decided to do at the end of the speech? Point to lines that support your thinking.

Part Two: Finding the Argument

1. Form small groups (4–5 students in each group).

2. Each group collaborates to break the soliloquy into a conversation between two alternating voices by marking lines on their scripts to indicate when the voice changes or highlighting the lines for the two sides in two different colors. At this point, students should consult one another, also sidenotes, glossaries, or dictionaries to learn more about unfamiliar words or phrases in the speech.

3. Write justifications for why you have assigned lines to each side in the margins of your copy of the speech.

[**TEACHER NOTE:** For example, a student might explain assigning *"What would he do had he the motive and the cue for passion that I have?"* to one speaker and *"He would drown the stage with tears [. . .]"* to another because one line asks a question and the other answers it.]

4. Next, groups decide on a direction for their two-voiced reading. Will one side whisper and one side shout? Will the volume increase as each line is read or decrease? Will the two sides step closer together with each line or farther apart? Students can decide. Each group should select one style for reading their two-voiced speech.

5. Two groups read their divided speeches. (If time allows, every group should perform.)

6. To conclude this exploration, discuss:

   a. Why did your group choose your delivery style? Which lines supported your choices?

   b. How do you think Hamlet has changed between the first speech of his that we studied and this one? How has he not changed?

    c. Do you think his idea about staging a play is a good one? Why or why not?

    d. In this speech, what narratives about identity has Hamlet reinvented or perpetuated? How?

Here's What Just Happened in Class

- Students learned more about Hamlet's internal conflict, a struggle to live up to his own expectations and the expectations he thinks others have of him.

- Students read a complex text aloud alongside their peers.

- Students recognized that by reading a text in different ways new meanings emerge.

- Students demonstrated how rereading a text aloud refines their understanding.

- Students made discoveries in a text without teacher explanation.

- Students collaborated to make decisions about performing a text without teacher direction.

- Students discussed how stories shape our understanding of ourselves and others.

- By questioning how effective Hamlet's "play's the thing" plan might be, students discussed the extent to which art can affect life.

RESOURCE #3.2

A Choral Reading of Hamlet's 2.2 Soliloquy

HAMLET: Now I am alone.

O, what a rogue and peasant slave am I!
Is it not monstrous that this player here,
But in a fiction, in a dream of passion,
Could force his soul so to his own conceit   580
That from her working all his visage wanned,
Tears in his eyes, distraction in his aspect,
A broken voice, and his whole function suiting
With forms to his conceit—and all for nothing!
For Hecuba!   585
What's Hecuba to him, or he to Hecuba,
That he should weep for her? What would he do
Had he the motive and the cue for passion
That I have? He would drown the stage with tears
And cleave the general ear with horrid speech,   590
Make mad the guilty and appall the free,
Confound the ignorant and amaze indeed
The very faculties of eyes and ears. Yet I,
A dull and muddy-mettled rascal, peak
Like John-a-dreams, unpregnant of my cause,   595
And can say nothing—no, not for a king
Upon whose property and most dear life
A damned defeat was made. Am I a coward?
Who calls me "villain"? breaks my pate across?
Plucks off my beard and blows it in my face?   600
Tweaks me by the nose? gives me the lie i' th' throat
As deep as to the lungs? Who does me this?
Ha! 'Swounds, I should take it! For it cannot be
But I am pigeon-livered and lack gall
To make oppression bitter, or ere this   605
I should have fatted all the region kites
With this slave's offal. Bloody, bawdy villain!
Remorseless, treacherous, lecherous, kindless
   villain!
O vengeance!   610
Why, what an ass am I! This is most brave,
That I, the son of a dear father murdered,
Prompted to my revenge by heaven and hell,
Must, like a whore, unpack my heart with words
And fall a-cursing like a very drab,   615
A stallion! Fie upon 't! Foh!

About, my brains!—Hum, I have heard
That guilty creatures sitting at a play
Have, by the very cunning of the scene,
Been struck so to the soul that presently   620
They have proclaimed their malefactions;
For murder, though it have no tongue, will speak
With most miraculous organ. I'll have these players
Play something like the murder of my father
Before mine uncle. I'll observe his looks;   625
I'll tent him to the quick. If he do blench,
I know my course. The spirit that I have seen
May be a devil, and the devil hath power
T' assume a pleasing shape; yea, and perhaps,
Out of my weakness and my melancholy,   630
As he is very potent with such spirits,
Abuses me to damn me. I'll have grounds
More relative than this. The play's the thing
Wherein I'll catch the conscience of the King.
He exits.

WEEK THREE: LESSON 3

"A Great Good to Be Diligently Sought": Hamlet and Frederick Douglass Speak Across Centuries

Here's What We're Doing and Why

Students will extend their exploration and learning about language, identity, and decision-making in *Hamlet* by reading Chapter 6 of *Narrative of the Life of Frederick Douglass* and drawing comparisons between his narrative and the Hamlet soliloquy we just read.

In yesterday's lesson on the "O, what a rogue" soliloquy, students explored how Hamlet's character is evolving, specifically how his identity is shaped by what the world expects of him and what he expects of and thinks of himself. In the *Narrative* excerpt, Douglass focuses on how social structures impact his identity. Hamlet's speech and Douglass's narrative side-by-side bring students to consider how this occurs across literature, geography, ethnicities, and history. Today's lesson also gives students another excellent example of another author talking back to Shakespeare," using a paired text to expand our thinking about Shakespeare's language and how we use language today. (We want students to talk back to Shakespeare, too.)

Hamlet uses the metaphor of enslavement to describe his obligation to and feelings about his quest for revenge. Shakespeare and other English readers in the Early Modern period would have understood the word *slave* to mean one who had an obligation to work to pay back a debt. Being such a "slave," however, did not deny one personhood, nor was it connected to one's race or ethnicity, nor did it mean that one was considered property. Douglass describes his personal experience as an enslaved man in the United States of America, the prisoner of an institution built on false ideas of economic and racial superiority. In this excerpt, he invites readers into his world with horrifying descriptions that illuminate his experience.

Douglass wrote this in 1845, and the Emancipation Proclamation became law in 1863. After the Proclamation, however, many white people retained an enslaver mindset, and engaged in social and judicial practices that continued to punish those who had been enslaved as well as their descendants.

[**TEACHER NOTE: Please take note of the pejorative language that appears in this passage.** We have purposely not removed it, but we have constructed this lesson so that neither teacher nor students will be reading this language aloud. The N-word is an obscenity that has been and still is a hurtful insult to African Americans and darker-skinned persons of other racial and ethnic groups when used by those who are not African American or darker-skinned people. Using the N-word in this way is often part of a racially motivated attack, whether verbal or physical. Sometimes members of the African American community and darker-skinned persons use the word themselves, to resist the hurt that this word brought to their ancestors and brings to them now. We want to completely avoid the spoken N-word, though, because its original intent was to cause profound injury to Black and brown people.

We feel that we cannot ignore or skirt conversation about this language because doing so allows the hate and prejudice of that language to fester and perpetuate. You know your students. Students' feelings and reactions to words depend on many factors, including demographics. Please take the time to handle with care conversations and questions that may come up.]

After reading a chapter from Douglass's narrative, students will, as he did, create a conversation between Douglass and Shakespeare. They can also create a mash-up soliloquy with lines from Douglass's narrative and Hamlet's soliloquy.

What Will I Need?

- Class copies of Hamlet's 2.2 soliloquy – **RESOURCE #3.3A**
- Chapter 6 of *Narrative of the Life of Frederick Douglass* – **RESOURCE #3.3B**
- Chapter 6 excerpted for mash-up purposes – **RESOURCE #3.3C**

How Should I Prepare?

- Read 2.2 of *Hamlet* and Chapter 6 of *Narrative of the Life of Frederick Douglass*
- Try making a dialogue or mash-up of your own from the choral reading scripts of both excerpts

Agenda (~ 45-minute period)

- ❑ Warm-up: 5 minutes
- ❑ Close-Reading of *Narrative of the Life of Frederick* Douglass: 15 minutes
- ❑ Mash-up making and sharing: 25 minutes

Here's What Students Hear (From You) and (Then What They'll) Do

Warm-up

1. Review your copy of Hamlet's 2.2. soliloquy and choose the line you consider most important.

2. Turn and talk with a partner about the line you chose and why.

3. Some students share lines and reasons for selecting them. Write the lines on the board or chart paper.

Part One: Reading and Discussion

1. What do we know about Frederick Douglass?

[TEACHER NOTE: You can fill in as needed or send students to research: He was an enslaved person who became an abolitionist. He was a well-known orator who alluded to Shakespeare in his speeches, and he participated in readings of Shakespeare's plays during meetings of Shakespeare clubs in the Washington, DC, area. Douglass was the most photographed American of the nineteenth century; there were more photographs of him than of President Abraham Lincoln. He was also known for his fine and widely read writing.]

Today, we're going to read an excerpt of his writing and use it to question and talk back to Shakespeare. Before we read, it's important for you to know that you will encounter some language in the passage that we will not say out loud. (See above note on pejorative language.)

2. Everyone will silently read Chapter 6 of *Narrative of the Life of Frederick Douglass*.

3. After the class has read, discuss:

    a. What do you think about this reading? What do you notice? What do you wonder?

    b. What conflicts (internal or external) can you hear in Frederick Douglass's words?

    c. What expectations did Mr. and Mrs. Auld (and, in turn, slaveholders) have for Douglass?

    d. What expectations did Frederick Douglass have for himself? Did those expectations change during the moments recorded in this chapter of the narrative? How?

    e. Do we see any lingering effects of Douglass's 1845 thinking today?

    f. In soliloquy, Hamlet calls himself a "rogue and peasant slave." Does Douglass's account of life in enslavement change the way you hear Hamlet's description of himself? How?

    g. In Hamlet's soliloquy, he makes a plan to assuage his feelings of guilt and frustration by staging a play that will incriminate Claudius. What plan has Douglass made to change his fate? How does he seem to feel about that plan?

Part Two: Write a Mash-up or Dialogue

1. Let's get Douglass (writing in 1845) and Shakespeare (writing *Hamlet* in about 1599, we think) talking to each other.

2. Organize into small groups.

3. Use lines from your choral reading scripts of Hamlet's 2.2 soliloquy and lines from Douglass's chapter to create either an 8-line dialogue between Hamlet and Douglass (4 lines from each speaker), or make a mash-up speech that incorporates lines from Shakespeare and Douglass.

[**TEACHER NOTE:** If working with smaller pieces of text is better for your students, RESOURCE #3.3C is a subsection of Douglass's chapter that might be more useful for them.]

4. When students have finished writing, invite some volunteers to share their speeches or conversations.

5. Following the dialogue and mash-up reading, discuss as a class:

    a. What do these two writers from different centuries, races, and places have to say to each other?

      b. What did you hear or see when you gave Douglass and Shakespeare the chance to talk to each other?

6. Conclude with rounds:

      a. I noticed . . .

      b. I wondered . . .

      c. I learned . . .

      d. Something I learned about myself . . .

Here's What Just Happened in Class

- Students read a complex text from American history.

- Students used Frederick Douglass's words and ideas to talk back to Shakespeare.

- Students made their own meaning of Douglass's and Shakespeare's words by bringing the writers in conversation.

RESOURCE #3.3A

Hamlet's 2.2 Soliloquy

HAMLET: Now I am alone.

   O, what a rogue and peasant slave am I!

   Is it not monstrous that this player here,

   But in a fiction, in a dream of passion,

   Could force his soul so to his own conceit   580

   That from her working all his visage wanned,

   Tears in his eyes, distraction in his aspect,

   A broken voice, and his whole function suiting

   With forms to his conceit—and all for nothing!

   For Hecuba!   585

   What's Hecuba to him, or he to Hecuba,

   That he should weep for her? What would he do

   Had he the motive and the cue for passion

   That I have? He would drown the stage with tears

   And cleave the general ear with horrid speech,   590

   Make mad the guilty and appall the free,

   Confound the ignorant and amaze indeed

   The very faculties of eyes and ears. Yet I,

   A dull and muddy-mettled rascal, peak

   Like John-a-dreams, unpregnant of my cause,   595

   And can say nothing—no, not for a king

   Upon whose property and most dear life

   A damned defeat was made. Am I a coward?

   Who calls me "villain"? breaks my pate across?

   Plucks off my beard and blows it in my face?   600

   Tweaks me by the nose? gives me the lie i' th' throat

   As deep as to the lungs? Who does me this?

   Ha! 'Swounds, I should take it! For it cannot be

   But I am pigeon-livered and lack gall

   To make oppression bitter, or ere this   605

   I should have fatted all the region kites

   With this slave's offal. Bloody, bawdy villain!

   Remorseless, treacherous, lecherous, kindless

      villain!

   O vengeance!   610

   Why, what an ass am I! This is most brave,

   That I, the son of a dear father murdered,

   Prompted to my revenge by heaven and hell,

   Must, like a whore, unpack my heart with words

   And fall a-cursing like a very drab,   615

   A stallion! Fie upon 't! Foh!

About, my brains!—Hum, I have heard
That guilty creatures sitting at a play
Have, by the very cunning of the scene,
Been struck so to the soul that presently   620
They have proclaimed their malefactions;
For murder, though it have no tongue, will speak
With most miraculous organ. I'll have these players
Play something like the murder of my father
Before mine uncle. I'll observe his looks;   625
I'll tent him to the quick. If he do blench,
I know my course. The spirit that I have seen
May be a devil, and the devil hath power
T' assume a pleasing shape; yea, and perhaps,
Out of my weakness and my melancholy,   630
As he is very potent with such spirits,
Abuses me to damn me. I'll have grounds
More relative than this. The play's the thing
Wherein I'll catch the conscience of the King.

RESOURCE #3.3B

Chapter 6, *Narrative of the Life of Frederick Douglass*

Chapter VI.

My new mistress proved to be all she appeared when I first met her at the door,—a woman of the kindest heart and finest feelings. She had never had a slave under her control previously to myself, and prior to her marriage she had been dependent upon her own industry for a living. She was by trade a weaver; and by constant application to her business, she had been in a good degree preserved from the blighting and dehumanizing effects of slavery. I was utterly astonished at her goodness. I scarcely knew how to behave towards her. She was entirely unlike any other white woman I had ever seen. I could not approach her as I was accustomed to approach other white ladies. My early instruction was all out of place. The crouching servility, usually so acceptable a quality in a slave, did not answer when manifested toward her. Her favor was not gained by it; she seemed to be disturbed by it. She did not deem it impudent or unmannerly for a slave to look her in the face. The meanest slave was put fully at ease in her presence, and none left without feeling better for having seen her. Her face was made of heavenly smiles, and her voice of tranquil music.

But, alas! this kind heart had but a short time to remain such. The fatal poison of irresponsible power was already in her hands, and soon commenced its infernal work. That cheerful eye, under the influence of slavery, soon became red with rage; that voice, made all of sweet accord, changed to one of harsh and horrid discord; and that angelic face gave place to that of a demon.

Very soon after I went to live with Mr. and Mrs. Auld, she very kindly commenced to teach me the A, B, C. After I had learned this, she assisted me in learning to spell words of three or four letters. Just at this point of my progress, Mr. Auld found out what was going on, and at once forbade Mrs. Auld to instruct me further, telling her, among other things, that it was unlawful, as well as unsafe, to teach a slave to read. To use his own words, further, he said, "If you give a nigger an inch, he will take an ell. A nigger should know nothing but to obey his master—to do as he is told to do. Learning would spoil the best nigger in the world. Now," said he, "if you teach that nigger (speaking of myself) how to read, there would be no keeping him. It would forever unfit him to be a slave. He would at once become unmanageable, and of no value to his master. As to himself, it could do him no good, but a great deal of harm. It would make him discontented and unhappy." These words sank deep into my heart, stirred up sentiments within that lay slumbering, and called into existence an entirely new train of thought. It was a new and special revelation, explaining dark and mysterious things, with which my youthful understanding had struggled, but struggled in vain. I now understood what had been to me a most perplexing difficulty—to wit, the white man's power to enslave the black man. It was a grand achievement, and I prized it highly. From that moment, I understood the pathway from slavery to freedom. It was just what I wanted, and I got it at a time when I the least expected it. Whilst I was saddened by the thought of losing the aid of my kind mistress, I was gladdened by the invaluable instruction which, by the merest accident, I had gained from my master. Though conscious of the difficulty of learning without a teacher, I set out with high hope, and a fixed purpose, at whatever cost of trouble, to learn how to read. The very decided manner with which he spoke, and strove to impress his wife with the evil consequences of giving me instruction, served to convince me that he was deeply sensible of the truths he was uttering. It gave me the best assurance that I might rely with the utmost confidence on the results which, he said, would flow from teaching me to read. What he most dreaded, that I most desired. What he most loved, that I most hated. That which to him was a great evil, to be carefully shunned, was to me a great good, to be diligently sought; and the argument which he so warmly urged, against my learning to read, only served to inspire me with a desire and determination to learn. In learning to read, I owe almost as much to the bitter opposition of my master, as to the kindly aid of my mistress. I acknowledge the benefit of both.

I had resided but a short time in Baltimore before I observed a marked difference, in the treatment of slaves, from that which I had witnessed in the country. A city slave is almost a freeman, compared with a slave on the plantation. He is much better fed and clothed, and enjoys privileges altogether unknown to the slave on the plantation. There is a vestige of decency, a sense of shame, that does much to curb and check those outbreaks of atrocious cruelty so commonly enacted upon the plantation. He is a desperate slaveholder, who will shock the humanity of his non-slaveholding neighbors with the cries of his lacerated slave. Few are willing to incur the odium attaching to the reputation of being a cruel master; and above all things, they would not be known as not giving a slave enough to eat. Every city slaveholder is anxious to have it known of him, that he feeds his slaves well; and it is due to them to say, that most of them do give their slaves enough to eat. There are, however, some painful exceptions to this rule. Directly opposite to us, on Philpot Street, lived Mr. Thomas Hamilton. He owned two slaves. Their names were Henrietta and Mary. Henrietta was about twenty-two years of age, Mary was about fourteen; and of all the mangled and emaciated creatures I ever looked upon, these two were the most so. His heart must be harder than stone, that could look upon these unmoved. The head, neck, and shoulders of Mary were literally cut to pieces. I have frequently felt her head, and found it nearly covered with festering sores, caused by the lash of her cruel mistress. I do not know that her master ever whipped her, but I have been an eye-witness to the cruelty of Mrs. Hamilton. I used to be in Mr. Hamilton's house nearly every day. Mrs. Hamilton used to sit in a large chair in the middle of the room, with a heavy cowskin always by her side, and scarce an hour passed during the day but was marked by the blood of one of these slaves. The girls seldom passed her without her saying, "Move faster, you black gip!" at the same time giving them a blow with the cowskin over the head or shoulders, often drawing the blood. She would then say, "Take that, you black gip!"—continuing, "If you don't move faster, I'll move you!" Added to the cruel lashings to which these slaves were subjected, they were kept nearly half-starved. They seldom knew what it was to eat a full meal. I have seen Mary contending with the pigs for the offal thrown into the street. So much was Mary kicked and cut to pieces, that she was oftener called "pecked" than by her name.

Douglass, Frederick. *Narrative of the Life of Frederick Douglass: An American Slave*. New York: Penguin Books, 1968. Print. https://docsouth.unc.edu/neh/douglass/douglass.html.

RESOURCE #3.3C

Chapter 6, *Narrative of the Life of Frederick Douglass*, further excerpted

These words sank deep into my heart, stirred up sentiments within that lay slumbering, and called into existence an entirely new train of thought. It was a new and special revelation, explaining dark and mysterious things, with which my youthful understanding had struggled, but struggled in vain. I now understood what had been to me a most perplexing difficulty—to wit, the white man's power to enslave the black man. It was a grand achievement, and I prized it highly. From that moment, I understood the pathway from slavery to freedom. It was just what I wanted, and I got it at a time when I the least expected it. Whilst I was saddened by the thought of losing the aid of my kind mistress, I was gladdened by the invaluable instruction which, by the merest accident, I had gained from my master. Though conscious of the difficulty of learning without a teacher, I set out with high hope, and a fixed purpose, at whatever cost of trouble, to learn how to read. The very decided manner with which he spoke, and strove to impress his wife with the evil consequences of giving me instruction, served to convince me that he was deeply sensible of the truths he was uttering. It gave me the best assurance that I might rely with the utmost confidence on the results which, he said, would flow from teaching me to read. What he most dreaded, that I most desired. What he most loved, that I most hated. That which to him was a great evil, to be carefully shunned, was to me a great good, to be diligently sought; and the argument which he so warmly urged, against my learning to read, only served to inspire me with a desire and determination to learn. In learning to read, I owe almost as much to the bitter opposition of my master, as to the kindly aid of my mistress. I acknowledge the benefit of both.

Douglass, Frederick. *Narrative of the Life of Frederick Douglass: An American Slave.* New York: Penguin Books, 1968. Print. https://docsouth.unc.edu/neh/douglass/douglass.html.

WEEK THREE: LESSON 4

Is That the Point or the Question? Exploring Many Ways "To Be" in Hamlet's Famous 3.1 Soliloquy

Here's What We're Doing and Why

If Shakespeare were a rock star, Hamlet's "To be or not to be" soliloquy in 3.1 would be one of his greatest hits. Words this famous can be intimidating . . . or can feel overdone. In this speech, Hamlet contemplates whether it's better for him to live with his current heartaches or die and face the unknown. Students will take on this speech from different perspectives, the way that actors, editors, and scholars do.

First, they will read Hamlet's speech in English, and because this speech is well-known the world over, they will be treated to speaking or hearing this famous speech in several different languages too. A few days before you teach this lesson, talk with your students and perhaps teachers in your World Languages department and other school staff about their languages beyond English. Ask a few of them if they would be willing to read all or part of "To be or not to be" in your class. Or perhaps a student—or a relative or a friend of a student—would be willing to record themselves reading all of part of the speech in a language other than English. Or find versions online in languages other than the ones provided in the resources. If they will be speaking, give them copies of the speech a few days before you plan to teach this lesson so they can practice.

Then, using archival materials from the Folger Library, students will make discoveries by comparing two of the earliest printed versions of *Hamlet*: the First Quarto (Q1), printed in 1603, and the First Folio (F1), printed in 1623. They'll discuss how language can change the meaning or mood of the speech. This lesson will give students ownership of the speech while they imagine new possibilities for what might have felt like a "permanent" text.

Comparing the differences in this speech as it appears in the First Quarto (Q1) and the First Folio (F1) is yet another way to practice close-reading and critical thinking. It also brings your students into the work of scholars, editors, and actors. Students will discuss the effects of contrasting words and lines in Q1 and F1 as they decide which version Hamlet should perform.

Agenda (~ 45-minute period)

❏ Choral Reading and the speech in translation: 15 minutes

❏ Quarto and Folio comparison: 30 minutes

What Will I Need?

- Copies of "To be or not to be" in several languages. We've shared here versions in English, Spanish, Mandarin, and Arabic – **RESOURCES #3.4A, #3.4B, #3.4C, and #3.4D**

- Class set of Q1/F1 comparison chart and accompanying Venn diagram – **RESOURCES #3.4E, #3.4F**

How Should I Prepare?

- Make copies of handouts and, if possible, find a way to project the quarto/folio comparison on a wall or whiteboard

Here's What Students Hear (From You) and (Then What They'll) Do

Part One/Warm-up: Fast Choral Reading and Global Reading

1. Gather everyone in a circle and read Hamlet's 3.1 soliloquy in unison twice.

2. What do you notice and understand about the speech? What is Hamlet thinking about?

[**TEACHER NOTE:** Students will notice that Hamlet contemplates suicide. To follow that observation, ask:

- Which details in the text lead you to that observation?
- What might be leading him to have these feelings?
- If Hamlet were a student at our school, what could he do or whom should he talk to for help? How could friends of Hamlet help him? (Here is an opportunity to reinforce the importance [and normalcy!] of talking about mental health and seeking help.)]

Students will notice that Hamlet struggles with the challenges of being human. To follow that observation, ask:

- Which details in the text lead you to that observation?
- Do any of the challenges he mentions resonate with you? Which ones?

3. Next, guest speakers (students and school staff) will read the speech in languages other than English, or play the audio versions they have found of these versions.

4. Ask the speakers to share their reactions to seeing/reading the speech in another of their languages. What did they notice?

5. What do you notice when hearing the speech delivered in another language? What do you wonder?

Part Two: Quarto/Folio Comparison

1. Let's look at the quarto/folio comparison chart. Generally, the First Folio gives us the texts of the plays that we are most familiar with, but in many cases, other early printed versions—like the quarto we're looking at today—offer interesting and sometimes mysterious alternate versions of some scenes or speeches.

2. Read both versions and work alone or in small groups to identify similarities and differences; mark these on the Venn diagram. Wait for students to note

differences like these:

    a. "That is the question" vs. "there's the point"

    b. The presence of "undiscovered country" in both speeches (Ask: What's powerful about that metaphor?)

    c. Difference in length between the two versions

    d. "Nymph" vs. "Lady"

    e. The "everlasting judge" in the Quarto is absent from the Folio

3. Once you have filled out the diagram, let's discuss (in small groups or as a class):

    a. What do you notice when you compare these versions of the speech? What do you wonder? What other questions do you have?

    b. How does the mood of the speech change when words are omitted or changed?

    c. How does your understanding of Hamlet change when words are omitted or changed?

4. To conclude, write a paragraph reflection for the following prompt:

    a. Which version of Hamlet's 3.1 soliloquy would be performed in a production of *Hamlet* that you are directing? Defend your choice with lines from the speech and lines or details from other scenes in the play.

Here's What Just Happened in Class

- Students learned that Hamlet is struggling to determine his purpose and a reason for living.

- Students explored what this iconic speech sounds like in languages other than English.

- Students collaborated to close-read Shakespeare by analyzing and comparing two of the earliest printed versions of the play.

- Students took ownership of Shakespeare's language by deciding which new version of Hamlet's soliloquy they would include in their own *Hamlet* production.

RESOURCE #3.4A

"To be or not to be" in Shakespeare's English

HAMLET

To be or not to be—that is the question:
Whether 'tis nobler in the mind to suffer   65
The slings and arrows of outrageous fortune,
Or to take arms against a sea of troubles
And, by opposing, end them. To die, to sleep—
No more—and by a sleep to say we end
The heartache and the thousand natural shocks   70
That flesh is heir to—'tis a consummation
Devoutly to be wished. To die, to sleep—
To sleep, perchance to dream. Ay, there's the rub,
For in that sleep of death what dreams may come,
When we have shuffled off this mortal coil,   75
Must give us pause. There's the respect
That makes calamity of so long life.
For who would bear the whips and scorns of time,
Th' oppressor's wrong, the proud man's contumely,
The pangs of despised love, the law's delay,   80
The insolence of office, and the spurns
That patient merit of th' unworthy takes,
When he himself might his quietus make
With a bare bodkin? Who would fardels bear,
To grunt and sweat under a weary life,   85
But that the dread of something after death,
The undiscovered country from whose bourn
No traveler returns, puzzles the will
And makes us rather bear those ills we have
Than fly to others that we know not of?   90
Thus conscience does make cowards of us all,
And thus the native hue of resolution
Is sicklied o'er with the pale cast of thought,
And enterprises of great pitch and moment
With this regard their currents turn awry   95
And lose the name of action.—Soft you now,
The fair Ophelia.—Nymph, in thy orisons
Be all my sins remembered.

RESOURCE #3.4B

"To be or not to be" in Spanish

Ser o no ser . . . He ahí el dilema.
¿Qué es mejor para el alma,
sufrir insultos de Fortuna, golpes, dardos,
o levantarse en armas contra el océano del mal,
y oponerse a él y que así cesen? Morir, dormir . . .
Nada más; y decir así que con un sueño
damos fin a las llagas del corazón
y a todos los males, herencia de la carne,
y decir: ven, consumación, yo te deseo. Morir, dormir,
dormir . . . ¡Soñar acaso! ¡Qué difícil! Pues en el sueño
de la muerte ¿qué sueño sobrevendrán
cuando despojados de ataduras mortales
encontremos la paz? He ahí la razón
por la que tan longeva llega a ser la desgracia.
¿Pues quién podrá soportar los azotes y las burlas del mundo,
la injusticia del tirano, la afrenta del soberbio,
la angustia del amor despreciado, la espera del juicio,
la arrogancia del poderoso, y la humillación
que la virtud recibe de quien es indigno,
cuando uno mismo tiene a su alcance el descanso
en el filo desnudo del puñal? ¿Quién puede soportar
tanto? ¿Gemir tanto? ¿Llevar de la vida una carga
Tan pesada? Nadie, si no fuera por ese algo tras la muerte
—ese país por descubrir, de cuyos confines
ningún viajero retorna—que confunde la voluntad
haciéndonos pacientes ante el infortunio
antes que volar hacia un mal desconocido.
La conciencia, así, hace a todos cobardes
y, así, el natural color de la resolución
se desvanece en tenues sombras del pensamiento;
y así empresas de importancia, y de gran valía,
llegan a torcer su rumbo al considerarse
para nunca volver a merecer el nombre
de la acción.

William Shakespeare. *Hamlet: edición bilingüe del Instituto Shakespeare.* Hicieron la versión definitiva Manuel Angel Conejero y Jenaro Taléns. Madrid: Cátedra, 1992.

RESOURCE #3.4C

"To be or not to be" in Mandarin

生存还是毁灭，这是一个值得考虑的问题；

默然忍受命运的暴虐的毒箭，

或是挺身反抗人世的无涯的苦难，

通过斗争把它们扫清，

这两种行为，哪一种更高贵？死了；睡着了；

什么都完了；要是在这一种睡眠之中，

我们心头的创痛，以及其他无数血肉之躯所不能避免的打击，

都可以从此消失，那正是我们求之不得的结局。死了；睡着了；

睡着了也许还会做梦；嗯，阻碍就在这儿：

因为当我们摆脱了这一具朽腐的皮囊以后，

在那死的睡眠里，究竟将要做些什么梦，

那不能不使我们踌躇顾虑。

人們甘心久困于患难之中，也就是为了这个缘故；

谁愿意忍受人世的鞭挞和讥嘲、

压迫者的凌辱、傲慢者的冷眼、

被轻蔑的爱情的惨痛、法律的迁延、

官吏的横暴和费尽辛勤所换来的小人的鄙视，

要是他只要用一柄小小的刀子，就可以清算他自己的一生？

谁愿意负着这样的重担，在烦劳的生命的压迫下呻吟流汗，

倘不是因为惧怕不可知的死后，

惧怕那从来不曾有一个旅人回来过的神秘之國，

是它迷惑了我们的意志，使我们宁愿忍受目前的磨折，

不敢向我们所不知道的痛苦飞去？

这样，重重的顾虑使我们全变成了懦夫，决心的赤热的光彩，

被审慎的思维盖上了一层灰色，

伟大的事业在这一种考虑之下，也会逆流而退，

失去了行动的意义。且慢！

美丽的奥菲利娅！——**女神，在你的祈祷之中，**

不要忘记替我忏悔我的罪孽。

Hamlet (哈姆萊特), trans. 朱生豪 Zhu, Shenghao (1912–1944)
(Prose lineated by Timothy Billings)

RESOURCE #3.4D

"To be or not to be" in Arabic

هاملت:

أَأَكون أم لا أكون؟ ذلك هو السؤال.
أَمِن الأنبل للنفس أن يصبر المرء على
مقاليع الدهر اللئيم وسهامه
أم يُشهر السلاح على بحر الهموم،
وبصدها ينهيها؟ نموت … ننام ..

وما من شيء بعد … أنقول بهذه النومة ننهي
لوعة القلب، وآلاف الصدمات التي
يتعرض لها الجسد من الطبيعة؟ تلك غايةٌ
ما أحرَّ ما تُشتهى. نموت… ننام…
ننام- وإذا حلمنا؟ أجل لعمري، هنا العقبة.

فما قد نراه في سبات الموت من رؤى،
وقد ألقينا بفانيات التلافيف هذه عنّا،
يوقفنا للتروي.
ذلك ما يجعل طامةً من حياة طويلة كهذه.
وإلا فمن ذا الذي يقبل صاغرًا سياط الزمان ومهاناته،
ويرضــخ لظلــم المســتبد، ويســكت عــن زرايــة
المتغطرس،
وأوجــاع الهــوى المــردود علــى نفســه، ومماطلات
القضاء
وصلافة أولي المناصب، والازدراء الذي
يلقاه ذو الجدارة والجلد من كل من لا خير فيه،
لو كان في مقدوره تسديد حسابه
بخنجرٍ مسلول؟ من منّا يتحمل عبأه الباهظ

لاهثًا، يعرق تحت وقر من الحياة،

لولا أن الخوف من أمرٍ قد يلي الموت،

ذلك القطر المجهول الَّذي من وراء حدوده

لا يعود مسافر، يثبط الإرادة فينا

ويجعلنا نؤثر تحمل المكروه الذي نعرفه

على الهرب منه إلى المكروه الذي لا نعرفه؟

ألا هكذا يجعل التأمل منّا جبناء جميعًا،

وما في العزم من لون أصيل يكتسي

بصفرة عليلة من التوجس والقلق،

ومشاريع الوزن والشأن ينثني

مجراها اعوجاجًا بذلك،

وتفقد اسم الفعل والتنفيذ؟

رويدك الآن!

أوفيليا الجميلة! أيتها الحورية، اذكري

في صلواتك خطاياي كلّها.

Shakespeare, William. *Hāmlit*. Trans. Jabrā Ibrāhīm Jabrā. Cairo: Dār al-Shurūq, 2015. 126–28. From the Global Shakespeare Collection, New York University Abu Dhabi Archives and Special Collections.

RESOURCE #3.4E

"To be or not to be": Comparing Q1 and F1

First Quarto (1603)

To be, or not to be, I there's the point,
To Die, to sleep, is that all? Aye all:
No, to sleep, to dream, aye marry there it goes,
For in that dream of death, when we awake,
And borne before an everlasting Judge,
From whence no passenger ever returned,
The undiscovered country, at whose sight
The happy smile, and the accursed damn'd.
But for this, the joyful hope of this,
Who'd bear the scorns and flattery of the world,
Scorned by the right rich, the rich cursed of the poor?
The widow being oppressed, the orphan wrong'd,
The taste of hunger, or a tyrants reign,
And thousand more calamities besides,
To grunt and sweat under this weary life,
When that he may his full Quietus make,
With a bare bodkin, who would this endure,
But for a hope of something after death?
Which puzzles the brain, and doth confound the sense,
Which makes us rather bear those evils we have,
Than fly to others that we know not of.
Aye that, O this conscience makes cowards of us all,
Lady in thy orisons, be all my sins remembered.

First Folio (1623)

To be, or not to be, that is the question:
Whether 'tis Nobler in the mind to suffer
The Slings and Arrows of outrageous Fortune,
Or to take Arms against a Sea of troubles,
And by opposing end them: to die, to sleep
No more; and by a sleep, to say we end
The Heart-ache, and the thousand Natural shocks
That Flesh is heir to? 'Tis a consummation
Devoutly to be wished. To die, to sleep,
To sleep, perchance to Dream; aye, there's the rub,
For in that sleep of death, what dreams may come,
When we have shuffled off this mortal coil,
Must give us pause. There's the respect
That makes Calamity of so long life:
For who would bear the Whips and Scorns of time,
The Oppressor's wrong, the poor man's Contumely,
The pangs of disprized Love, the Law's delay,
The insolence of Office, and the Spurns
That patient merit of the unworthy takes,
When he himself might his Quietus make
With a bare Bodkin? Who would these Fardels bear,
To grunt and sweat under a weary life,
But that the dread of something after death,
The undiscovered Country, from whose bourn
No Traveller returns, Puzzles the will,
And makes us rather bear those ills we have,
Than fly to others that we know not of.
Thus Conscience does make Cowards of us all,
And thus the Native hue of Resolution
Is sicklied o'er, with the pale cast of Thought,
And enterprises of great pith and moment,
With this regard their Currents turn away,
And lose the name of Action. Soft you now,
The fair Ophelia? Nymph, in thy Orisons
Be all my sins remembered.

Created by University of Oregon, published to accompany *First Folio! The Book That Gave Us Shakespeare*, the Folger Library's national First Folio Tour in 2016.

Venn Diagram for Comparing Q1/F1

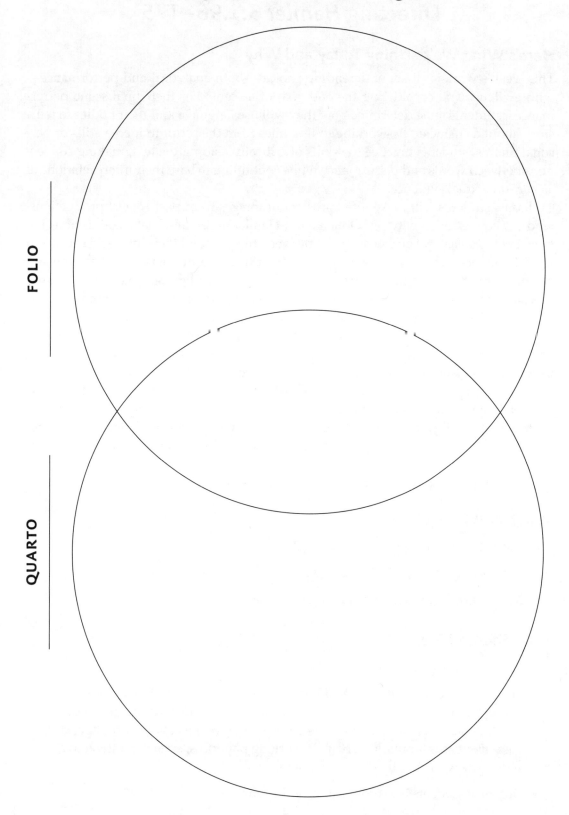

FOLIO

QUARTO

"Get thee to a nunnery": Directing *Hamlet* 3.1.96–175

Here's What We're Doing Today and Why

This week's work is all about defending choices—both analytical and performance—with evidence and considering the end goal of a scene. For their final scene performances, students must determine how they will use language and their bodies to tell a story about a character. By working to link lines from the script to media stills or personal photos, students practice the skills of critically reading the text, making connections between words and performance while continuing to base their interpretations of *Hamlet* on textual evidence.

Today, students will make inferences about images from past *Hamlet* productions, read the conversation between Ophelia and Hamlet in 3.1, and make connections between both *Hamlet* text and images and between the play and their lives and society. In the 3.1 conversation, Hamlet tells Ophelia, "Get thee to a nunnery." At that time and place, "nunnery" could have meant either a place where religious women live or used as a slang term for a house of prostitution. The ambiguity of Hamlet's comment opens opportunities to explore subtext—the real meaning or feeling that lies beneath spoken words. It's also a chance for students to explore the impact of single words on the mood of a line and a scene. And this Hamlet-Ophelia conversation raises questions about the different expectations society has for men and women.

The last step of the lesson (Part Three) asks students to pair a line from this scene with an image from "your world today." We imagine that image coming from one of a few sources: ideally, students will search for their own images on their devices either in class or earlier at home. Or you can create a collection of images (advertisements, media stills, images from news stories) that might pair well with lines from the scene. Overall, a goal of today's work is to make Shakespeare's text visual.

What Will I Need?

- Excerpt from 3.1 of *Hamlet* – **RESOURCE #3.5A**

- Images of *Hamlet* – **RESOURCE #3.5B**

- A collection of contemporary images (see above)

How Should I Prepare?

- Read 3.1.96 on your own

- Make copies of **RESOURCE #3.5B**, the images of Hamlet and Ophelia, or prepare to project these images. If working with hard copies, print the image handout for students and place larger copies of the images on pieces of chart paper or on whiteboards around the room. If working paperless, create an interactive slideshow with one slide for each image.

- Organize students into groups of three or four

Agenda (~ 45-minute period)

❏ Introduction: 5 minutes

❏ Read the Scene and Check for Understanding: 20 minutes

❏ Pair Images with Texts: 10 minutes

❏ Pair Text with Image and Write: 10 minutes

Here's What Students Will Hear (From You) and (Then What They'll) Do

Introduction

1. Today, we will look at a conversation between Hamlet and Ophelia that can be (and has been!) interpreted in many ways. In the conversation, Hamlet tells Ophelia, "Get thee to a nunnery." Could someone share what the sidenotes in our text tell us about the word *nunnery*? Let's hear your ideas about that. Because a nunnery and a brothel (a place where prostitutes lived) were the two places where large groups of single women lived together in Shakespeare's day, one became a slang term for the other. Using the text and some images from past productions, you will make your own interpretation about what Hamlet means when he says this line. The conversation we're about to read also raises questions about the differences in what society expects from men and from women.

Part One: Read the Scene and Check for Understanding

1. Let's look at the script of 3.1.96–175. Read the scene around the room, changing readers after each speaker or end punctuation mark. We may need to read the scene twice. You'll be studying this scene more closely in small groups, so you'll have time after these readings to develop your understanding further.

2. After the class has read the scene, show your understanding using our finger system.

3. Discuss:

   a. What seems to be happening in this scene?

[**TEACHER NOTE:** Students should recognize that Ophelia is returning some of Hamlet's love tokens and that Hamlet is upset with Ophelia.]

   b. Which words or phrases are still difficult to understand, especially given what you already understand about the scene?

[**TEACHER NOTE:** Answers may vary, but you may want to draw attention to the double meaning of "honest" and "fair" as well as Hamlet's comments about marriage and what he might be implying when he describes "your paintings."]

   c. What do you notice about this scene?

  d. How do you react to the scene?

  e. When Hamlet commands Ophelia, "Get thee to a nunnery!," do you think he is trying to protect her, hurt her, or something else? Point to the lines that support your interpretation.

  f. Hamlet and Ophelia speak to each other here, but do they "hear" each other? Do they seem to understand each other? How do you know?

  g. What are your reactions to Hamlet's command?

  h. What connections can you make between Ophelia and Hamlet's conversation here and Ophelia's conversation with her brother and father? How do you react to the connections that these scenes share?

[**TEACHER NOTE:** It's important to examine the gender dynamics of this play. While Ophelia's father, brother, and suitor's interest in her chastity might be historically accurate, we are reading these plays today so we question and urge students to point out and question the differences—why something so personal to Ophelia is any of their business or something they should try to control. This conversation is an opportunity to discuss double standards in expectations connected to gender and sexuality, then and now, and across different cultures. *Don't skip the next question!*]

  i. Do you see or hear gender-focused conversations like the one in this scene happening today? Where? How?

Part Two: Gallery Walk: Pair Images with Text

1. Look at the images of Hamlet and Ophelia in **RESOURCE #3.5B**.

2. Caption each image with a quote from this scene.

3. Now, let's look at these images together and share our captions. What are your reasons for pairing these images and lines?

Part Three: Pair Text with Image

1. Choose a powerful line from the scene.

2. Select an image from your world today that amplifies or resonates with the line you've chosen.

3. Write a one-paragraph explanation or defense of your line/image pairing.

Here's What Just Happened in Class

- Students made inferences about characters and conflicts based on the characters' movements and expressions.

- Students close-read Shakespeare's text in order to make informed interpretive analysis of a scene.

- Students supported their interpretation of images with evidence from Shakespeare's text.

- Students made connections between their lives and society and Shakespeare's text.

- Students learned how, even in Shakespeare, words can wound or warn.

- Students learned that Hamlet and Ophelia's relationship is complicated!

- Students explored what they understand about the gender-based expectations in their own lives.

Hamlet and Ophelia, 3.1.96–175

HAMLET —Soft you now,
    The fair Ophelia.—Nymph, in thy orisons
    Be all my sins remembered.

OPHELIA Good my lord,
    How does your Honor for this many a day?   100

HAMLET I humbly thank you, well.

OPHELIA
    My lord, I have remembrances of yours
    That I have longèd long to redeliver.
    I pray you now receive them.

HAMLET
    No, not I. I never gave you aught.   105

OPHELIA
    My honored lord, you know right well you did,
    And with them words of so sweet breath composed
    As made the things more rich. Their perfume
       l ost,
    Take these again, for to the noble mind   110
    Rich gifts wax poor when givers prove unkind.
    There, my lord.

HAMLET Ha, ha, are you honest?

OPHELIA My lord?

HAMLET Are you fair?   115

OPHELIA What means your Lordship?

HAMLET That if you be honest and fair, your honesty
    should admit no discourse to your beauty.

OPHELIA Could beauty, my lord, have better commerce
    than with honesty?   120

HAMLET Ay, truly, for the power of beauty will sooner
   transform honesty from what it is to a bawd than
   the force of honesty can translate beauty into his
   likeness. This was sometime a paradox, but now
   the time gives it proof. I did love you once.   125

OPHELIA Indeed, my lord, you made me believe so.

HAMLET You should not have believed me, for virtue
   cannot so inoculate our old stock but we shall
   relish of it. I loved you not.

OPHELIA I was the more deceived.   130

HAMLET Get thee to a nunnery. Why wouldst thou be
   a breeder of sinners? I am myself indifferent honest,
   but yet I could accuse me of such things that it
   were better my mother had not borne me: I am
   very proud, revengeful, ambitious, with more offenses   135
   at my beck than I have thoughts to put them
   in, imagination to give them shape, or time to act
   them in. What should such fellows as I do crawling
   between earth and heaven? We are arrant knaves
   all; believe none of us. Go thy ways to a nunnery.   140
   Where's your father?

OPHELIA At home, my lord.

HAMLET Let the doors be shut upon him that he may
   play the fool nowhere but in 's own house. Farewell.

OPHELIA O, help him, you sweet heavens!   145

HAMLET If thou dost marry, I'll give thee this plague
   for thy dowry: be thou as chaste as ice, as pure as
   snow, thou shalt not escape calumny. Get thee to a
   nunnery, farewell. Or if thou wilt needs marry,
   marry a fool, for wise men know well enough what   150
   monsters you make of them. To a nunnery, go, and
   quickly too. Farewell.

OPHELIA Heavenly powers, restore him!

HAMLET I have heard of your paintings too, well
   enough. God hath given you one face, and you   155
   make yourselves another. You jig and amble, and
   you lisp; you nickname God's creatures and make

your wantonness your ignorance. Go to, I'll no
more on 't. It hath made me mad. I say we will have
no more marriage. Those that are married already,   160
all but one, shall live. The rest shall keep as they are.
To a nunnery, go.   *He exits.*

OPHELIA
    O, what a noble mind is here o'erthrown!
    The courtier's, soldier's, scholar's, eye, tongue,
        sword,   165
    Th' expectancy and rose of the fair state,
    The glass of fashion and the mold of form,
    Th' observed of all observers, quite, quite down!
    And I, of ladies most deject and wretched,
    That sucked the honey of his musicked vows,   170
    Now see that noble and most sovereign reason,
    Like sweet bells jangled, out of time and harsh;
    That unmatched form and stature of blown youth
    Blasted with ecstasy. O, woe is me
    T' have seen what I have seen, see what I see!   175

RESOURCE #3.5B

Images from *Hamlet*

CAPTION:

CAPTION:

CAPTION:

CAPTION:

CAPTION:

CAPTION:

CAPTION:

CAPTION:

CAPTION:

"This show imports the argument of the play": Turning Language into Action with a Dumb-Show

Here's What Will Happen Today and Why

Today's lesson explores how the language of Shakespeare's text guides movement and how movement can tell its own story. It also introduces students to the historical theater convention of a dumb-show.

Early medieval plays were often performed without the actors speaking, and this tradition continued into the Early Modern period when Shakespeare was writing. They were called dumb-shows, short plays performed without words. Characters in the play mimed what was about to happen, so audiences would be ready for the action when it took place. In Shakespeare's time, the word *dumb* had only one meaning: "without words" or "silent." We don't use that definition for "dumb" anymore; if we could go backward in history, we would call what happens in a dumb-show a "mime" or "pantomime."

The "play-within-a-play" in *Hamlet* is called *The Murder of Gonzago*. The dumb-show that precedes it was well-known. Students will read and perform it, and afterward will compare the text and their performance to King Hamlet's account of his own murder. They will determine how closely the two descriptions mirror each other. They will also explore whether seeing these actions without words has a different impact than reading the words without seeing the actions.

What Will I Need?

- Copies of *Hamlet*'s dumb-show text (3.2.145–156) – **RESOURCE #4.1A**

- Copies of side-by-side dumb-show text and King Hamlet's description of his own death – **RESOURCE #4.1B**

- Props to aid the performance of the dumb-show: maybe crowns, a vial, a shawl, and/or students' creativity?

How Should I Prepare?

- Organize your class into groups of 4–5 students (3 can do in a pinch)

Agenda (~ 45-minute period)

- ❏ Small Group Dumb-show Study and Performance: 20 minutes
- ❏ Dumb-show Reflection: 5 minutes
- ❏ Side-by-side Text Comparison: 15 minutes
- ❏ Closing: 5 minutes

Here's What Students Hear (From You) and (Then What They'll) Do

Part One: Dumb-show Study and Reflection

1. Today, we'll read and perform the "dumb-show," or mime, from the traveling players' performance of *The Murder of Gonzago*. As Ophelia explains in 3.2, in theater of that day, a dumb-show preceded the performance of a play in order to "import the argument," or provide a heads up on the action that would follow. After performing the dumb-show, you'll compare the dumb-show from *The Murder of Gonzago* to King Hamlet's account of his own murder.

2. Organize the class into groups of four (1 narrator, 3 actors).

3. Pass out the script for the *Murder of Gonzago* dumb-show. Give groups 10 minutes to rehearse.

[**TEACHER NOTE:** See how students work out unfamiliar words in the script by themselves, by defining/talking them through together. Observe how they perform those words and phrases, and then talk together about how they determined the definition of the words or phrases.]

4. After all groups have performed, discuss:

   a. What did you *notice* while watching or preparing the performance?

   b. What do you *wonder* after watching or preparing the performance?

Part Two: Text Comparison: Compare Murder Plots

1. Pass out the side-by-side scripts of King Hamlet's death and the dumb-show from *The Murder of Gonzago*.

2. Read King Hamlet's account of his own death by moving from speaker to speaker, changing at each end punctuation mark.

3. Discuss:

   a. What do you notice?

   b. What do you wonder?

   c. Which lines in the dumb-show script and King Hamlet's account of his death share similarities?

   d. How do the two descriptions of the murders differ? In what lines do you see the difference?

   e. What do you think about those similarities and differences?

   f. What is the effect of SEEING the actions that King Hamlet described (as we did with the dumb-show from *The Murder of Gonzago*) rather than HEARING about them?

   g. Claudius calls, "Give me some light, away!" before Hamlet's play is finished. If you were playing Claudius, how would you say that line?

   h. When in your life has it been important to witness something happen rather than hear about it? What effect did that experience have on you?

4. Conclude class with rounds:

    a. I observed . . .

    b. I discovered . . .

    c. I learned . . .

Here's What Just Happened in Class

- Students close-read Shakespeare's text.

- Students collaborated to find movement in Shakespeare's text.

- Students made decisions about a scene performance by assigning movement to Shakespeare's words.

- Students interpreted a scene using evidence from the text.

- Students learned that Claudius was responsible for King Hamlet's murder, and they saw how closely the plot of Hamlet's play as revealed in the dumb-show resembles his father's account of his own murder.

The Dumb-Show:
Hamlet 3.2.145–156

Directions: In your small group, act out the scene described below. During your dumb-show performance, one group member should serve as the narrator and read the script below aloud as the actions are performed by the others.

Enter a King and a Queen, very lovingly, the Queen embracing him and he her. She kneels and makes show of protestation unto him. He takes her up and declines his head upon her neck. He lies him down upon a bank of flowers. She, seeing him asleep, leaves him. Anon	145
comes in another man, takes off his crown, kisses it, pours poison in the sleeper's ears, and leaves him. The Queen returns, finds the King dead, makes passionate action. The poisoner with some three or four come in again, seem to condole with her. The dead body is carried away. The	150
poisoner woos the Queen with gifts. She seems harsh awhile but in the end accepts his love.	155

Side-by-Side Text Versions of King Hamlet's Murder

Dumb-Show 3.2.145–156

Enter a King and a Queen, very lovingly, the
Queen embracing him and he her. She kneels
and makes show of protestation unto him.
He takes her up and declines his head upon
her neck. He lies him down upon a bank of
flowers. She, seeing him asleep, leaves him.
Anon comes in another man, takes off his
crown, kisses it, pours poison in the sleeper's
ears, and leaves him. The Queen returns,
finds the King dead, makes passionate action.
The poisoner with some three or four come
in again, seem to condole with her. The dead
body is carried away. The poisoner woos the
Queen with gifts. She seems harsh awhile but
in the end accepts his love.

King Hamlet's Speech 1.5.49–87

Ay, that incestuous, that adulterate beast,
With witchcraft of his wits, with traitorous gifts— 50
O wicked wit and gifts, that have the power
So to seduce!—won to his shameful lust
The will of my most seeming-virtuous queen.
O Hamlet, what a falling off was there!
From me, whose love was of that dignity 55
That it went hand in hand even with the vow
I made to her in marriage, and to decline
Upon a wretch whose natural gifts were poor
To those of mine. [. . .]
Sleeping within my orchard,
My custom always of the afternoon,
Upon my secure hour thy uncle stole,
With juice of cursèd hebona in a vial
And in the porches of my ears did pour 70
The leprous distilment, whose effect
Holds such an enmity with blood of man
That swift as quicksilver it courses through
The natural gates and alleys of the body,
And with a sudden vigor it doth posset 75
And curd, like eager droppings into milk,
The thin and wholesome blood. So did it mine,
And a most instant tetter barked about,
Most lazar-like, with vile and loathsome crust
All my smooth body. 80
Thus was I, sleeping, by a brother's hand
Of life, of crown, of queen at once dispatched,
Cut off, even in the blossoms of my sin,
Unhouseled, disappointed, unaneled,
No reck'ning made, but sent to my account 85
With all my imperfections on my head.
O horrible, O horrible, most horrible!

Examining Rare Materials in Order to Explore Claudius's "Double Business": *Hamlet* 3.3.40–102

Here's What We're Doing Today and Why

This week is all about directing Shakespeare, and so today we will create a director's promptbook. A promptbook is a Folger Essential because in creating one, a student (and in the theater, a director) pulls together the text with annotations that indicate line cuts, entrances and exits, stage movement, the set, props and costumes, and generally how the scene should be performed. Students will create promptbooks for their final scenes; this one around Claudius's speech is a great learning opportunity.

We will start by taking a look at images of 3 rare *Hamlet* promptbooks from the Folger collection, then exploring Claudius's powerful soliloquy in 3.3. It starts off "O, my offense is rank." Speeches like this one—with lots of contradictions and ambiguity—are made to be put into students' hands! Get out of their way as they show you what they see, and why they see it that way.

Students will read Claudius's soliloquy and manifest their understanding of his character—does he feel guilty? Is he unrepentant?—in the promptbook of his speech, starting with the text and indicating cuts, stage movement, vocal changes, and other performance choices.

What Will I Need?

- Copies of Claudius's speech – **RESOURCE #4.2A**

- Guidelines for creating a promptbook – **RESOURCE #4.2B**

- Images from three rare *Hamlet* promptbooks from the Folger collection to share/ display – **RESOURCE #4.2C**

- Pencils and erasers

How Should I Prepare?

- Make copies of materials

- Review the soliloquy and lesson plan

- Organize the class into pairs and arrange your room to facilitate partner work (desks in pairs or spaces opened up for students to meet and work together)

Agenda (~ 45-minute period)

❏ Introduction: 5 minutes

❏ Read the Scene: 10 minutes

❏ Promptbook: 25 minutes

❏ Reflection: 5 minutes

Here's What Students Hear (From You) and (and Then What They'll) Do

Introduction

1. Let's take a look at these historical images of directors' promptbooks from the Folger collection.

2. What do you notice, and what do you wonder, about these pages?

3. Today, we will create promptbooks for Claudius's 3.3 soliloquy. He delivers this speech after abruptly leaving in the middle of the performance of *The Murder of Gonzago*.

Part One: Read the Scene

Pass out copies of Claudius's soliloquy

1. In pairs, read the text aloud together.

2. Read the text aloud again.

3. Decide together what is happening in the speech and how you think Claudius feels delivering it.

4. Discuss as a class:

   a. How would you summarize this passage in one sentence?

   b. How does Claudius seem to feel about King Hamlet's death? How do you know?

   c. How do you interpret that last couplet of the speech, "My words fly up, my thoughts remain below / Words without thoughts never to heaven go"?

   d. How does language shape the audience's perceptions of Claudius?

Part Two: Make a Promptbook

1. Let's look at the guidelines for creating a promptbook—**RESOURCE #4.2B**—and get busy. I'm going to tell you how much time you have.

2. Once pairs have completed their promptbooks, discuss as a class:

   a. Which line was most difficult to assign an action to? Why?

   b. What is your most inventive direction? What led you to make it?

3. Close out the lesson with rounds:

    a. I noticed . . .

    b I learned . . .

    c. I appreciated . . .

    d. Something I learned about myself . . .

Here's What Just Happened in Class

- Students had a chance to examine digitized versions of rare materials.

- Students pulled together meaning, movement, vocal inflection, and more into a full treatment of the speech.

- Students made collaborative decisions about staging the play without your help.

- Students reflected on how their staging choices impact the audience's interpretation of the scene.

RESOURCE #4.2A

Claudius's Speech, 3.3.40–102

KING

O, my offense is rank, it smells to heaven;   40
It hath the primal eldest curse upon 't,
A brother's murder. Pray can I not,
Though inclination be as sharp as will.
My stronger guilt defeats my strong intent,
And, like a man to double business bound,   45
I stand in pause where I shall first begin
And both neglect. What if this cursèd hand
Were thicker than itself with brother's blood?
Is there not rain enough in the sweet heavens
To wash it white as snow? Whereto serves mercy   50
But to confront the visage of offense?
And what's in prayer but this twofold force,
To be forestallèd ere we come to fall,
Or pardoned being down? Then I'll look up.
My fault is past. But, O, what form of prayer   55
Can serve my turn? "Forgive me my foul murder"?
That cannot be, since I am still possessed
Of those effects for which I did the murder:
My crown, mine own ambition, and my queen.
May one be pardoned and retain th' offense?   60
In the corrupted currents of this world,
Offense's gilded hand may shove by justice,
And oft 'tis seen the wicked prize itself
Buys out the law. But 'tis not so above:
There is no shuffling; there the action lies   65
In his true nature, and we ourselves compelled,
Even to the teeth and forehead of our faults,
To give in evidence. What then? What rests?
Try what repentance can. What can it not?
Yet what can it, when one cannot repent?   70
O wretched state! O bosom black as death!
O limèd soul, that, struggling to be free,
Art more engaged! Help, angels! Make assay.
Bow, stubborn knees, and heart with strings of steel
Be soft as sinews of the newborn babe.   75
All may be well.   *He kneels.*

[Hamlet enters, speaks, and exits.]

KING, *rising*

My words fly up, my thoughts remain below;   101
Words without thoughts never to heaven go.
He exits.

RESOURCE #4.2B

Guidelines on Creating a Promptbook

The transition to sharing and reflection will be facilitated by the teacher.

GROUP TASK

Collaborate to make a promptbook with annotations that show how your group would stage the text. All your choices must be supported by your understanding of the text. Write clear, detailed notes in the margins and on the text marking specific words and lines. Note your group decisions about the elements listed below.

1. **Mood / Tone**
   a. overall
   b. key moments

2. **Acting:** describe what each character is doing
   a. movement (gestures, exits, entrances, facial expressions)
   b. voice (tone, stress, volume)
   c. emotion (nervous, angry, curious, elated, etc.)
   d. nonverbal human sound (laughter, sigh, cry, scream, etc.)

3. **Design:** as simple or involved as time allows
   a. set
   b. costumes and props
   c. lighting
   d. sound effects

Director's Vision: Include in your promptbook a few paragraphs about the group's vision (interpretation) of the scene. Describe how your staging choices reflect the text.

SHARE: At the end, each group will share their promptbooks in short presentations.

REFLECTION ROUND (as done in previous activities):
   I observed . . .
   I learned . . .
   I wonder . . .

RESOURCE #4.2C

Come into the Folger Vault!: Promptbooks in the Folger Collection

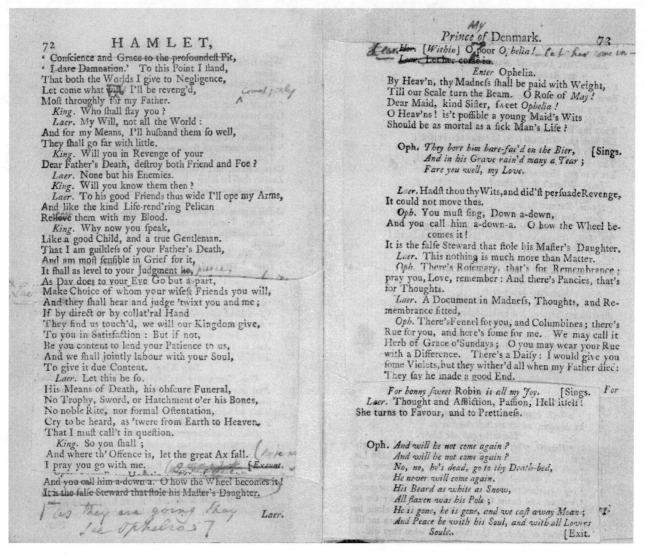

Pages 72 and 73 of a promptbook in the making, from David Garrick's 1747 production of *Hamlet* at the Drury Lane Theatre in London. Garrick was a very famous actor, director, playwright, and theater manager in his day who often rewrote the Shakespeare plays that he produced. From the collection of the Folger Shakespeare Library in Washington, DC.

4

(After Ophelia is in her position, Hamlet looks
up and sees her, slowly rises)
                    Soft you now;
The fair Ophelia;
        (Hamlet indicates an impulse to speak, then to
        escape unobserved. Then changing his mind cross-
        es R and above her)
                    Nymph, in thy orizons
Be all my sins remember'd.

                        Ophelia
        Good, my lord,
        (Ophelia speaks with an assumed indifference)
How does your honour for this many a day?

                        Hamlet
        (Hamlet indicating surprise at Ophelia's tone
        immediately adopts a formal attitude)
I humbly thank you; well,
        (Hamlet turns his head away. Ophelia takes a
        step upstage)
                    well, well
        (Hamlet crosses in front of her down L. Ophelia
        lets the book fall at her side)

                        Ophelia
    My lord, I have remembrances of yours
That I have longed to re-deliver;
I pray you, now receive them.
        (Ophelia offers the casket to Hamlet)

                        Hamlet
        No, not I;
I never gave you aught.

                        Ophelia
    My honour'd Lord, you know right well you did,
And with them words of so sweet breath compos'd
As made the things more rich; their perfume lost,
Take these again, for to the noble mind
Rich gifts wax poor when givers prove unkind.
        (Ophelia places casket directly in front of
        Hamlet)
There, my lord.

                        Hamlet
        (Hamlet takes casket, crosses in front of
        Ophelia to center. She gives a small sob as
        he is R of her, Hamlet suddenly turns to her)
Ha, ha; are you honest?

Page of a promptbook from an early twentieth-century American production of *Hamlet* that played in New York in 1921, and across the United States during this period. E. H. Sothern played Hamlet and Julia Marlowe, Ophelia; they were a popular pair of actors who toured this and other Shakespeare plays. From the collection of the Folger Shakespeare Library in Washington, DC.

The back page and inside back cover of the promptbook from John Barrymore's *Hamlet*, produced in New York in 1922–23, and that moved to London the next year. Barrymore was a very famous actor. This promptbook was put together by Lark Taylor, who, on the lower right-hand page, notes that after the first performance of the play, the director gave him an additional part as well. Noted in detail on the facing page is the choreography for the Hamlet-Laertes fight at the end of the play. From the collection of the Folger Shakespeare Library in Washington, DC.

"Now I'll do it": Determining the What and Where of Hamlet's Words and Locations

Here's What We're Doing Today and Why

In the middle of Claudius's 3.3 soliloquy, Hamlet delivers a soliloquy of his own! Today, students will read Hamlet's 3.3 speech, then compare the speech to others they have heard from Hamlet to see whether or how Hamlet has changed in three acts. They'll also consider how Hamlet's words shape our reception of Claudius's words. They'll dive deep into Hamlet's words by cutting his speeches, and then students will assign a location to each of Hamlet's soliloquies. They will map these locations and defend their choices with evidence from the text, as they must also do with their final scenes.

What Will I Need?

- Printed or projected image from a production of *Hamlet* – **RESOURCE #4.3A**
- Copies of Hamlet's soliloquies – **RESOURCE #4.3B**

How Should I Prepare?

- Make copies of materials
- Organize the class into groups of four and arrange your room for group work

Agenda (~ 45-minute period)

- ❏ Warm-up: 5 minutes
- ❏ Part One: Hamlet's 3.3 speech: 10 minutes
- ❏ Part Two: Speech Cutting and Locating: 25 minutes
- ❏ Part Three: Reflection: 5 minutes

What Students Hear (From You) and (Then What They'll) Do

Warm-up

1. Look at this image from a 2020 production of *Hamlet* – **RESOURCE #4.3A**

   a. What do you notice about this image?

   b. What do you wonder?

   c. Where do you imagine this scene happening?

   d. What does this place look like?

   e. What does it smell like? Sound like? How do you know?

[**TEACHER NOTE:** The image is of actor Ruth Negga as Hamlet, in the Gate Theatre production at St. Ann's Warehouse, New York City.]

    f. The character in the image is Hamlet.

    g. What do you wonder about the image now that you know this information?

    h. What else do you notice as you look at the image again?

    i. Does this Hamlet look like the Hamlet you imagine? Why or why not?

Part One: Speech Study

1. Read Hamlet's 3.3 soliloquy by changing readers at each end punctuation mark.

2. Discuss:

    a. What do you notice? What do you wonder?

    b. What conflicts do you hear in Hamlet's speech?

    c. What decision does Hamlet reach by the end of the speech? How do you react to that decision?

    d. How do you react to Claudius's last couplet ("My words fly up, my thoughts remain below; / Words without thoughts never to heaven go") knowing that Hamlet's speech is delivered before it?

Part Two: Getting Down to Business—Cutting the Text

1. Here are copies of Hamlet's three previous soliloquies – **RESOURCE #4.3B**

2. Organize the class into groups so that at least two groups are assigned to each speech.

3. Work in groups to cut each speech down to the most important five lines. YOU (each group) get to decide what "important" means here; have spirited conversations about which are the most important five lines.

4. Below your cut script, write a brief defense of your group's choice.

5. As a group, select the ideal location for each speech to be delivered. Justify why these are the best locations. Consider:

    a. What sort of places does the language of the passage evoke?

    b. What do these places look like?

    c. What do they smell like? Sound like? How do you know?

6. Once groups have made their cuts, each group will share the five lines they kept for one speech. Compare and contrast the kept lines from the groups that cut the same speeches.

Part Three: Reflection

1. Based on Hamlet's words and choices in his soliloquies, how has he changed over the course of the play so far? Does he surprise you? Why or why not? Use lines from the soliloquies to explain your answer.

2. To conclude, do rounds:
   - I observed . . .
   - I discovered . . .
   - I wondered . . .
   - Something I learned about myself . . .

Here's What Just Happened in Class

- Students analyzed a production image while expanding their view of casting.

- Students made connections between speeches and across scenes to analyze Hamlet's character.

- Students collaborated to cut Shakespeare's text and, in doing so, read the text closely and analyzed (or argued) the value and effects of language.

- Students discovered that a scene can be set in any place and that setting contributes to an interpretation of character and plot.

RESOURCE #4.3A

Hamlet's Four Soliloquies

HAMLET'S 3.3 SPEECH

Now might I do it pat, now he is a-praying,
And now I'll do 't.   *He draws his sword.*
And so he goes to heaven,
And so am I revenged. That would be scanned: 80
A villain kills my father, and for that,
I, his sole son, do this same villain send
To heaven.
Why, this is hire and salary, not revenge.
He took my father grossly, full of bread,   85
With all his crimes broad blown, as flush as May;
And how his audit stands who knows save heaven.
But in our circumstance and course of thought
'Tis heavy with him. And am I then revenged
To take him in the purging of his soul,   90
When he is fit and seasoned for his passage?
No.
Up sword, and know thou a more horrid hent.
                    He sheathes his sword.
When he is drunk asleep, or in his rage,
Or in th' incestuous pleasure of his bed,   95
At game, a-swearing, or about some act
That has no relish of salvation in 't—
Then trip him, that his heels may kick at heaven,
And that his soul may be as damned and black
As hell, whereto it goes. My mother stays.   100
This physic but prolongs thy sickly days.
                    Hamlet exits.

HAMLET'S 1.2 SPEECH

O, that this too, too sullied flesh would melt,
Thaw, and resolve itself into a dew,
Or that the Everlasting had not fixed   135
His canon 'gainst self-slaughter! O God, God,
How weary, stale, flat, and unprofitable
Seem to me all the uses of this world!
Fie on 't, ah fie! 'Tis an unweeded garden
That grows to seed. Things rank and gross in nature   140
Possess it merely. That it should come to this:

But two months dead—nay, not so much, not two.
So excellent a king, that was to this
Hyperion to a satyr; so loving to my mother
That he might not beteem the winds of heaven   145
Visit her face too roughly. Heaven and Earth,
Must I remember? Why, she would hang on him
As if increase of appetite had grown
By what it fed on. And yet, within a month
(Let me not think on 't; frailty, thy name is woman!),   150
A little month, or ere those shoes were old
With which she followed my poor father's body,
Like Niobe, all tears—why she, even she
(O God, a beast that wants discourse of reason
Would have mourned longer!), married with my   155
    uncle,
My father's brother, but no more like my father
Than I to Hercules. Within a month,
Ere yet the salt of most unrighteous tears
Had left the flushing in her gallèd eyes,   160
She married. O, most wicked speed, to post
With such dexterity to incestuous sheets!
It is not, nor it cannot come to good.
But break, my heart, for I must hold my tongue.

HAMLET'S 2.2 SPEECH

Now I am alone.
O, what a rogue and peasant slave am I!
Is it not monstrous that this player here,
But in a fiction, in a dream of passion,
Could force his soul so to his own conceit   580
That from her working all his visage wanned,
Tears in his eyes, distraction in his aspect,
A broken voice, and his whole function suiting
With forms to his conceit—and all for nothing!
For Hecuba!   585
What's Hecuba to him, or he to Hecuba,
That he should weep for her? What would he do
Had he the motive and the cue for passion
That I have? He would drown the stage with tears
And cleave the general ear with horrid speech,   590
Make mad the guilty and appall the free,
Confound the ignorant and amaze indeed
The very faculties of eyes and ears. Yet I,
A dull and muddy-mettled rascal, peak
Like John-a-dreams, unpregnant of my cause,   595
And can say nothing—no, not for a king
Upon whose property and most dear life

A damned defeat was made. Am I a coward?
Who calls me "villain"? breaks my pate across?
Plucks off my beard and blows it in my face?   600
Tweaks me by the nose? gives me the lie i' th' throat
As deep as to the lungs? Who does me this?
Ha! 'Swounds, I should take it! For it cannot be
But I am pigeon-livered and lack gall
To make oppression bitter, or ere this   605
I should have fatted all the region kites
With this slave's offal. Bloody, bawdy villain!
Remorseless, treacherous, lecherous, kindless
    villain!
O vengeance!   610
Why, what an ass am I! This is most brave,
That I, the son of a dear father murdered,
Prompted to my revenge by heaven and hell,
Must, like a whore, unpack my heart with words
And fall a-cursing like a very drab,   615
A stallion! Fie upon 't! Foh!
About, my brains!—Hum, I have heard
That guilty creatures sitting at a play
Have, by the very cunning of the scene,
Been struck so to the soul that presently   620
They have proclaimed their malefactions;
For murder, though it have no tongue, will speak
With most miraculous organ. I'll have these players
Play something like the murder of my father
Before mine uncle. I'll observe his looks;   625
I'll tent him to the quick. If he do blench,
I know my course. The spirit that I have seen
May be a devil, and the devil hath power
T' assume a pleasing shape; yea, and perhaps,
Out of my weakness and my melancholy,   630
As he is very potent with such spirits,
Abuses me to damn me. I'll have grounds
More relative than this. The play's the thing
Wherein I'll catch the conscience of the King.
                                                    He exits.

HAMLET'S 3.1 SPEECH

To be or not to be—that is the question:
Whether 'tis nobler in the mind to suffer   65
The slings and arrows of outrageous fortune,
Or to take arms against a sea of troubles
And, by opposing, end them. To die, to sleep—
No more—and by a sleep to say we end
The heartache and the thousand natural shocks   70

That flesh is heir to—'tis a consummation
Devoutly to be wished. To die, to sleep—
To sleep, perchance to dream. Ay, there's the rub,
For in that sleep of death what dreams may come,
When we have shuffled off this mortal coil,   75
Must give us pause. There's the respect
That makes calamity of so long life.
For who would bear the whips and scorns of time,
Th' oppressor's wrong, the proud man's contumely,
The pangs of despised love, the law's delay,   80
The insolence of office, and the spurns
That patient merit of th' unworthy takes,
When he himself might his quietus make
With a bare bodkin? Who would fardels bear,
To grunt and sweat under a weary life,   85
But that the dread of something after death,
The undiscovered country from whose bourn
No traveler returns, puzzles the will
And makes us rather bear those ills we have
Than fly to others that we know not of?   90
Thus conscience does make cowards of us all,
And thus the native hue of resolution
Is sicklied o'er with the pale cast of thought,
And enterprises of great pitch and moment
With this regard their currents turn awry   95
And lose the name of action.—Soft you now,
The fair Ophelia.—Nymph, in thy orisons
Be all my sins remembered.

WEEK FOUR: LESSONS 4 + 5

Performing *Hamlet* 3.4 in Relay: "Words like daggers"

Lesson 4: Introduction and Rehearsal
Lesson 5: Performance

Here's What We're Doing Today and Why

We're moving toward preparation and performance of final scenes, so now is a good time to revisit the cold-reading and collaborative staging that takes place in the 3D Lit Essential. At the beginning of this unit, your students put a fresh scene on its feet with just a little guidance from you; now, it's time to revisit the strategy so that they can get busy and you can get out of the way.

Today, students will perform 3.4 in relay: They'll break this long scene into smaller pieces and each small group will perform a section, passing along a costume like a relay baton from one Hamlet, Gertrude, Polonius, and King Hamlet to the next. Think of this relay as a test run for the final performance project. As you observe groups at work, ask yourself: Which skills (close-reading, cutting, line tossing, making a promptbook) can students perform on their own? Which skills might need to be revisited before final performance work begins?

[**TEACHER NOTE:** Be sure to check out your own homework assignment for next week at the end of this lesson. We've also included it in the first lesson next week too—**RESOURCE #5.1A.**]

What Will I Need?

- Texts for each performance group – **RESOURCE #4.4**

  Do you need more roles or scenes? Discover the free, online Folger Shakespeare (folger.edu/shakespeares-works) to find scenes—maybe 4.5, when Ophelia sings to the court?

- Some props and costumes that will serve as your relay "batons." (Examples: a tiara for Gertrude, a sword for Hamlet, a sash for Polonius, a crown for the ghost, or everyday items that could be used creatively!)

How Should I Prepare?

- Organize the class into small groups as indicated on the relay scripts
- Make copies of the scripts for the small groups

Agenda (~ TWO class periods)

Lesson 4 (one 45-minute period)

- ❑ Warm-up: 5 minutes
- ❑ Small group study and rehearsal: 40 minutes

Lesson 5 (one 45-minute period)

- ❑ Quick Rehearsal and Get Organized: 10 minutes
- ❑ Performance: 30 minutes
- ❑ Wrap-up Reflection: 5 minutes

Here's What Students Hear (From You) and (Then What They'll) Do

Lesson 4: Warm-up

1. Think, from Gertrude's perspective, of all that has happened in the play so far. She has lost her husband, married a new husband, wondered what is making her son behave so strangely, and watched a performance of a play that closely mirrored her quick marriage. Her husband interrupted and ended that performance in the middle of a scene!

2. Write a brief diary entry from Gertrude. She hasn't had a lot to say in the play, but what might she be thinking about all that she has witnessed?

3. Share your diary entries.

Lesson 4: Preparation for the Relay!

1. Get into small groups and I'll pass out the relay text to each group. The texts are your plays. Your assignment is that you as a group will read your scene, you'll cut the number of lines in half, you'll make a promptbook, and you'll rehearse your plays and then perform them tomorrow.

2. Use the techniques we have been using all along. Read the passage end-punctuation to end-punctuation.

3. Work together to determine what's going on and what's being expressed.

4. Work together to cut the number of lines in half.

5. Groups cast the parts. Make decisions about how to move based on the words on the page. Pull all of this together into a promptbook.

6. Rehearse.

Lesson 5: Quick Rehearsal and Get Organized

1. Each group will have 20 minutes to rehearse.

2. Determine the order before you start, so you'll know who you follow.

Lesson 5: Performance!

Start with 3.4.1–25 and carry on from there. Use the costume "batons" to help the audience follow the characters from scene to scene. As each group finishes, applaud wildly!

Lesson 5: Wrap-up Reflection

1. Conclude with some questions:

   a. If Gertrude wrote another diary entry after this scene, how might she reflect on what just happened?

   b. What did you discover?

   c. What did it make you think about?

   d. What did you learn about Hamlet from performing and watching this scene?

   e. What did you learn about Gertrude?

   f. What did you learn about yourselves?

Here's What Just Happened in These Two Classes

- Students collaborated to cut their scene and stage it.

- Students demonstrated understanding of the characters, dialogue, and conflict through performance.

- Students saw and demonstrated how grief affects family members differently.

- Students saw Hamlet kill Polonius, an action that will complicate his relationships with everyone in the play.

In anticipation of next week, teacher's homework: **RESOURCE #5.1A** at the end of this lesson!

RESOURCE #4.4

Scripts for *Hamlet* Relay

3.4.1–25 (three actors)

Enter Queen and Polonius.

POLONIUS
 He will come straight. Look you lay home to him.
 Tell him his pranks have been too broad to bear
  with
 And that your Grace hath screened and stood
  between   5
 Much heat and him. I'll silence me even here.
 Pray you, be round with him.

HAMLET, *within* Mother, mother, mother!

QUEEN I'll warrant you. Fear me not. Withdraw,
 I hear him coming.   10
          Polonius hides behind the arras.
          Enter Hamlet.

HAMLET Now, mother, what's the matter?

QUEEN
 Hamlet, thou hast thy father much offended.

HAMLET
 Mother, you have my father much offended.

QUEEN
 Come, come, you answer with an idle tongue.

HAMLET
 Go, go, you question with a wicked tongue.   15

QUEEN
 Why, how now, Hamlet?

HAMLET What's the matter now?

QUEEN
 Have you forgot me?

HAMLET No, by the rood, not so.
> You are the Queen, your husband's brother's wife,   20
> And (would it were not so) you are my mother.

QUEEN
> Nay, then I'll set those to you that can speak.

HAMLET
> Come, come, and sit you down; you shall not budge.
> You go not till I set you up a glass
> Where you may see the inmost part of you.   25

3.4.26–60 (3 actors)

QUEEN
> What wilt thou do? Thou wilt not murder me?
> Help, ho!

POLONIUS, *behind the arras* What ho! Help!

HAMLET
> How now, a rat? Dead for a ducat, dead.
>> *He kills Polonius by thrusting a rapier*
>> *through the arras.*

POLONIUS, *behind the arras*
> O, I am slain!   30

QUEEN O me, what hast thou done?

HAMLET Nay, I know not. Is it the King?

QUEEN
> O, what a rash and bloody deed is this!

HAMLET
> A bloody deed—almost as bad, good mother,
> As kill a king and marry with his brother.   35

QUEEN
> As kill a king?

HAMLET Ay, lady, it was my word.
>> *He pulls Polonius's body from behind the arras.*
> Thou wretched, rash, intruding fool, farewell.
> I took thee for thy better. Take thy fortune.
> Thou find'st to be too busy is some danger.   40

To Queen. Leave wringing of your hands. Peace, sit
  you down,
And let me wring your heart; for so I shall
If it be made of penetrable stuff,
If damnèd custom have not brazed it so   45
That it be proof and bulwark against sense.

QUEEN
What have I done, that thou dar'st wag thy tongue
In noise so rude against me?

HAMLET Such an act
That blurs the grace and blush of modesty,   50
Calls virtue hypocrite, takes off the rose
From the fair forehead of an innocent love
And sets a blister there, makes marriage vows
As false as dicers' oaths—O, such a deed
As from the body of contraction plucks   55
The very soul, and sweet religion makes
A rhapsody of words! Heaven's face does glow
O'er this solidity and compound mass
With heated visage, as against the doom,
Is thought-sick at the act.   60

3.4.61–105 (2 actors)

QUEEN Ay me, what act
That roars so loud and thunders in the index?

HAMLET
Look here upon this picture and on this,
The counterfeit presentment of two brothers.
See what a grace was seated on this brow,   65
Hyperion's curls, the front of Jove himself,
An eye like Mars' to threaten and command,
A station like the herald Mercury
New-lighted on a heaven-kissing hill,
A combination and a form indeed   70
Where every god did seem to set his seal
To give the world assurance of a man.
This was your husband. Look you now what follows.
Here is your husband, like a mildewed ear
Blasting his wholesome brother. Have you eyes?   75
Could you on this fair mountain leave to feed
And batten on this moor? Ha! Have you eyes?
You cannot call it love, for at your age

The heyday in the blood is tame, it's humble
And waits upon the judgment; and what judgment 80
Would step from this to this? Sense sure you have,
Else could you not have motion; but sure that sense
Is apoplexed; for madness would not err,
Nor sense to ecstasy was ne'er so thralled,
But it reserved some quantity of choice 85
To serve in such a difference. What devil was 't
That thus hath cozened you at hoodman-blind?
Eyes without feeling, feeling without sight,
Ears without hands or eyes, smelling sans all,
Or but a sickly part of one true sense 90
Could not so mope. O shame, where is thy blush?
Rebellious hell,
If thou canst mutine in a matron's bones,
To flaming youth let virtue be as wax
And melt in her own fire. Proclaim no shame 95
When the compulsive ardor gives the charge,
Since frost itself as actively doth burn,
And reason panders will.

QUEEN O Hamlet, speak no more!
   Thou turn'st my eyes into my very soul, 100
   And there I see such black and grainèd spots
   As will not leave their tinct.

HAMLET Nay, but to live
   In the rank sweat of an enseamèd bed,
   Stewed in corruption, honeying and making love 105
   Over the nasty sty!

3.4.106–148 (3 actors)

QUEEN O, speak to me no more!
   These words like daggers enter in my ears.
   No more, sweet Hamlet!

HAMLET A murderer and a villain, 110
   A slave that is not twentieth part the tithe
   Of your precedent lord; a vice of kings,
   A cutpurse of the empire and the rule,
   That from a shelf the precious diadem stole
   And put it in his pocket— 115

QUEEN No more!

HAMLET A king of shreds and patches—

Enter Ghost.

Save me and hover o'er me with your wings,
You heavenly guards!—What would your gracious
　　figure?   120

QUEEN Alas, he's mad.

HAMLET

Do you not come your tardy son to chide,
That, lapsed in time and passion, lets go by
Th' important acting of your dread command?
O, say!   125

GHOST Do not forget. This visitation

Is but to whet thy almost blunted purpose.
But look, amazement on thy mother sits.
O, step between her and her fighting soul.
Conceit in weakest bodies strongest works.   130
Speak to her, Hamlet.

HAMLET How is it with you, lady?

QUEEN Alas, how is 't with you,

That you do bend your eye on vacancy
And with th' incorporal air do hold discourse?   135
Forth at your eyes your spirits wildly peep,
And, as the sleeping soldiers in th' alarm,
Your bedded hair, like life in excrements,
Start up and stand an end. O gentle son,
Upon the heat and flame of thy distemper   140
Sprinkle cool patience! Whereon do you look?

HAMLET

On him, on him! Look you how pale he glares.
His form and cause conjoined, preaching to stones,
Would make them capable. *To the Ghost.* Do not
　　look upon me,   145
Lest with this piteous action you convert
My stern effects. Then what I have to do
Will want true color—tears perchance for blood.

3.4.149–176 (3 actors)

QUEEN To whom do you speak this?

HAMLET Do you see nothing there?   150

QUEEN
  Nothing at all; yet all that is I see.

HAMLET Nor did you nothing hear?

QUEEN No, nothing but ourselves.

HAMLET
  Why, look you there, look how it steals away!
  My father, in his habit as he lived!   155
  Look where he goes even now out at the portal!
                                 Ghost exits.

QUEEN
  This is the very coinage of your brain.
  This bodiless creation ecstasy
  Is very cunning in.

HAMLET Ecstasy?   160
  My pulse as yours doth temperately keep time
  And makes as healthful music. It is not madness
  That I have uttered. Bring me to the test,
  And I the matter will reword, which madness
  Would gambol from. Mother, for love of grace,   165
  Lay not that flattering unction to your soul
  That not your trespass but my madness speaks.
  It will but skin and film the ulcerous place,
  Whiles rank corruption, mining all within,
  Infects unseen. Confess yourself to heaven,   170
  Repent what's past, avoid what is to come,
  And do not spread the compost on the weeds
  To make them ranker. Forgive me this my virtue,
  For, in the fatness of these pursy times,
  Virtue itself of vice must pardon beg,   175
  Yea, curb and woo for leave to do him good.

3.4.177–202 (2 actors)

QUEEN

    O Hamlet, thou hast cleft my heart in twain!

HAMLET

    O, throw away the worser part of it,
    And live the purer with the other half!
    Good night. But go not to my uncle's bed.   180
    Assume a virtue if you have it not.
    That monster, custom, who all sense doth eat,
    Of habits devil, is angel yet in this,
    That to the use of actions fair and good
    He likewise gives a frock or livery   185
    That aptly is put on. Refrain tonight,
    And that shall lend a kind of easiness
    To the next abstinence, the next more easy;
    For use almost can change the stamp of nature
    And either . . . the devil or throw him out   190
    With wondrous potency. Once more, good night,
    And, when you are desirous to be blest,
    I'll blessing beg of you. For this same lord
                              Pointing to Polonius.
    I do repent; but heaven hath pleased it so
    To punish me with this and this with me,   195
    That I must be their scourge and minister.
    I will bestow him and will answer well
    The death I gave him. So, again, good night.
    I must be cruel only to be kind.
    This bad begins, and worse remains behind.   200
    One word more, good lady.

QUEEN What shall I do?

3.4.203–End (2 actors)

HAMLET

    Not this by no means that I bid you do:
    Let the bloat king tempt you again to bed,
    Pinch wanton on your cheek, call you his mouse,   205
    And let him, for a pair of reechy kisses
    Or paddling in your neck with his damned fingers,
    Make you to ravel all this matter out
    That I essentially am not in madness,

But mad in craft. 'Twere good you let him know,   210
For who that's but a queen, fair, sober, wise,
Would from a paddock, from a bat, a gib,
Such dear concernings hide? Who would do so?
No, in despite of sense and secrecy,
Unpeg the basket on the house's top,   215
Let the birds fly, and like the famous ape,
To try conclusions, in the basket creep
And break your own neck down.

QUEEN
Be thou assured, if words be made of breath
And breath of life, I have no life to breathe   220
What thou hast said to me.

HAMLET
I must to England, you know that.

QUEEN Alack,
I had forgot! 'Tis so concluded on.

HAMLET
There's letters sealed; and my two schoolfellows,   225
Whom I will trust as I will adders fanged,
They bear the mandate; they must sweep my way
And marshal me to knavery. Let it work,
For 'tis the sport to have the enginer
Hoist with his own petard; and 't shall go hard   230
But I will delve one yard below their mines
And blow them at the moon. O, 'tis most sweet
When in one line two crafts directly meet.
This man shall set me packing.
I'll lug the guts into the neighbor room.   235
Mother, good night indeed. This counselor
Is now most still, most secret, and most grave,
Who was in life a foolish prating knave.—
Come, sir, to draw toward an end with you.—
Good night, mother.   240
        They exit, Hamlet lugging in Polonius.

RESOURCE #5.1A

Teacher's Overview

Introducing the Final Week and the Final Project: Make *Hamlet* Your Own

The Final Project's Learning Goals

This project is the culmination of everything your students have been doing all unit long. Students will work in groups to make a scene from *Hamlet* entirely their own, demonstrating all that they have learned during this unit.
By the end of this project every student will have:

- Pulled together all the pieces of this unit, particularly essential practices like cutting a scene, creating a promptbook and 3D Lit , in order to get inside of and create a scene from Act 4 or 5 of *Hamlet*.

- Moved collaboratively through a complex process of reading, rereading, editing, adapting, embodying, imagining, reediting, rehearsing, performing, deciding, and defending.

- Used the text to make choices about how to edit, adapt, and stage the scene.

- Performed their original interpretation of their *Hamlet* scene for an audience.

- Written and presented a group rationale for the text-based decisions that led to this performance (edits, additions, staging, etc.).

- Written a brief personal reflection on the experience of completing this project.

- Grappled with the whole play (Acts 1–5) through work in class up to now and collaborative group work on Acts 4 and 5 this week.

Both the students and you, the teacher, should walk away with resounding evidence that everyone in your class can make meaning from Shakespeare's language—from complex texts—on their own.

Advice and Reminders

These final projects are the unit exam.

Time. This learning experience is designed to take roughly 5 class periods of 45 minutes each. However, depending on your teaching context, it might take a longer or shorter time. For example, this plan is written with one day for final performances, but if you need more time and have the time, take more time!

Chaos. Since it's all about turning the language and the learning over to the students, you can expect the process to get somewhat messy and noisy. As long as students are making *their own way* through their scenes, it's all good. As you have been doing right along, resist the urge to explain the text to your students. Trust the process—and trust your students to ask questions, find answers, create interpretations, and make meaning on their own, as they have been. (If they don't do this, then they're missing the project.) Throughout this process and this week, students are tracking their cutting, adding, promptbooking decisions and preparing to present, along with their scene performance, an oral defense of their key decisions.

Time and Less Chaos. It works out best if you can decide how much time your schedule allows you for the final performances and scene rationales on the final day of the project. Then work backward to schedule your groups within that time.

An example: If you have 45 minutes of class time and 20 students, you might have 5 performing groups with 4 students each. That could mean each group would have 7–8 minutes to share their work (their performance + the defense of their decisions). 8 minutes x 5 groups = 40 minutes, leaving 5 minutes for a whole-class reflection round. If this feels tight to you, give each group 7 minutes.

Flexibility and Creativity. You'll see that on the menu of scenes for this project, some scenes involve more than 4 actors, and some fewer than 4. Students will add their own creativity to the mix by double-casting parts or using other means to make sure there is full participation.

For You, Suggested Guidance on Assessing the Projects: A Seven-Point Checklist

1. Does the performance demonstrate a grasp of what the characters are saying and wanting?

2. Does the performance make strategic use of voice and body to convey effective tone and feeling?

3. Does the defense summarize the scene clearly, concisely, and accurately?

4. Does the defense comment on the scene's importance in the overall play and our world today?

5. Does the defense justify key decisions to cut, add, and perform language in this particular way? Is there strong and relevant textual evidence for this performance overall?

6. Does the defense describe how this process shaped new or different understandings of this play?

7. Does the personal reflection consider specific things that the student has learned, contributed, and discovered?

WEEK FIVE: LESSON 1

Your Final Projects!

Here's What We're Doing This Week and Why

Today kicks off the culminating project, the student-driven process of making Shakespeare thoroughly their own, by collaborating on creating for each other the last acts of *Hamlet.* By the end of this lesson, students will understand what's expected of them and why—both as individuals and as project groups. They will also have gathered with their group mates and their assigned scene for this project. Although we've divided the final project into 5 days, it's really one unified, cumulative process, so please **make whatever pacing adjustments your students need.** Different groups might be at different steps of the process on different days, and that's okay.

What Will I Need?

- Final Project: Teacher Overview – **RESOURCE #5.1A** (Perhaps you got an early start and have read this already!)

- Final Project: Student Overview and Assignment – **RESOURCE #5.1B**

- The menu of *Hamlet* scenes for you to assign from, or for groups to choose from – **RESOURCE #5.1C**

How Should I Prepare?

- Make copies of the student overview and assignment for everyone in class.

- Make a plan for grouping students.

- Make a plan for matching groups to scenes. (It's up to you whether you want to assign them scenes that you feel are key to the play or allow them to make their own choices.)

- Figure out how much time students will have for their scenes and their defense so you can let them know today (see Teacher Overview, **RESOURCE #5.1A**).

- Prepare yourself to get out of the way and let students figure things out on their own. You're assessing their ability to do exactly that.

Agenda (~ 45-minute period)

- ❏ Intro to the assignment and scene menu: 20 minutes
- ❏ Groups meet for the first time: 25 minutes

Here's What Students Hear (From You) and (Then What They'll) Do

Part One: Project Introduction

1. Give students the project assignment.

2. Check for understanding with reflection rounds:

   a. I notice . . .

   b. I wonder . . .

3. Assign scenes, answer any wonderings, and fill in any details that students missed.

Part Two: Group Work

Students work in their groups and get started!

Here's What Just Happened in Class

- Students met their final project and started working in groups to tackle the assignment!

- Every student read out loud some *Hamlet* new to them as groups started to befriend their scenes.

RESOURCE #5.1A

Teacher's Overview

Introducing the Final Week and the Final Project: Make *Hamlet* Your Own

The Final Project's Learning Goals

This project is the culmination of everything your students have been doing all unit long. Students will work in groups to make a scene from *Hamlet* entirely their own, demonstrating all that they have learned during this unit.

By the end of this project every student will have:

- Pulled together all the pieces of this unit, particularly essential practices like cutting a scene, creating a promptbook, and 3D Lit, in order to get inside of and create a scene from Act 4 or 5 of *Hamlet*.

- Moved collaboratively through a complex process of reading, rereading, editing, adapting, embodying, imagining, reediting, rehearsing, performing, deciding, and defending.

- Used the text to make choices about how to edit, adapt, and stage the scene.

- Performed their original interpretation of their *Hamlet* scene for an audience.

- Written and presented a group rationale for the text-based decisions that led to this performance (edits, additions, staging, etc.).

- Written a brief personal reflection on the experience of completing this project.

- Grappled with the whole play (Acts 1–5) through work in class up to now and collaborative work on Acts 4 and 5 this week.

Both the students and you, the teacher, should walk away with resounding evidence that everyone in your class can make meaning from Shakespeare's language—from complex texts—on their own.

Advice and Reminders

Time. This learning experience is designed to take roughly 5 class periods of 45 minutes each. However, depending on your teaching context, it might take a longer or shorter time. For example, this plan is written with one day for final performances, but if you need more time and have the time, take more time!

Chaos. Since it's all about turning the language and the learning over to the students, you can expect the process to get somewhat messy and noisy. As long as students are making *their own way* through their scenes, it's all good. As you have been doing right along, resist the urge to explain the text to your students. Trust the process—and trust your students to ask questions, find answers, create interpretations, and make meaning on their own, as they have been. (If they don't do this, then they're missing all of this juicy learning.) Throughout this process and this week, students are tracking their cutting, adding, promptbooking decisions and preparing to present, along with their scene performance, an oral defense of their key decisions.

Time and Less Chaos. It works out best if you can decide how much time your schedule allows you for the final performances and scene rationales on the final day of the project. Then work backward to schedule your groups within that time.

An example: If you have 45 minutes of class time and 20 students, you might have 5 performing groups each with 4 students each. That could mean that each group would have 7–8 minutes to share their work (their performance + the defense of their decisions). 8 minutes x 5 groups = 40 minutes, leaving 5 minutes for a whole-class reflection round. If this feels tight to you, give each group 7 minutes.

Flexibility and Creativity. You'll see that on the menu of scenes for this project, some scenes involve more than 4 actors, and some fewer than 3 actors. Students will add their own creativity to the mix by double-casting parts, or using other means to make sure they have full participation.

Suggested Guidance on Assessing the Projects: A Seven-Point Checklist

1. Does the performance demonstrate a grasp of what the characters are saying and wanting?

2. Does the performance make strategic use of voice and body to convey effective tone and feeling?

3. Does the defense summarize the scene clearly, concisely, and accurately?

4. Does the defense comment on the scene's importance in the overall play and our world today?

5. Does the defense justify key decisions to cut, add, and perform language in this particular way? Is there strong and relevant textual evidence for this performance overall?

6. Does the defense describe how this process shaped new or different understandings of this play?

7. Does the personal reflection consider specific things that the student has learned, contributed, and discovered?

RESOURCE #5.1B

Student's Overview and Assignment

Introducing the Final Week and the Final Project: Make *Hamlet* Your Own

You will work in groups to make a scene from Act 4 or Act 5 of *Hamlet* entirely your own. This project is the culmination of everything you have been doing all unit long, and you will be demonstrating all that you have learned this week!

By the end of this project, you will have:

- Put together all the pieces of this unit, particularly essential practices like cutting a scene, creating a promptbook, and 3D Lit in order to get inside of and create a scene from Act 4 or 5 of *Hamlet*. The end of *Hamlet*!

- Moved collaboratively through a complex process of reading, rereading, editing, adapting, embodying, imagining, re-editing, rehearsing, performing, deciding, and defending.

- Used the text to make choices about how to edit, adapt, and stage the scene.

- Performed your original interpretation of the scene for an audience.

- Written and presented a group rationale for the text-based decisions that led to this performance (edits, additions, staging, etc.).

- Written a brief personal reflection on the experience of completing this project.

- Grappled with the whole play (Acts 1–5) through work in class up to now and collaborative work on Acts 4 and 5 this week.

You, your classmates, and your teacher will walk away with resounding evidence that YOU can make meaning from Shakespeare's language—from complex texts—on your own.

What You Will Produce

1. A performed scene from Act 4 or Act 5 of *Hamlet* (in a group)

2. A defense of your scene, delivered orally and in writing (in a group)

3. A personal reflection on this project (from you, as an individual)

Your Action Steps

1. **Get your group and scene assignment** from your teacher.

2. Next, before anything else: with your group, **dive deeply into your scene**. Read it out loud as a group, just as we have done in class. Take notes on all of this—these will come in handy later. Collaboratively as a group, figure out

    - what's happening in the scene
    - what the characters are saying
    - what each of the characters wants
    - why the scene is important in the play
    - why someone should care about this scene today

3. Next, **consider the end goal**: Your group is making a scene of **X** minutes and an oral defense of the scene that is no longer than **X** minutes. Your teacher will tell you the timing that you—like any group of actors—must work with. Keep this in mind as you work through the scene.

4. Next, work to **be directors and put the scene on its feet**. Each member of the group should be **creating a promptbook** for the scene along the way so that you're all working from the same script with the same notes. Together, make—and note—decisions about the following and be prepared to explain to your audience what in the text (and in your personal experience of reading it) motivated you to cut, add, and perform as you did.

    - **Cutting the scene.** Perhaps you must cut it so that it fits your time limit and still makes sense. What must stay? What can go?

    - **Locating the scene.** Where is it happening? What does this place look like? Feel like? Smell like? Sound like? How do you know this?

    - **Adding to the scene.** You may want to choose one to two outside texts to mash up with your scene. If you do, what is gained by putting these texts into your Shakespeare scene? What made you choose this/these text(s)? Why and where do they work best? If you choose to add outside texts, be sure that at least 80 percent of your scene is *Hamlet*.

    - **Getting ready to perform the scene.** Cast the parts. Which of you plays whom? Every group member must speak. What does each character want and think and feel? How can the audience tell? Who is moving where on what line, and why? Get on your feet and start moving because some of these questions are answered when you get a scene on its feet. As you know, this is not about acting talent; it is about knowing what you are saying and doing as you bring life to this scene.

    - As you go, you're documenting your decisions and preparing your oral defense of the scene. What are the most significant or original decisions your group made? What drove those decisions? Let the audience in to your interpretive process, your minds, ever so concisely. Your defense should involve every group member and do the following:
        - Summarize your scene
        - Comment on the scene's importance in the overall play

- Justify your cutting, adding, and performing choices with textual evidence
- Conclude by describing how the process of preparing this performance shaped new or different understandings of *Hamlet*

5. **Rehearse**. Yes, you should memorize your lines, though you can ask someone to serve as your prompter, as we think Shakespeare's company might have. Repeat: This is not about acting talent.

6. **Perform your scene and present your scene rationale** during your scheduled class period. After your performance, present your rationale for your scene. As with your performance, every group member must speak. Focus on just the most significant decisions and stick to your time limit. We will all watch the final project scenes together so that we can celebrate wrapping up *Hamlet* with YOUR voices.

7. At that time, you will **submit the 2 written documents**:
   - The written version of your group's defense of your scene.
   - An individual reflection (400–500 words) reflecting on the experience—both the process and what you feel were your own contributions to the project.

Menu: Juicy Act 4 and Act 5 Scenes From *Hamlet*

Act & Scenes	Lines	# of Characters
4.2	all	3
4.3	all	3
4.7	122–186	2
5.1	119–223	3
5.1	224–319	6
5.2	209–285	5–6
5.2	286–end of play	5–6

WEEK FIVE: LESSONS 2, 3, AND 4

Your Final Project: Making *Hamlet* Your Own

Here's What We're Doing and Why

We're here! Groups are making their way through the final project this week. They are working on scenes from Acts 4 and 5, demonstrating as they go what they have learned in terms of making the language, characters, and action their own—all infused with their own energy and creativity. They are also presenting Acts 4 and 5 to each other as we wrap up *Hamlet*.

Agenda for Lessons 2, 3, and 4 (~ THREE 45-minute periods)

Lesson 2:

❏ Introduction/Warm-up: 10 minutes

❏ Cutting the Scene/Group Work: 35 minutes

Lesson 3:

❏ Introduction: 10 minutes

❏ Promptbook the newly edited scene and add outside texts if you choose to/ Group Work: 35 minutes

Lesson 4:

❏ Frozen Scenes/Warm-up – **RESOURCE #5.4**: 10 minutes

❏ Rehearsing the scene and writing the scene rationale/Group Work: 35 minutes

What Will I Need for These Lessons?

- Some print copies of the Folger Shakespeare edition of the play for student reference

- A few dictionaries or Shakespeare glossaries for student reference

- Space and time for students to make their way through this project

- Strength to resist the urge to explain or interpret the text for students (you're a pro by now)

- Access to outside books, songs, poems, films, etc., if they choose to add outside material to their scene

- A discreet eye to observe students as they work

How Should I Prepare for These Lessons?

- As long as every student understands the task at hand, you're good. Students are doing the hard work now!

Lesson 2: Here's What Students Hear (From You) and (Then What They'll) Do

Part One: Introduction/Warm-up

1. Choose your favorite line from your scene.

2. Count off by 4. Meet with the other students with the same number.

3. Toss your lines in a circle; everyone should say their line three times. (Say it differently each time!)

4. Discuss as a class: Given the lines you heard in your circle, what do you think is happening in the scenes you all are performing? Which delivery of your line felt like the best fit for your character or scene? Why?

Part Two: Cutting the Scene/Group Work

Groups are reading, rereading, and cutting their final scenes. They are also cooperating to compose a rationale for their unique performance of the scene. For a closer look at the steps in this process, please refer to the Student's Overview and Assignment—**RESOURCE #5.1B.**

[**TEACHER NOTE:** Students typically need to take this work home with them, especially the 2 writing tasks: the group rationale and the personal reflection. Check in with your students during each class period to see where they are in the process, and help them set realistic goals for homework and classwork.]

Lesson 3: Here's What Students Hear (From You) and (Then What They'll) Do

Part One: Introduction/Warm-up

1. In your groups, agree on a song that best represents your scene.

2. Discuss with your small group. Share with the class.

Part Two: Group Work

Groups are cutting, adapting, promptbooking, and rehearsing their final scenes. If they are including an outside text(s) they should decide what and how today. For a closer look at the steps in this process, please refer to the Student's Overview and Assignment—**RESOURCE #5.1B.**

Once again, check in with your students during period to see where they are in the process, and help them set realistic goals for homework and classwork and ensure that they have a plan to complete the 2 writing tasks.

Lesson 4: Here's What Students Hear (From You) and (Then What They'll) Do

Part One: Frozen Scenes/Warm-up

1. Pass out a frozen scene text to each group—**RESOURCE #5.4.** These frozen scenes will wrap up Ophelia's plot.

2. Groups have five minutes to read the text and create a "frozen scene," one frame of a dumb-show to represent the action described. Then, they should select one line to caption their frozen scene.

3. Gather the class back together; each group will freeze in their formation and say their line.

4. Discuss in groups: What did you notice about Ophelia in these scenes? What do you wonder about her? How did the language of the text lead you to arrange your "frozen scene"?

Part Two: Rehearsing the scene and writing the scene rationale/Group Work

Groups are rehearsing their final scenes. They are also cooperating to compose a rationale for their unique performance of their scene. For a closer look at the steps in this process, please refer to the Student's Overview and Assignment—**RESOURCE #5.1B.**

Students typically need to work at home on these, especially the two writing tasks: the group rationale and the personal reflection. Check in with your students each class to see where they are in the process, and help them set realistic goals for homework and classwork.

Here's What Just Happened in These Three Classes

- You observed a class full of students in a state of flow, deeply engaged in the process of making a scene from *Hamlet* their own!

- You watched peers help one another by asking good questions, building comprehension, citing textual evidence, and encouraging creativity.

RESOURCE #5.4

Ophelia's Frozen Scenes

FROZEN SCENE #1

Ophelia's Description of Hamlet's Visit to Her Chambers: 2.1.95–175

OPHELIA

My lord, as I was sewing in my closet,
Lord Hamlet, with his doublet all unbraced,
No hat upon his head, his stockings fouled,
Ungartered, and down-gyvèd to his ankle,   90
Pale as his shirt, his knees knocking each other,
And with a look so piteous in purport
As if he had been loosèd out of hell
To speak of horrors—he comes before me.
[. . .]
He took me by the wrist and held me hard.
Then goes he to the length of all his arm,   100
And, with his other hand thus o'er his brow,
He falls to such perusal of my face
As he would draw it. Long stayed he so.
At last, a little shaking of mine arm,
And thrice his head thus waving up and down,   105
He raised a sigh so piteous and profound
As it did seem to shatter all his bulk
And end his being. That done, he lets me go,
And, with his head over his shoulder turned,
He seemed to find his way without his eyes,   110
For out o' doors he went without their helps
And to the last bended their light on me.

FROZEN SCENE #2

A member of the court describes Ophelia's reaction to Polonius's death: 4.5.5–16

GENTLEMAN

[Ophelia] speaks much of her father, says she hears   5
There's tricks i' th' world, and hems, and beats her
    heart,
Spurns enviously at straws, speaks things in doubt
That carry but half sense. Her speech is nothing,
Yet the unshapèd use of it doth move   10
The hearers to collection. They aim at it
And botch the words up fit to their own thoughts;

Which, as her winks and nods and gestures yield
   them,
Indeed would make one think there might be   15
   thought,
Though nothing sure, yet much unhappily.

FROZEN SCENE #3

Gertrude describes the death of Ophelia: 4.7.190–208

QUEEN
   There is a willow grows askant the brook   190
   That shows his hoar leaves in the glassy stream.
   Therewith fantastic garlands did she make
   Of crowflowers, nettles, daisies, and long purples [. . .]
   There on the pendant boughs her coronet weeds
   Clamb'ring to hang, an envious sliver broke,
   When down her weedy trophies and herself
   Fell in the weeping brook. Her clothes spread wide,   200
   And mermaid-like awhile they bore her up,
   Which time she chanted snatches of old lauds,
   As one incapable of her own distress
   Or like a creature native and endued
   Unto that element. But long it could not be   205
   Till that her garments, heavy with their drink,
   Pulled the poor wretch from her melodious lay
   To muddy death.

The Final Project: Your Own *Hamlet*, Performed!

Here's What We're Doing and Why

It's showtime! Watch and listen as your students demonstrate their ability to grapple with, respond to, and perform Shakespeare's language. Hear why they staged things as they did. Celebrate how far your students have come, not just as Shakespeareans but as thinkers and readers and makers. Don't forget to save time for a whole-class reflection round after all the performances. This is often just as, if not more, enlightening as the scenes themselves.

What Will I Need?

- Space and time for all groups to present their performances and rationales

- A notepad or digital doc to take notes on all the great learning you're witnessing. These notes will come in handy when you provide student feedback. (Revisit the 7-point checklist and the learning goals of the final project when it's time for feedback.)

- Space and time for everyone to gather in a circle for a reflection round

How Should I Prepare?

- Create and share the "run of show" for today. At the beginning of class, groups should know when they're on.

- Arrange your space so everyone can see each scene. A giant circle is our favorite.

- It's always nice to have a lighthearted but clear way to call "time" on a scene, too. Some teachers rely on a phone timer. Your call.

Agenda (~ 45-minute period)

- ❏ Part One: Groups get organized: 5 minutes
- ❏ Part Two: Scenes performed and defenses presented: 35 minutes
- ❏ Part Three: Whole class reflection: 10 minutes

Here's What Students Will Do

Part One: Groups Get Organized

- Students meet in their groups to organize props or make quick, last-minute changes for their scene.

Part Two: Performances

- Each group presents their work to thunderous applause

- Collect whatever project documentation you need to assess student learning

Part Three: Reflection Round

To conclude the performances, respond to the following prompts *thinking just about your work this week including this performance experience.*

1. I observed . . .

2. I discovered . . .

3. I expect that . . .

4. *If responses stay focused on the language and activities, teachers should add:* What did you learn about yourself?

Here's What Just Happened in Class

- Massive learning in action, all set up by you. WOW!

Teaching Shakespeare—and *Hamlet*—with English Learners

Christina Porter

I am Christina Porter and for the past 20 years I have worked in an urban school community right outside of Boston, Massachusetts. I began as an English teacher, then a literacy coach, and currently I am the district curriculum director for the humanities. I first started working with English Learners in 2006 when I became the literacy coach. Prior to that, I had little experience with these phenomenal students.

Also prior to working with them, I knew the general assumptions about ELs. For as long as they have sat in U.S. classrooms, ELs most often have been considered "other," having many "deficits" that need to be overcome. The "deficits" tend to be their native language and culture—seen as roadblocks that should be surmounted so that EL students can more closely match prevailing assumptions of "American" culture—white, middle-class, and English-speaking. In my work with EL students, I soon learned that this mindset can manifest itself in many ugly ways in schools, and that can be both culturally and academically destructive.

Something I observed early on was that while our white, middle-class, English-speaking students were reading Shakespeare—the real thing, not that watered-down summarized stuff—our English Learners were not. Not even a watered-down version of Shakespeare! By "real Shakespeare" I mean his words in all their glorious Early Modern English (both with the full text of a play as well as in edited scenes from a play). Initially, I had the incorrect assumption myself: I assumed, like so many others, that because students were developing English, Shakespeare was probably too difficult for them to handle. I learned that this is incorrect. What I learned instead was that once we adults dismissed our own deficit-based thinking—and allowed our EL students to read, create, design, and imagine—the results were tremendous, with Shakespeare as well as with many other complex texts.

Coinciding with my start as a literacy coach, I spent a summer at the Folger Library's Teaching Shakespeare Institute. I learned about so many of the student-centered, get-them-on-their-feet methods that are one of the backbones of this book. As the new literacy coach at the high school, I was so excited to get into a classroom and use these, especially because I had the unique opportunity to work with many teachers in the building. One of the first colleagues to reach out was an English as a Second Language (ESL) teacher. We met to brainstorm, and I described how I had spent my summer at the Folger Library learning all of these innovative methods of engaging students. She was immediately onboard. Specifically, she wanted to tackle Shakespeare (again, REAL Shakespeare). Over the course of several years, we taught many plays together, and I did the same with other colleagues in the ESL department. Our ELs consistently destroyed any concern I or others could have had about their ability to read and perform something as intricate and complex as Shakespeare. Just one example: one of the first things I learned was that these students are uniquely attuned to the intricacy of language; it's how they exist on a daily basis! Sometimes when teaching a play with my native speakers, I found that they would want to rush. In this rushing, they would miss the depth and beauty of the words. ELs, on the other hand, take time with language—with the word, the line, the speech, and the scene. This is only one of the many strengths these students bring to working with Shakespeare, and other authors too.

Because the Folger understands the importance of ELs, I have been asked to share some of the knowledge I've gained working with these unique, intelligent, and resilient EL students and Shakespeare. My suggestions are based on years of scholarly research regarding second language acquisition coupled with my knowledge and experience working with ELs, Shakespeare, and the Folger Method. I am excited to share both what I've taught and what I've learned from EL students!

One important and perhaps obvious note here is that English Learners are not a monolith. You may have students in your class who have had exposure to English in their native country, you may also have students who have experienced gaps in schooling, and more. Though most of this chapter is focused on ELs generally, when I have found an approach that is particularly helpful for a specific subgroup of ELs, I point that out.

I build here on principles and classroom practices that you will find throughout this book and this series. Since teachers are the busiest people on the planet, this material is organized so that you can find what you need quickly:

- ❏ **Part One: ELs at Home in the Folger Method**
- ❏ **Part Two: Shakespeare with English Learners**
- ❏ **Part Three: *Hamlet* with English Learners**

Part One: ELs at Home in the Folger Method

Many of the Folger Essentials are *already* excellent supports for ELs. Folger Essentials like choral reading, rereading, focusing on single words and lines and then building to speeches and scenes—all of these support fluency and comprehension. In addition, these Teaching Guides include plot summaries and play maps, and the lesson plans include lots of other active instructional approaches.

When reading Shakespeare with ELs, I always give the option to read the scene summary in advance. I do this because it balances accessibility with giving them a chance to grapple with a complex text. Remember, Shakespeare borrowed most of his plots, so the plot is the least of our concern. We never want the story to become the roadblock to working with the words. The Folger Shakespeare, both in print and online, includes brief play and scene synopses for all the plays. The play maps may be helpful to ELs who may have had interruptions in their prior schooling or ELs who have not previously read a drama. It can be another structural support to "unveil" the characters and plot. You may choose to spend some time deconstructing the structure of a drama—discussing, for example, scenes, acts, and character lists. For some students, drama may be completely new, for others this quick activity can serve as an activator of prior knowledge.

Understanding text features is a solid support for comprehension. It is easy to assume that by high school when most students are reading this play, they have been exposed to drama, but this is not always the case, depending on the backgrounds of individual students.

Part Two: Shakespeare with English Learners

With the Folger Method as my base, I build in additional resources to support English Learners in my urban school. This is because working with ELs *is* different from working with native English speakers. Equity is removing barriers. Equity is giving students what *they* need to be successful. Thus, I have come to four Truths that prevail when diving into Shakespeare—and other complex texts, too—with EL students:

- TRUTH #1: **ELs need support with classroom practices.** We cannot assume that our ELs have had the same experience in classrooms as our other students. We need to offer specific guidance and support for common classroom practices such as having a small group discussion, acting out a piece of drama, or other Folger Essentials. Being clear in our expectations, our directions, and offering scaffolds (for example, sentence starters for small group discussions) is good for all students and essential for ELs.

- TRUTH #2: **ELs need additional support in order to grapple with complex texts.** ELs are capable of reading Shakespeare. ELs also need supports for language comprehension. Important supports include: chunking a scene/speech into smaller parts and using edited scenes or plays. To be clear, we always use Shakespeare's text (rather than the "simplified" versions), and we want to offer accessibility to those words through appropriate support for students who are in the process of acquiring English.

- TRUTH #3: **ELs need to have space for their unique language and culture to live in our classrooms.** Students' funds of knowledge are an asset, not a deficit. They need to bring their selves and their whole native culture to Shakespeare. This truth echoes the Folger principle about the importance of student voice.

- TRUTH #4: **ELs need support with the specific aspects of the English language and how words function** (individually, in a sentence, and more). This helps them build academic vocabulary, in written as well as oral language.

Continuing from Truth #4 and parts of the Folger Method, I introduce my students to what I call the "actor's arsenal"—a toolbox of five elements of communication that actors (and all of us) have at their disposal in English: stress, inflection, pause, nonverbal communication, and tone. At its simplest, it looks like this, and my students appreciate this visual:

STRESS: Emphasis placed on a **WORD** (or word, or word)

INFLECTION: The way the voice goes ^up^ or ~down~ when a word is pronounced

PAUSE: A break ..... in reading for emphasis

NONVERBAL COMMUNICATION: Without words, the gestures, posture, presence or absence of eye contact

TONE: The *emotional* sound in your voice

These five tools deserve attention because *they are not the same in all languages.* In some languages, some of these tools are nonexistent or used in different ways than they are in English. I have a distinct memory of teaching a lesson on tone for the first time to a class of ELs. Generally, students really enjoy practicing a word/line with varying tones of voice. In this class, I couldn't help but notice one student who had a puzzled look on his face. I didn't want to embarrass him in his small group, so I sought guidance from the ESL teacher I was working with. She explained to me that tone did not work the same way in his native language as it did in English. In some languages—Hmong, for example—tone alone literally changes the meaning of a word, while in other languages—English, for one—tone accompanied by nonverbal communication alters the subtext of a word/phrase.

When working with students who have varying language backgrounds, additional attention to tone and nonverbal communication is very helpful. I typically introduce this "arsenal" as a part of our prereading. Tone and Stress, the first Folger Essential, includes visuals and practice rounds, and is recommended for all students beginning their journey with Shakespeare's language. Learn more about it in the Folger Method chapter. What I describe here can be an additional and introductory support for EL students.

I often begin this communication work by asking students to consider a universal teenage dilemma—having a disagreement with your parents or caregivers. (I have found, after working with students from all over the world, that this is one of the few situations that transcend language and culture for most adolescents.) I then ask them to brainstorm all the different ways they can "show" their displeasure with words or actions. The list they generate generally includes items like volume, eye rolling, silence, additional gestures, and tone of voice. I then introduce the concept of tone vocabulary and include visuals with each element to further support comprehension. We pay particular attention to tone, as the English language offers infinite options for impacting the meaning of a word or phrase with tone alone. We define *tone* as the emotional sound in our voice, and I offer a specific list of tones for students' reference: love, hate, anger, joy, fear, and sorrow. While certainly not comprehensive of all the tones available in English, these six seem to capture the fundamentals. Students always enjoy taking a phrase like "That's great!" and applying these tones in small groups. For students coming from language backgrounds where tone is not utilized in the same way as it is in English, this activity offers additional practice in and added awareness of how tone functions in English. Using the Folger Essential, students practice with the word *Oh!*, saying it in a variety of tones (happy, sad, angry, surprised, and more). Students on their own will automatically add accompanying nonverbal communication, crossing their arms if the tone is angry, for example.

In addition, you can use a film clip of a scene from a Shakespeare play to further explore tone. (There is a wide variety of clips online, and be sure to check out folger .edu.) Initially, I hand out a copy of the scene to the students and I play the clip *audio only*. Students can work individually or they can work in small groups. They listen to the audio only, following along with the lines. As they listen, I instruct them to focus on one character and note any tone of voice they hear (anger, love, joy, and more). Next, we watch the scene *video only*, with no audio at all. They continue to track the same character and note any nonverbal communication. Finally, we watch the scene *with audio and video*, and add any additional notes on tone, stress, nonverbal communication, inflection, or pause. After this, students share their notes and findings either in a pair (if they have been working individually) or with another small group. Later, when we get up on our feet as a class we are able to draw on this kind of analysis to support our version of the play!

Part Three: *Hamlet* with English Learners

Two of my four Truths around EL students and Shakespeare focus on students' need for additional supports when working with complex texts (Truth #2) and EL students' need for an invitation to include their language and culture (Truth #3). Born from these Truths and backed up by the Folger Method, I share here approaches and practices that I have used most frequently when reading *Hamlet* with EL students. You will find that these strategies are useful for all students but *essential for ELs*!

ELs' need additional support in order to grapple with complex texts. Chunking the text is the breaking of a scene or a speech into smaller parts based on changes in the scene or speech: a new character is entering, or a character's mood is changing, a character may be finally getting something they want, or a new topic of conversation is starting. Or more. In *Hamlet*, we chunk both scenes and Hamlet's soliloquys. To chunk a text, I literally draw lines across the page to mark these chunks and these changes. I also add short titles to each chunk to summarize what is going on. Chunking text is a strategy that supports comprehension, analysis, and the ultimate goal—performance!

Chunking is first done by the teacher as a reading comprehension support. YOU chunk the text for students to support their reading. The end goal is that students will eventually chunk the text themselves. Initially, when you hand students a chunked text, remember to first distribute and read together a scene summary. (Remember, the Folger print and digital editions—folger.edu/shakespeares-works—have scene summaries. If you are chunking a speech or soliloquy, provide students with a brief (one to two lines) synopsis in advance. When students do the chunking themselves—either individually or in small groups—it becomes a textual analysis tool for them. Again, the ultimate goal is for students to understand all that is taking place in a particular scene so that they can make well-informed choices as they prepare for performance.

Let's look at *Hamlet* 2.2.576–634. This is Hamlet's second soliloquy—the one that starts "O, what a rogue and peasant slave am I!"—and it's lengthy. Chunking it into 3 parts supports comprehension and aids in analysis and performance. The first time we chunk a text, I do the work, and offer it to my students already chunked and titled. The second time we look at a chunked text, however, they do more work. We start with the speech on which I had drawn the lines and titled the first few chunks. After we read the text together, students add titles to the final few. Ultimately, students read the summary, read the scene as a group, and then chunk and title it in their groups.

HAMLET CRITICIZES HIMSELF AND MAKES A PLAN

Chunk	What's Happening?
Chunk #1 **(2.2.575–593)** Now I am alone. O, what a rogue and peasant slave am I! Is it not monstrous that this player here, But in a fiction, in a dream of passion, Could force his soul so to his own conceit That from her working all his visage wann'd, Tears in his eyes, distraction in's aspect, A broken voice, and his whole function suiting With forms to his conceit? and all for nothing! For Hecuba! What's Hecuba to him, or he to Hecuba, That he should weep for her? What would he do, Had he the motive and the cue for passion That I have? He would drown the stage with tears And cleave the general ear with horrid speech, Make mad the guilty and appal the free, Confound the ignorant, and amaze indeed The very faculties of eyes and ears.	The actor has more passion for acting than Hamlet has for revenge

Chunk #2 (2.2.593–617) **("Yet I," to "About, my brains!")** Yet I, A dull and muddy-mettled rascal, peak, Like John-a-dreams, unpregnant of my cause, And can say nothing; no, not for a king, Upon whose property and most dear life A damn'd defeat was made. Am I a coward? Who calls me villain? breaks my pate across? Plucks off my beard, and blows it in my face? Tweaks me by the nose? gives me the lie i' the throat, As deep as to the lungs? who does me this? Ha! 'Swounds, I should take it: for it cannot be But I am pigeon-liver'd and lack gall To make oppression bitter, or ere this I should have fatted all the region kites With this slave's offal: bloody, bawdy villain! Remorseless, treacherous, lecherous, kindless villain! O, vengeance! Why, what an ass am I! This is most brave, That I, the son of a dear father murder'd, Prompted to my revenge by heaven and hell, Must, like a whore, unpack my heart with words, And fall a-cursing, like a very drab, A stallion! Fie upon't! foh!	Hamlet criticizes himself. Why? Doubts himself?
Chunk #3 (2.2.617–634) ("I have heard" to **"catch the conscience of the king")** I have heard That guilty creatures sitting at a play Have by the very cunning of the scene Been struck so to the soul that presently They have proclaim'd their malefactions; For murder, though it have no tongue, will speak With most miraculous organ. I'll have these players Play something like the murder of my father Before mine uncle: I'll observe his looks; I'll tent him to the quick: if he but blench, I know my course. The spirit that I have seen May be the devil: and the devil hath power To assume a pleasing shape; yea, and perhaps Out of my weakness and my melancholy, As he is very potent with such spirits, Abuses me to damn me: I'll have grounds More relative than this: the play's the thing Wherein I'll catch the conscience of the king.	Hamlet's plan for revenge

Truth #3: The role of students' own lives and cultures in the study of *Hamlet*. Connecting reading to students' lives is a critical component of engagement. The day-by-day lesson plans elsewhere speak to *Hamlet* as a play in which characters are driven by concerns about family, identity, guilt, the supernatural, and so much more. *Hamlet* offers EL students a great deal of space to bring their whole selves and culture to the work in class.

In working with *Hamlet* with students from all over the world, I have seen that family relationships and beliefs regarding the supernatural are two great topics that generate real interest in my students, and that warrant additional time for processing and self-reflection. Just as with everything else I suggest, they are a good "grappling opportunity" for all students; when you are fortunate enough to work with students who come from a wide range of cultures, it adds an even more interesting dimension to these conversations. Before beginning discussions of this nature with students, it is critical to have in place classroom norms that outline ways in which to respectfully disagree, and that allow space for a variety of backgrounds and opinions.

Hamlet is a play about familial relationships: Hamlet's relationship with his father (dead and alive), Hamlet's relationship with his mother, Ophelia's relationship with her father, her brother, and more. I give students time to reflect on their own family structure so they can draw on that while reading and performing the play, and I do this on a daily basis. It can be in the form of a quick write at the beginning of class ("Who do you consider your family and why?"), or a turn-and-talk based on discussing "blood is thicker than water" with a partner, or a discussion of something larger with the whole class. In Act 1, I always ask students to construct a map of their family. I explain that this map can certainly include people who are not related by blood or marriage. They can illustrate this as a pyramid, a map, or a graph. I also ask them to indicate who has a say in how decisions are made in their family. Is it one person, two people, a group? This comes in very handy when examining a number of actions in the play, beginning with Gertrude's hasty marriage to Claudius.

Another rich topic that we spend time discussing is ghosts—and belief in ghosts. I always start by asking students if they believe that ghosts exist. If they do, I ask them in what ways, if any, are ghosts able to interact with the living. The action of the play is predicated on the fact that Hamlet believes what the ghost tells him (maybe more so after the dumb-show confirms it).

To begin this conversation I ask students to take a few minutes to write their thoughts on ghosts. Depending on their level of language development, you can offer stem starters ("I definitely believe in ghosts because . . ." and "I do not believe in ghosts because . . .") if that is helpful. After students share what they believe in pairs, they share in small groups, keeping the classroom norms in mind. Then we divide the room into two groups—those who believe in the supernatural and those who do not. They then share their reasons why, keeping classroom norms in mind. Students often engage in impassioned and wonderful debate on this topic. Conversations like these open up very important space for students to share their backgrounds and cultures with their peers. Several students of Mexican heritage have had the opportunity to teach us all about traditions such as Día de los Muertos and beliefs surrounding deceased relatives' ability to visit and interact with the living. One year, students set their production of

Hamlet in Mexico. They included an opening silent scene of Hamlet visiting an *ofrenda* (an altar for a deceased relative with pictures, offerings of food, and decorations of flowers). As Hamlet walked offstage, the ghost entered, picked up his photo, and then followed Hamlet offstage . . . It was absolutely brilliant!

In another class, one of my students got so passionate about his beliefs in the supernatural world that he invited his grandfather, a healer, to visit our class and share his thoughts. It is quite an impressive sight to see a room of teenagers fall silent, astounded to hear the truth of a powerful storyteller.

All that we have discussed here will make for a rich experience with *Hamlet* and more broadly with Shakespeare—for EL students and for you, too! Working with ELs and Shakespeare (and the Folger too) is a joy. You're on your way!

Teaching Shakespeare—and *Hamlet*—with Students with Learning Differences

Roni DiGenno

I am Roni DiGenno, a special education teacher with 10 years' experience teaching ninth- through twelfth-grade English in a District of Columbia public high school. My students' reading levels range from pre-primer to college level and their special education classifications include specific learning disabilities, ADHD, auditory disabilities, autism, as well as intellectual and emotional disabilities. I teach self-contained pull-out classes, each of about fifteen students, all with IEPs (Individualized Education Programs). Sometimes I have a teaching assistant; most often I do not.

I love teaching. I love my students. And I love teaching Shakespeare to my students. I put to use what I have learned at the Folger; I use Shakespeare to inspire my students to believe in themselves. Most importantly, my students begin to see themselves as learners because I trust them with the hard stuff, the challenging content. I believe we can do it together, and my students know this. My passion for teaching these kids, who at times seem unreachable, comes from my own experience growing up with a reading difficulty. I could not sound out words, but this had nothing to do with my value or my intellect. My students, and all students, deserve the best, most engaging, intellectually stimulating lessons possible.

Shakespeare Rewrites How Students See Themselves Learning

For the past several years, I have taught exclusively some of the most difficult students in my school—those with very large learning gaps, usually reading 5–8 years below grade level, and with emotional disturbances that make it difficult to build positive peer and adult relationships. They arrive in my classroom plagued with low expectations of themselves and of school because for years other people have had low expectations of them. They are used to passing just by showing up and doing minimal work. Some have been through the criminal justice system, which adds another layer of low expectations. My first priority is to help my students see themselves as capable and valued members of our classroom community. I do this by teaching lessons that empower them—lessons based on the Folger's philosophy. As a result, my students grow in exciting and surprising ways that no one could have anticipated.

I teach students like Armando, who had serious trust issues. He cut class frequently and was involved in groups that negatively influenced him in school. He repeated grades because he refused to do the work, and he cursed teachers out regularly. In addition to being in and out of the criminal justice system, he was also a target of violent crime, which left him hospitalized for weeks and suffering from post-traumatic stress disorder. Through our class's collaborative work using Folger methods, Armando slowly began to discover and enjoy his strengths. He felt welcomed into the learning process and started to trust himself and others. He eventually became a peer leader who helped facilitate lessons.

I also taught Martin, a student who had such severe dyslexia that early on in my class he was reading at a kindergarten level. He was withdrawn and shied away from participating for fear of judgment. Here again, by incorporating Folger principles and practices, I was able to give Martin the safe learning environment he needed and the confidence to try reading aloud. He learned to trust his peers and he began to take risks—reading parts, participating, and giving amazing insight into discussion topics.

The Folger Method supports students like Armando and Martin, who have vastly different learning needs but who may also be in the same class. The teaching strategies offer students multiple entry points—tactical, visual, and aural—through which to engage and enjoy complex texts. Differentiation and scaffolding are built into the Folger's interactive lessons so students build a positive association with challenging texts. This is hugely important for students with learning differences and emotional difficulties. If content or concepts are overwhelming, or not taught in a way that they can grasp them, students will build a negative association. No one wants to struggle or feel like they can't learn something, which is often the root cause of behavior issues within classrooms. The Folger Method meets students' social and emotional learning needs through building a supportive and collaborative classroom community. Through the process, students begin to work through conflict, solve problems, and accept and support one another's learning differences.

How the Folger Method Works for Students with IEPs

In the Folger Method chapter and in the *Hamlet* lessons in this book, you'll find the Folger Essentials that will throw your students right into the text through powerful practices like tossing words and phrases, two-line scenes, choral reading, and 3D Lit. Each Essential gives students exposure to the language and removes a barrier to learning and comprehension. Each builds on the others, increasing cognitive demand. Students master each step before moving to the next—words before lines, lines before scenes, choral reading before acting and reading parts solo. They don't feel left behind because they learn the content and the skills to understand it simultaneously.

Every year, my students look forward to our unit on Shakespeare. Typically about 10 weeks long, the unit allows us to slow down and dig into the text. Instead of skipping over difficult parts, we want to conquer them! It is important for us to embrace the struggle because it is an inevitable part of the learning process. In the Folger work, struggle is about joyful investigation and thinking hard together rather than a feeling of inadequacy. Students question, try out, and connect with the words and each other and so they learn that there is no one right answer but rather a whole new way to discover a text. The Essentials get the language in the students' mouths, encourage collaboration, and shift focus away from the teacher so that students can practice navigating themselves through their learning. It's a different way of teaching and a different way of learning. At first, they are hesitant: They resist, they laugh, they feel weird, they are unsure, they can't believe they are talking this much in class—and I am encouraging all of it. Within a week or two, students are more willing to experiment and take risks with the language by reading really strange words they have never seen or heard before. And soon, students are reading Shakespeare and enjoying it.

Reading Shakespeare can be a great equalizer. While scholars, directors, and actors never tire of decoding, interpreting, and defining Shakespeare, the truth is that no one knows exactly what Shakespeare *really* meant. He left no diary or notes. Everyone is entitled to their own interpretation. We also have no idea how the words were spoken because we have no recordings of the play performances in the Globe Theatre. The "funny" English (my students' term) in Shakespeare's works puts us all on the same playing field. Be vulnerable, mess up some words, and have fun! The students will ask, "How do you say this word?" and my only response is, "Not sure, let's figure it out." It's okay to do your best and sound "funny." We are all in this together and repeating that idea to students builds bridges.

The Folger Method gives students the scaffolding and tools needed to launch them from struggling readers to invested readers. Martin, my student with severe dyslexia and on a Beginning Reader level, struggled with sight words. As the rest of his class became more comfortable reading Shakespeare's words, he remained unsure. Could he read and understand Shakespeare? But he can't read! But he has a learning disability! But . . . *nothing*! Martin found his voice and his courage to try to read and read he did. One day we were using the Folger Essential 3D Lit to explore a scene, and when his turn came to read, he chose *not* to pass. Previously, he'd always politely declined to read aloud, and the class and I obliged. On this day though, he did not pass. Slowly, he began to read the words. Fumbling often, he kept reading, with the encouragement and support of his peers. They helped him sound out words when he didn't know how to start. He finished reading, and the room applauded him. Martin entered center stage that day because he had developed both belief in himself and trust in his peers. He wanted to join them and believed he could do it. Shakespeare is truly for everyone, and everyone is capable of "getting it." Martin "got it" not because he read the text flawlessly and was able to analyze the motifs in an essay. He got it because he was able to understand the text through a series of activities that led to his comprehension.

Shakespeare and other excellent complex texts are so important, especially for students who have IEPs, because they deserve an enriching learning experience with real, challenging content. Giving students access to appropriate grade-level material is essential to meeting their IEP goals, regardless of the educational setting (resource, pull-out, or inclusion). More than teaching Shakespeare, the Folger Method is about instilling confidence in students about the reality that they can do much of this work themselves. Even if it takes a while, even if they need a little help here and there—*they can do it.*

My Students and *Hamlet*

Connecting the play to their own lives

In general, multiple connections to any text build interest and improve comprehension. I have found that when my students connect elements of Shakespeare's plays to their own lives, they become more engaged in what they read and build stronger bonds with the text. In my classes, through the Folger approach, we have been building a safe, trusting community all along that makes it possible to explore these big ideas in the text.

Hamlet offers students any number of connections to their own lives. Here are a few, and ways in which you might use these in class.

Death and Grief: Not only is there death throughout *Hamlet*, but there is also murder and grief. Hamlet mourns his father's murder and then he himself murders others. Ophelia dies, and we're not quite sure why. Students may have experienced the loss of an adult or peer, or they may have been witness to violence.

Idea for Class: Students can share their experiences of loss in small circles or groups. Place students in small groups, no more than four per group. In this activity, only one student speaks at a time while the others listen. There are three rounds to this activity. Round 1: The first person in the group has 30 seconds to share their experience with grief or loss. No one can talk while another student is speaking. Then, each student takes their turn sharing their example in 30 seconds as well. This continues until all students have shared. Round 2: Students have another 30 seconds to share more about their experiences, again talking one at a time. Round 3: Students now relate their own experience to what Hamlet experienced. This time, they take turns in their group to talk for 1 minute each. Following this speaking and listening activity, they each journal or write down their connections to Hamlet. The writing can be in paragraph form with evidence or just student reflections. If students are not comfortable sharing experiences aloud, they can use the timed periods to reflect independently in their journals.

Mental Health: It is sometimes debated whether Hamlet pretends to act insane or actually is insane. It's generally thought that Ophelia commits suicide, and we know from Hamlet himself that he considers suicide. The topics of mental health, depression, and suicide are important and timely ones for students to talk about—they are present in their everyday lives.

Idea for Class: Students participate in a gallery walk with information about mental health, depression, and suicide. Each station has different information that attempts to dispel common misconceptions and offers resources for getting help to remain mentally healthy, treat depression, and avoid suicide. Ideas for stations can be the symptoms of depression, warning signs of suicide among students, what students can do to support one another, types of professionals who can support them, or types of mental illnesses. During the gallery walk, students write down what they have learned at each station. Using this model presents play-related content as well as develops the practice of active reading of expository text.

Parents and Stepparents: Hamlet has to work through the murder of his father, and the quick remarriage of his mother to his uncle, his father's brother. Then there's his relationship with his mother. Nearly a quarter of all students experience the divorce of a parent, one in ten experience multiple divorces, and many may have no father in their lives.

Idea for Class: Students can share their experiences of divorce, remarriage, or parental dating in small circles or groups. These groups work as described in the section above on Death and Grief.

Focus on Key Scenes

The lessons in this book focus on key scenes and use the Folger Essentials to actively and immediately involve students. The choice of key scenes is up to you. In *Hamlet*, I tend to focus on the opening scene (1.1); the family scene (1.2); father and daughter, Polonius and Ophelia (2.1); the play-within-the-play (3.2), and the final scene—the duel (5.2).

I pay attention to these important guidelines:

Prioritize depth over breadth. It is more important that students learn the skills to dig deep into a text, especially independently, than it is to read every line in the play. It may take your class of students with IEPs the same amount of time to analyze 4 key scenes as it takes your general education class to analyze 7. That's okay. Give your students the time they need to do this important work rather than rush through the text. The scripts we create and use in class are without footnotes or explanatory glosses. This allows students to decipher meaning on their own or collaboratively, and removes distractions that impede their understanding.

Keep the original language. Always use Shakespeare's original language and *not* the modernized, made-easy versions. Do not substitute simplified language to make it easier. For one thing, it doesn't make it easier. More important, students with IEPs need to be given access to the original language and be able to make sense of it. And they can.

Shorten the scenes if you need to. You can cut key scenes to include just the most important information. Don't worry about cutting Shakespeare. For as long as Shakespeare's been performed, his plays have been cut by directors and editors. To guide you, ask yourself these questions: What do I want students to understand from this scene? In what part of the scene does that idea happen? Below is the cut version of 1.1 that I used in my class.

Annotate the text

When I say "annotate," I mean making any notes about what is happening in the text; this practice helps students remember what is happening. Some may call this "marking the text." It's all the same. Encourage students to take notes directly on the text during discussions because it leads them to analysis. **Make it purposeful.** Ensure that each time students annotate, they relate the underlined parts of the text to what is happening in the discussion. The annotations can be used for writing assignments.

Show them what an annotated scene or speech looks like and how it's useful. Model for students by annotating and thinking aloud with them. You can do this by using a projector or smartboard, or by distributing copies of your own annotations. The example below is a student's annotation of Act 1, Scene 5.

Act I   Hamlet Annotation Sample

SCENE V. Another part of the platform.

Enter GHOST and HAMLET

HAMLET
Where wilt thou lead me? speak; I'll go no further.   *Hamlet does not trust the Ghost*

Ghost
Mark me.

HAMLET
I will.

Ghost
My hour is almost come,
When I to sulphurous and tormenting flames
Must render up myself.

HAMLET
Alas, poor ghost!

Ghost
Pity me not, but lend thy serious hearing   *— Going to tell a story*
To what I shall unfold.

HAMLET
Speak; I am bound to hear.   *— Hamlet will believe him*

Ghost
So art thou to revenge when thou shalt hear.   *— Why would Hamlet want revenge?*

HAMLET
What?

Ghost
I am thy father's spirit   *— King Hamlet - Hamlet's father's ghost*
Doom'd for a certain term to walk the night,
And for the day confined to fast in fires,
Till the foul crimes done in my days of nature
Are burnt and purged away. But that I am forbid
To tell the secrets of my prison-house,
I could a tale unfold whose lightest word
Would harrow up thy soul, freeze thy young blood,
But this eternal blazon must not be
To ears of flesh and blood. List, list, O, list!
If thou didst ever thy dear father love--

HAMLET
O God!

Ghost
Revenge his foul and most unnatural murder.   *— Kill the father's murderer?*

HAMLET
Murder!

Ghost

Murder most foul, as in the best it is;
But this most foul, strange and unnatural.

HAMLET

Haste me to know't, that I, with wings as swift — Hamlet will do it!
As meditation or the thoughts of love,
May sweep to my revenge.

Ghost

Now, Hamlet, hear: —————————— Listen closely
'Tis given out that, sleeping in my orchard,
A serpent stung me; so the whole ear of Denmark
Is by a forged process of my death
Rankly abused: but know, thou noble youth,
The serpent that did sting thy father's life — The guy who killed him is now the King
Now wears his crown.

HAMLET

O my prophetic soul! My uncle! — King Hamlet's brother and Hamlet's uncle is now the King.

Ghost

Ay, that incestuous, that adulterate beast,
With witchcraft of his wit, with traitorous gifts,--
So to seduce!--won to his shameful lust — Uncle married the queen to become the King.
The will of my most seeming-virtuous queen:
But, soft! methinks I scent the morning air;
Brief let me be. Sleeping within my orchard,
My custom always of the afternoon,
Upon my secure hour thy uncle stole,
With juice of cursed hebenon in a vial,
And in the porches of my ears did pour
The leperous distilment; whose effect
Holds such an enmity with blood of man
Thus was I, sleeping, by a brother's hand — yes, it was the brother
Of life, of crown, of queen, at once dispatch'd:
O, horrible! O, horrible! most horrible!
Let not the royal bed of Denmark be
A couch for luxury and damned incest.
Adieu, adieu! Hamlet, remember me.

Exit

Spread the Shakespeare love. You and your students are on a Shakespeare journey together. As with everything you teach, the energy you give is the energy you get back. The more you LOVE teaching Shakespeare, the more your students will love it too. Keep in mind it may take time, so fake it until you make it. When I started using the Folger Method, my students thought I was way too excited about Shakespeare. Over time, the energy is contagious, and they are just as excited to learn as I am to teach. Shakespeare has always been my favorite unit because it demonstrates that powerful literature belongs to them, and my students look forward to it because it is fun. From calling each other "greasy onion-eyed nut-hook" and "rank rump-fed giglet" to fake sword play with foam weapons and adding "thee" and "thou" to those words, I can see through their actions that they have fallen for Shakespeare as well.

Starting this journey with your students isn't always easy, but it is worth it. You are expecting more from them and teaching them more. Believe they can do the work and they will start to believe in themselves. Forgive yourself if a day does not work out. We are all works in progress, and it may take some tweaking to find out what extra things your students may need. Teaching Shakespeare or any other complex text using the Folger Method may be an adjustment to the way you teach now, so the more you do it, the better you will get at it. Students will become the drivers of the classroom, so get yourself ready for the show.

So, to my students who pop in to ask, "Hey Ms. DiGenno, you still doing that Shakespeare thing?" "Yes, I am, and so are you," I always say back as they rush out of the classroom. Usually their last word: "Cool!"

Pairing Texts:
Hamlet Off the Pedestal and in
Conversation with Other Voices

Donna Denizé

Something wildly important happens when we teach two very different works or authors together—like *Macbeth* and writings of Frederick Douglass; *Hamlet* and something by Claudia Rankine; *Othello* and the poetry of George Moses Horton, or *Taming of the Shrew* and the poems of Audre Lorde.

Paired texts are two texts that you and your students dive into at the same time. Both texts have equal weight; each is strong and can stand fully on its own. You can pair whole works or segments of works, selected narratives, scenes, or stanzas. But there is no "primary" and "secondary" or "supplemental" hierarchy—ever. Two voices, two points of view, two writing styles, two characters . . . and each will illuminate the other.

It's important to note here, since we are in the world of Shakespeare, that a Shakespeare play and an adaptation of a Shakespeare play or plot are *not* paired texts. That's a primary text and most often some kind of supplemental one. Together, they don't have the power or the payoff of a set of paired texts.

Why pair texts? Because, taken together, they illuminate each other in powerful and surprising ways. Looking closely at paired works gives kids a sense of the sweep of literature and allows them to consider together two authors who wrote in vastly different times, places, cultures, genders, races, religions—you name it. These juxtapositions allow them to notice that in many cases, writers have been asking the same big questions for some time: about human identity—how we define ourselves through culture, our moral choices, or how we navigate power or powerlessness, and more. In other instances, they are on very different wavelengths . . . and what might be the reasons for that?

I developed my love for paired texts in my thirty-eight years teaching in a variety of secondary school settings—public, private, urban, and rural—and in serving a term on the advisory board for all vocational schools in the state of Virginia. I currently teach at St. Albans School for Boys in Washington, DC, where I chair the English Department. I love working with paired texts because two strong texts working together produce something marvelous in class: They create a space for meaningful conversations that come from students' experiences and questions, and this creates not just good analysis but empathy. Since students today must navigate an incredibly complex global society, they can only benefit by considering a sweep of literature that helps them deepen their empathy for others.

I've found that the more specific or particular the pairing, the better, since this inspires students' creativity and establishes new ways of thinking about both texts. It also strengthens students' analytical skills and increases their capacity for understanding complexity—qualities that are essential for navigating current human challenges and the promise of an ever-evolving world—and the worlds students inhabit.

The following section is set up in two parts: the first to give you examples and a fuller sense of how paired texts work, and the second to recommend a range of text pairs that in my experience pair very well with *Hamlet*.

Part One: Examples of Paired Texts in General and How They Have Worked in Class

1. Pairing **Macbeth's "If it were done" soliloquy** (1.7.1–28, Macbeth weighs plans to murder King Duncan) with the passage from **Frederick Douglass's** *Narrative of the Life of Frederick Douglass: An American Slave* in which Douglass sits on a hillside watching freely moving ships while his movement is confined by slavery and its laws and customs.

Macbeth (1.7.1–28)	*Narrative of the Life of Frederick Douglass*
MACBETH If it were done when 'tis done, then 'twere well It were done quickly. If th' assassination Could trammel up the consequence and catch With his surcease success, that but this blow Might be the be-all and the end-all here, But here, upon this bank and shoal of time, We'd jump the life to come. But in these cases We still have judgment here, that we but teach Bloody instructions, which, being taught, return To plague th' inventor. This even-handed justice Commends th' ingredience of our poisoned chalice To our own lips. He's here in double trust: First, as I am his kinsman and his subject, Strong both against the deed; then, as his host, Who should against his murderer shut the door, Not bear the knife myself. Besides, this Duncan Hath borne his faculties so meek, hath been So clear in his great office, that his virtues Will plead like angels, trumpet-tongued, against The deep damnation of his taking-off;	Our house stood within a few rods of the Chesapeake Bay, whose broad bosom was ever white with sails from every quarter of the habitable globe. Those beautiful vessels, robed in purest white, so delightful to the eye of freemen, were to me so many shrouded ghosts, to terrify and torment me with thoughts of my wretched condition. I have often, in the deep stillness of a summer's Sabbath, stood all alone upon the lofty banks of that noble bay, and traced, with saddened heart and tearful eye, the countless number of sails moving off to the mighty ocean. The sight of these always affected me powerfully. My thoughts would compel utterance; and there, with no audience but the Almighty, I would pour out my soul's complaint, in my rude way, with an apostrophe to the moving multitude of ships:— "You are loosed from your moorings, and are free; I am fast in my chains, and am a slave! You move merrily before the gentle gale, and I sadly before the bloody whip! You are freedom's swift-winged angels, that fly round the world; I am confined in

And pity, like a naked newborn babe
Striding the blast, or heaven's cherubin horsed
Upon the sightless couriers of the air,
Shall blow the horrid deed in every eye,
That tears shall drown the wind. I have no spur
To prick the sides of my intent, but only
Vaulting ambition, which o'erleaps itself
And falls on th' other.

bands of iron! O that I were free! O, that I were on one of your gallant decks, and under your protecting wing! Alas! betwixt me and you, the turbid waters roll. Go on, go on. O that I could also go! Could I but swim! If I could fly! O, why was I born a man, of whom to make a brute. The glad ship is gone; she hides in the dim distance. I am left in the hottest hell of unending slavery. O God, save me! God, deliver me! Let me be free! Is there any God? Why am I a slave? I will run away. I will not stand it. Get caught, or get clear, I'll try it. I had as well die with ague as the fever. I have only one life to lose. I had as well be killed running as die standing. Only think of it; one hundred miles straight north, and I am free! Try it? Yes! God helping me, I will. It cannot be that I shall live and die a slave. I will take to the water. This very bay shall yet bear me into freedom. The steamboats steered in a north-east course from North Point. I will do the same; and when I get to the head of the bay, I will turn my canoe adrift, and walk straight through Delaware into Pennsylvania. When I get there, I shall not be required to have a pass; I can travel without being disturbed. Let but the first opportunity offer, and, come what will, I am off. Meanwhile, I will try to bear up under the yoke. I am not the only slave in the world. Why should I fret? I can bear as much as any of them. Besides, I am but a boy, and all boys are bound to some one. It may be that my misery in slavery will only increase my happiness when I get free. There is a better day coming."

Thus I used to think, and thus I used to speak to myself; goaded almost to madness at one moment, and at the next reconciling myself to my wretched lot.

In class, we started with a definition of *ambition*. The kids looked it up in various dictionaries. They came up with definitions like these:

- an earnest desire for some type of achievement or distinction, as power, honor, fame, or wealth, and the willingness to strive for its attainment

- the object, state, or result desired or sought after

- to seek after earnestly

- aspire to

I asked a few simple questions to start them off:

1. What is the ambition of each man? What is it driving him toward? What is he seeking?

2. What are they both wrestling against and with—morally and socially?

3. What solutions, if any, does each one reach?

A discussion developed that connected the word *ambition* with some of the other topics that they found in both texts: isolation; self-perception; moral dilemmas; questions about freedom and justice. My students came up with valuable comparisons and contrasts that I list here in no particular order:

- Both are wrestling in the mind, the imagination alive, the struggle with consequences, moral right and wrong.

- In *Macbeth*, the moral wrong is in the individual; in the Douglass, the moral wrong is in the larger society.

- Both bring isolation, pain, and suffering; Macbeth's isolation leads to his destruction; Douglass's isolation leads him to being an orator and a major voice in the cause for the abolition of slavery.

- Macbeth's ambition has a negative outcome while Douglass's has a positive outcome.

- Both search for justice—Macbeth to avoid it and Douglass to have justice manifest.

- Macbeth has social and political power, while Douglass—a slave—is marginalized, without social and political power.

- Both are seeking freedom. Macbeth imagines freedom from consequences. Douglass imagines the consequences of freedom.

These two texts—Shakespeare's *Macbeth* and Frederick Douglass's *Narrative of the Life of Frederick Douglass: An American Slave*—are separated by time, space, culture, and geopolitics, and yet my students made wonderful connections between both, identifying isolation, self-perception, and moral dilemmas. They also asked big questions about freedom and justice, and the function of the human imagination, and ambition.

2. Pairing **Iago's speech in *Othello*** (3.3.367–382, he plots to use Desdemona's handkerchief to stoke Othello's jealousy) with **"Troubled with the Itch and Rubbing with Sulphur," a poem by George Moses Horton**, a contemporary of Frederick Douglass. This is a more unusual pairing, and one that is focused on language.

A note here on George Moses Horton (ca.1798–ca.1883): He was a slave in North Carolina who taught himself to read with the help of spelling books, a Bible, and a book of hymns. His master soon realized that there was money to be made sending Horton on errands to deliver produce to students and staff at the University of North Carolina in Chapel Hill. That is where Horton became a little like a celebrity; students befriended him because he created love poems that enabled them to get dates. Since Horton could not yet write, the students would write the poems down as he dictated them; they paid him in either money or books. In this way he acquired the complete works of Shakespeare, a collection of works by Lord Byron, Samuel Johnson's *Dictionary of the English Language*, Homer's *Iliad*, and many more. Once paid, Horton tried to save enough to purchase his freedom, but his attempt was unsuccessful. Horton lived long enough to see the end of slavery, though, so he was freed eventually. After his first book, *Poems by a Slave* (1837), newspapers began calling him "the colored bard of Chapel Hill." In 1997, Horton was named Historic Poet Laureate of Chatham County, North Carolina.

Othello (3.3.367–382)	*"Troubled with the Itch and Rubbing with Sulphur"* **by George Moses Horton**

IAGO
Be not acknown on 't.
I have use for it. Go, leave me.
                   Emilia exits.
I will in Cassio's lodging lose this napkin
And let him find it. Trifles light as air
Are to the jealous confirmations strong
As proofs of holy writ. This may do something.
The Moor already changes with my poison;
Dangerous conceits are in their natures poisons,
Which at the first are scarce found to distaste,
But with a little act upon the blood
Burn like the mines of sulfur
                   Enter Othello.
I did say so.
Look where he comes. Not poppy nor mandragora
Nor all the drowsy syrups of the world
Shall ever medicine thee to that sweet sleep
Which thou owedst yesterday.
	'Tis bitter, yet 'tis sweet;
	   Scratching effects but transient ease;
	Pleasure and pain together meet
	     And vanish as they please.
	
	My nails, the only balm,
	   To every bump are oft applied,
	And thus the rage will sweetly calm
	     Which aggravates my hide.
	
	It soon returns again:
	   A frown succeeds to every smile;
	Grinning I scratch and curse the pain
	     But grieve to be so vile.
	
	In fine, I know not which
	   Can play the most deceitful game:
	The devil, sulphur, or the itch.
	     The three are but the same.
	
	The devil sows the itch,
	   And sulphur has a loathsome smell,
	And with my clothes as black as pitch
	     I stink where'er I dwell.
	
	Excoriated deep,
	   By friction played on every part,
	It oft deprives me of my sleep
	     And plagues me to my heart.

In class, we read both pieces aloud first, and then I asked students to look up the word *sulfur* and its purposes. From various online sources, both medical and agricultural, they learn that, at least in the Mississippi Delta, sulfur is an important substance in yielding maximum cotton crops. Yet, applied to the skin, sulfur can both cause pain and provide relief from itching and burning and rashes, even though as Horton points out, it stinks.

Then, I asked students to make as many connections between the two texts as possible. Where does sulfur come in? What does sulfur do?

- Sulfur can heal or burn or both.

- In both texts, it seems like the thing that is meant to heal and at first brings relief (sulfur) is also the thing that brings the pain again.

I had to do little to keep the discussion going. My students had this to say about Horton:

- Even if he's free, which means he can make his own choices and his own money, Horton is still not a citizen, not part of society, and the self is torn between two worlds—as an established reader and writer in a world that denies Blacks literacy and education.

- Horton has no way to vote or own property. In fact, he's part of a larger society where slavery exists and the laws as well as the social practices deny his equality with white citizens.

- For the whites, Horton's existence is problematic: He's supposed to be inferior intellectually, morally, but he has demonstrated the opposite, and it's difficult to reconcile the contradiction he creates through the racial lens. These contradictions create moral dilemmas. Irrational Othello, on the other hand, is looking to solve a moral dilemma, seeking a way out of his suffering, and believing Iago is the one to heal his fears and insecurity about Desdemona's infidelity. Students saw pretty quickly that Othello thinks that Iago will bring freedom from these worries, but in reality, Iago is the cause—the sulfur that burns, and not the healing balm.

In both cases, my students have seen clearly the corrosive effects of prejudice, of racism. With matters of prejudice, whether it's class, gender, race, or religion, there are no quick solutions, no easy balms to apply. Moreover, if we do not see the "other," we cannot see the self and cannot understand the self.

Part Two: Pairing Various Texts with *Hamlet*

1. Pairing *Hamlet* (1.5.14–28, the speech in which the ghost of Hamlet's father speaks to him) with the *final paragraph in* **"No Name Woman," a chapter in Maxine Hong Kingston's** *The Woman Warrior: Memoirs of a Girlhood Among Ghosts.*

Hamlet 1.5.14–28	*The Woman Warrior: Memoirs of a Girlhood Among Ghosts;* **Chapter 1: "No Name Woman"**
GHOST I am thy father's spirit, Doomed for a certain term to walk the night And for the day confined to fast in fires Till the foul crimes done in my days of nature Are burnt and purged away. But that I am forbid To tell the secrets of my prison house, I could a tale unfold whose lightest word Would harrow up thy soul, freeze thy young blood, Make thy two eyes, like stars, start from their spheres, Thy knotted and combinèd locks to part, And each particular hair to stand an end, Like quills upon the fearful porpentine. But this eternal blazon must not be To ears of flesh and blood. List, list, O list!	My aunt haunts me—her ghost drawn to me because now, after fifty years of neglect, I alone devote pages of paper to her, though not origamied into houses and clothes. I do not think she always means me well. I am telling on her, and she was a spite suicide, drowning herself in the drinking water. The Chinese are always very frightened of the drowned one, whose weeping ghost, wet hair hanging and skin bloated, waits silently by the water to pull down a substitute.

My students made great connections between these two texts: Both have ghosts, of course, and that's always interesting. But unlike Hamlet's father, the aunt in Kingston's novel drowns herself. She does, however—like the ghost in Hamlet—haunt the novel's narrator who confesses to readers, "I do not think she always means me well." Much as they do in terms of the ghost's relationship to young Hamlet, students immediately raised questions about the ghostly aunt's intentions, too. They dug into the fact that both ghosts have questionable motives.

Some of my Chinese American students shared their cultural traditions and beliefs regarding ghosts and the afterlife. They wanted to discuss how their culture viewed the supernatural as well as the relationship of the dead to the living. They noted how both texts involved complicated family relations as well as the community's history and past misdeeds, whether real or imagined. Finally, both texts, they said, gave them a way to discuss the power or powerlessness of women in a society that was both hierarchical and patriarchal. Here, again, are two works separated by time and space and yet what appears are the same big questions about gender, family, and community.

2. Pairing *Hamlet* (3.4.40–240 edited, the closet scene between Hamlet and his mother, Gertrude) with **"Poem III" from Claudia Rankine's *Citizen: An American Lyric*. "Poem III" is often referred to as "the Don Imus poem" because it focuses on the radio host's racial insults directed to the 2007 Rutgers all-Black women's basketball team.**

Shakespeare's plays are a powerful way to address the complicated history of prejudice. Pairing *Hamlet* with Claudia Rankine sheds new and different light on the mangled matter of race relations, gender erasure, and the corrosive effects of not questioning the nature of our reality. To bring forward for student discovery the moral conflicts and societal dilemmas that racism and conflict share across centuries with *Hamlet*, I paired a cut version of the closet scene in *Hamlet* (3.4.41–240) with "Poem III"—the "Don Imus poem"—in Rankine's poetry collection, *Citizen: An American Lyric*. Even though several other Rankine poems also work with the closet scene—"Stop and Frisk," "Affirmative Action," and "Neighbor who Called the Police"—I most often use this pairing.

Hamlet 3.4.40–240 (edited)	"Poem III"
HAMLET *[To Queen]* Leave wringing of your hands. Peace, sit you down, And let me wring your heart; for so I shall If it be made of penetrable stuff. QUEEN What have I done, that thou dar'st wag thy tongue In noise so rude against me? HAMLET Look here upon this picture and on this, The counterfeit presentment of two brothers. See what a grace was seated on this brow . . . This was your husband. Look you now what follows. Here is your husband, like a mildewed ear Blasting his wholesome brother. Have you eyes? . . . O shame, where is thy blush? Rebellious hell, . . . QUEEN O Hamlet, speak no more! Thou turn'st my eyes into my very soul, And there I see such black and grainèd spots As will not leave their tinct. HAMLET Nay, but to live In the rank sweat of an enseamèd bed, Stewed in corruption, honeying and making love Over the nasty sty! QUEEN O, speak to me no more! These words like daggers enter in my ears. No more, sweet Hamlet! HAMLET A murderer and a villain, A slave that is not twentieth part the tithe Of your precedent lord; a vice of kings, A cutpurse of the empire and the rule, That from a shelf the precious diadem stole And put it in his pocket— QUEEN No more! HAMLET A king of shreds and patches— *Enter Ghost.*	You are rushing to meet a friend in a distant neighborhood of Santa Monica. This friend says, as you walk toward her, You are late, you nappy-headed ho. What did you say? you ask. though you have heard every word. This person has never before referred to you like this in your presence, never before code-switched in this manner. What did you say? She doesn't, perhaps physically cannot, repeat what she has just said. Maybe the content of her statement is irrelevant and she only means to signal the stereotype of "black people time" by employing what she perceives to be "black people language." Maybe she is jealous of whoever kept you and wants to suggest you are nothing or everything to her. Maybe she wants to have a belated conversation about Don Imus and the women's basketball team he insulted with this language. You don't know. You don't know what she means. You don't care what response she expects from you nor do you care. For all your previous understandings, suddenly incoherent feels violent. You both experienced this cut, which she keeps insisting is a joke, a joke stuck in her throat, and like any other injury, you watch it rupture along its suddenly exposed suture.

Save me and hover o'er me with your wings,
You heavenly guards!—What would your gracious figure?

QUEEN Alas, he's mad.

HAMLET
Do you not come your tardy son to chide,
That, lapsed in time and passion, lets go by
Th' important acting of your dread command?
O, say!

GHOST Do not forget. This visitation
Is but to whet thy almost blunted purpose.
But look, amazement on thy mother sits.
O, step between her and her fighting soul.
Conceit in weakest bodies strongest works.
Speak to her, Hamlet.

HAMLET How is it with you, lady?

QUEEN Alas, how is 't with you,
That you do bend your eye on vacancy
And with th' incorporal air do hold discourse? . . .
O gentle son,
Upon the heat and flame of thy distemper
Sprinkle cool patience! Whereon do you look?

HAMLET
On him, on him! Look you how pale he glares.
His form and cause conjoined, preaching to stones,
Would make them capable. [*To the Ghost.*] Do not
look upon me,
Lest with this piteous action you convert
My stern effects. Then what I have to do
Will want true color—tears perchance for blood.

QUEEN To whom do you speak this?

HAMLET Do you see nothing there?

QUEEN Nothing at all; yet all that is I see.

HAMLET Nor did you nothing hear?

QUEEN No, nothing but ourselves.

HAMLET
Why, look you there, look how it steals away!
My father, in his habit as he lived!
Look where he goes even now out at the portal!
                              Ghost exits.

QUEEN
This is the very coinage of your brain.
This bodiless creation ecstasy
Is very cunning in.

HAMLET Ecstasy? . . .
It is not madness
That I have uttered. Bring me to the test,
And I the matter will reword, which madness
Would gambol from. Mother, for love of grace,
Lay not that flattering unction to your soul
That not your trespass but my madness speaks.
. . . Confess yourself to heaven,
Repent what's past, avoid what is to come,
And do not spread the compost on the weeds
To make them ranker.

QUEEN
O Hamlet, thou hast cleft my heart in twain!

HAMLET
O, throw away the worser part of it,
And live the purer with the other half!
Good night. But go not to my uncle's bed.
Assume a virtue if you have it not.
. . . Refrain tonight,
And that shall lend a kind of easiness
To the next abstinence, the next more easy; . . .
I must be cruel only to be kind.
This bad begins, and worse remains behind.

One word more, good lady.

QUEEN What shall I do?

HAMLET
Not this by no means that I bid you do:
Let the bloat king tempt you again to bed,
Pinch wanton on your cheek, call you his mouse,
And let him, for a pair of reechy kisses
Or paddling in your neck with his damned fingers,
Make you to ravel all this matter out
That I essentially am not in madness,
But mad in craft. . . .

QUEEN
Be thou assured, if words be made of breath
And breath of life, I have no life to breathe
What thou hast said to me.

When I asked my students what similarities they saw between the scene in which Hamlet confronts his mother and the Rankine poem, they all became fully engaged. They began a difficult conversation about feeling like an outsider or an "other" in one's native land, and sometimes in one's family. This pairing also helped them address questions about identity—cultural or individual. They noted that both texts revealed an absurd situation in which one person is meant to feel crazy, irrational, angry, confused, and they were keenly aware that misreading the predicament in both texts led to silence, moral dilemma, and violent emotion. More of their comments centered around:

- the dangers of inaction—on the part of both individuals and traditional institutions;

- accumulated humiliations that create painful moments of intense self-awareness;

- the absurdities that racism, moral dilemmas, and other prejudices create for both the recipient and perpetrator/aggressor; and

- the moral courage and strength of character it takes for the "other" and/or their allies to perform a decisive act, one which results in self-determination and true moral identity.

3. Pairing *Hamlet* (4.7.187–208, Gertrude's speech on Ophelia's death) and **"Pilgrimage" by Natasha Trethewey**.

Hamlet 4.7.187–208	"Pilgrimage"

QUEEN
One woe doth tread upon another's heel,
So fast they follow. Your sister's drowned, Laertes.
 	
LAERTES
Drowned? O, where?
 	
QUEEN
There is a willow grows askant the brook
That shows his hoar leaves in the glassy stream.
Therewith fantastic garlands did she make
Of crowflowers, nettles, daisies, and long purples,
That liberal shepherds give a grosser name,
But our cold maids do "dead men's fingers" call
    them.
There on the pendant boughs her coronet weeds
Clamb'ring to hang, an envious sliver broke,
When down her weedy trophies and herself
Fell in the weeping brook. Her clothes spread wide,
And mermaid-like awhile they bore her up,
Which time she chanted snatches of old lauds,
As one incapable of her own distress
Or like a creature native and endued
Unto that element. But long it could not be
Till that her garments, heavy with their drink,
Pulled the poor wretch from her melodious lay
To muddy death.
	Vicksburg, Mississippi
	
	Here, the Mississippi carved
	    its mud-dark path, a graveyard
	
	for skeletons of sunken riverboats.
	    Here, the river changed its course,
	
	turning away from the city
	    as one turns, forgetting, from the past—
	
	the abandoned bluffs, land sloping up
	    above the river's bend—where now
	
	the Yazoo fills the Mississippi's empty bed.
	    Here, the dead stand up in stone, white
	
	marble, on Confederate Avenue. I stand
	    on ground once hollowed by a web of caves;
	
	they must have seemed like catacombs,
	    in 1863, to the woman sitting in her parlor,
	
	candlelit, underground. I can see her
	    listening to shells explode, writing herself
	
	into history, asking *what is to become
	    of all the living things in this place?*
	
	This whole city is a grave. Every spring
	    Pilgrimage—the living come to mingle

with the dead, brush against their cold shoulders
in the long hallways, listen all night

to their silence and indifference, relive
their dying on the green battlefield.

At the museum, we marvel at their clothes—
preserved under glass—so much smaller

than our own, as if those who wore them
were only children. We sleep in their beds,

the old mansions hunkered on the bluffs, draped
in flowers—funereal—a blur

of petals against the river's gray.
The brochure in my room calls this

living history. The brass plate on the door reads
Prissy's Room. A window frames

the river's crawl toward the Gulf. In my dream,
the ghost of history lies down beside me,

rolls over, pins me beneath a heavy arm.

In her poetry collection *Native Guard*, Natasha Trethewey's "Pilgrimage" is an interesting study in imagery, diction, and theme when paired with Gertrude's speech about Ophelia's tragic demise. "Pilgrimage" is a poetic retelling of the moral confusion created by those white soldiers who were fighting for the Confederacy in the name of "honor" contrasted with the dark history of Mississippi in terms of racial equality for Blacks. Southern soldiers were fighting for "honor"; Black soldiers were fighting for equality.

After reading both texts, my students raised questions about the imagery: both include water that is dark and muddy; both reflect on tragic loss of life before its time, and both are lyrical expressions of deep feeling. In Trethewey's poem, a single speaker in a museum views the tragic loss of young life in a war that is both spiritual and literal. Her poem poses the big questions raised by Laertes about Ophelia's passing—what will best commemorate the dead, and what is an appropriate and sincere remembrance? Students connected the images that appear in both Gertrude's speech and "Pilgrimage": clothes, glass, flowers, gray, and ghost. The poem deals as much with the muddy nature of human memory (its "weedy trophies") as it does with revealing the speaker's capacity for unresolved grief.

Additionally, my students—remember, I teach in a boys' school—wanted to discuss women, objectified in this male-dominated society. They focused on a side of Gertrude's character they had not seen earlier, noticing that she can express grief, an emotion she did not seem to have for her first husband, Hamlet's father. They noted that Gertrude's drawn-out description at the loss of Ophelia and the end of innocence in the play revealed emotion that the men—at least those concerned with power and status like Claudius—are incapable of expressing. At least she has compassion, they said. Men seem more interested in their need for material power. For Gertrude, there's real emotion present.

When pairing Shakespeare's plays with unusual and perhaps surprising works, Ophelia's line "we know what we are but know not what we may be" (4.5.48–49) seems very appropriate. Juxtaposed paired texts often force sophisticated analysis and make a space for conversations that I as a teacher sometimes didn't realize needed to be had. May you have the same pleasure! Learning should expand our consciousness and give students—and teachers too—the chance to discover insights in realities and mysteries that heretofore have been veiled. If we as teachers are thoughtful about lifting these veils, we will move forward as a society and a human race to discover, that in pairing two very different texts, "[t]here are more things in heaven and earth . . . Than are dreamt of in your philosophy" (1.5.187–188).

Sources

Douglass, Frederick. *Narrative of the Life of Frederick Douglass: An American Slave.* New York: Penguin Books, 1968. Print. https://docsouth.unc.edu/neh/douglass/douglass.html.

Horton, George M. (1845). *The Poetical Works of George M. Horton, the colored bard of North-Carolina: to which is prefixed the life of the author, written by himself.* Hillsborough, North Carolina.

Kingston, Maxine Hong. *The Woman Warrior: Memoirs of a Girlhood Among Ghosts.* New York: Random House, 1989.

Rankine, Claudia. *Citizen: An American Lyric.* Minneapolis, MN: Graywolf Press, 2014, 41–42.

Trethewey, Natasha D. *Native Guard.* Boston: Houghton Mifflin, 2007.

PART FOUR

Five More Resources for You

- *Folger Teaching*—**folger.edu/teach**—The Folger's online universe for teachers! Search lesson plans, podcasts, videos, and other classroom resources. Connect with like-minded colleagues and experts. Access on-demand teacher workshops and participate in a range of live professional development opportunities from hour-long sessions to longer courses, all offering CEU credit. Complete access to *Folger Teaching* is one of many benefits of joining the Folger as a **Teacher Member**.

- *Folger Shakespeare* online—**folger.edu/shakespeares-works**—Shakespeare's complete works free and online, and all downloadable in various formats that are particularly useful for teachers and students. The Folger texts are the most up-to-date available online; behind the scenes, they have been encoded to make the plays easy to read, search, and index. Also available here are audio clips of selected lines performed.

- *Folger Shakespeare* in print—Shakespeare's plays and sonnets in single-volume paperbacks and in ebooks. The texts are identical to those of *Folger Shakespeare* online; the books, however, are all in a format featuring the text on the right-hand page with glosses and definitions on the left. Used in many, many classrooms, the *Folger Shakespeare* in print is published by Simon & Schuster and available from booksellers everywhere.

- *The Folger Shakespeare Library*—**folger.edu**—The online home of the wide world of the Folger Shakespeare Library, offering all kinds of experiences and resources from the world's largest Shakespeare collection. We're waiting for you, your class, and your family! Explore the Folger collection, enjoy the magic of music and poetry, participate in a workshop, see a play! We're a great opportunity for lively and satisfying engagement with the arts and humanities.

- *Shakespeare Documented*—**shakespearedocumented.folger.edu**—A singular site that brings together digitized versions of hundreds of the known primary source documents pertaining to Shakespeare—the playwright, actor, and stakeholder; the poet; and the man engaged in family and legal matters. A destination for curious students! Convened by the Folger, this collection is a collaboration among the Folger and Shakespeare Birthplace Trust, the National Archives of Great Britain, the Bodleian Library at Oxford, and the British Library.

ACKNOWLEDGMENTS

Seven or eight years ago, Mark Miazga, an exceptional high school teacher from Baltimore—and a Folger teacher—said, "We should make a series of books where we lay out for teachers key specifics about the play, and then how to teach the whole play using the Folger Method."

Ignition.

An important idea with a huge scope: five books, each focused on a single play—*Hamlet*, *Macbeth*, *Romeo and Juliet*, *Othello*, and *A Midsummer Night's Dream*. Each one a pretty revolutionary dive into basic info, scholarship, and the how of teaching each of the plays to *all* students. *Every* student. This demanded assembling an extraordinarily strong array of knowledge, expertise, and experience and moving it into action.

It is finally time to name and celebrate this crowd of people who, with generosity of all kinds, had a hand in creating the book that you are reading right now:

Folger director Michael Witmore, a deep believer in the importance of learning, teaching, and the power of the Folger to support both for all and at all levels, has been a fan and a wise advisor from the start.

The generosity of the Carol and Gene Ludwig Family Foundation—and in particular our fairy godmother, Carol Ludwig—has fueled every part of the creation of this series, including making certain that every English teacher in Washington, DC, has their own set of books *gratis*. I express the gratitude of the Folger as well as that of teachers in DC and beyond.

None of these volumes would exist without Folger Education's extraordinary Katie Dvorak, who, from the first minute to the last, herded not cats but our many authors, contracts, editorial conferences, publisher meetings, the general editor, and a series of deadlines that *never ever* stopped changing. Much of this was accomplished as Covid covered all lives, work, families, everything. Katie's persistence, along with her grace, humor, empathy, and patience kept us moving and was the glue we never did not need.

We appreciate the support and guidance of our team at Simon & Schuster: Irene Kheradi, Johanna Li, and Amanda Mulholland.

All along, the overall project benefited from the wisdom and support of these key players: Skip Nicholson, Heather Lester, Michael LoMonico, Corinne Viglietta, Maryam Trowell, Shanta Bryant, Missy Springsteen-Haupt, and Jessica Frazier . . . and from the creative genius of Mya Gosling.

Major gratitude to colleagues across the Folger who contributed to building these books in terms of content and business support. Our thanks to Erin Blake, Caroline Duroselle-Melish, Beth Emelson, Abbey Fagan, Esther French, Eric Johnson, Adrienne

Jones, Ruth Taylor Kidd, Melanie Leung, Mimi Newcastle, Rebecca Niles, Emma Pol-track, Sara Schliep, Emily Wall, and Heather Wolfe.

We are in debt to the schoolteachers and scholars who generously shared their time and wisdom as we got started, helping us to map our path and put it in motion—all along the intersections where scholarship and teaching practice inform each other. Massive gratitude to Patricia Akhimie, Bernadette Andreas, Ashley Bessicks, David Sterling Brown, Patricia Cahill, Jocelyn Chadwick, Ambereen Dadabhoy, Eric DeBarros, Donna Denizé, Ruben Espinosa, Kyle Grady, Kim Hall, Caleen Sinnette Jennings, Stefanie Jochman, Heather Lester, Catherine Loomis, Ellen McKay, Mark Miazga, Noémie Ndiaye, Gail Kern Paster, Amber Phelps, Katie Santos, Ian Smith, Christina Torres, and Jessica Cakrasenjaya Zeiss.

It's impossible to express our thanks here without a special shout-out to Ayanna Thompson, the scholarly powerhouse who has been nudging Folger Education for the last decade. Know that nudges from Ayanna are more like rockets . . . always carrying love and a challenge. We could not be more grateful for them, or for her.

With endless admiration, I give the close-to-last words and thanks to the working schoolteachers who authored major portions of these books. First here, I honor our colleague Donnaye Moore, teacher at Brookwood High School in Snellville, Georgia, who started on this project teaching and writing about *Othello* but succumbed to cancer far too soon. None of us have stopped missing her or trying to emulate her brilliant practicality.

I asked working teachers to take on this challenge because I know that no one knows the "how" of teaching better than those who do it in classrooms every day. The marvels I am about to name were teaching and living through all the challenges that Covid presented in their own lives *and* thinking about your students too, putting together (and testing and revising) these lessons for you who will use these books. Over a really loud old-fashioned PA system, I am shouting the names of Ashley Bessicks, Noelle Cammon, Donna Denizé, Roni DiGenno, Liz Dixon, David Fulco, Deborah Gascon, Stefanie Jochman, Mark Miazga, Amber Phelps, Vidula Plante, Christina Porter, and Jessica Cakrasenjaya Zeiss! You rock in every way possible. You honor the Folger—and teachers everywhere—with your wisdom, industry, and generosity.

Finally, I wrap up this project with humility, massive gratitude to all, for all, and—perhaps amazingly in the complicated days in which we are publishing—relentless HOPE. Hamza, Nailah, and Shazia O'Brien, Soraya Margaret Banta, and gazillions of children in all parts of the world deserve all we've got. Literature—in school, even!—can get us talking to, and learning from, one another in peace. Let's get busy.

—Peggy O'Brien,
General Editor

ABOUT THE AUTHORS

Ashley Bessicks is a leadership coach who partners with school administrators, coaches, and teachers to implement evidence-based instructional practices and increase student engagement. After spending nearly a decade in the classroom serving Washington, DC, students in grades 9–12, Ashley works on teams to help schools redesign teacher professional learning models to include conversations about equity. A Buffalo, New York, native, Ashley spends her time reading and exploring the world with family.

Dr. Catherine Loomis holds a PhD in Renaissance Literature from the University of Rochester, and an MA in Shakespeare and Performance from the Shakespeare Institute. She is the author of *William Shakespeare: A Documentary Volume* (Gale, 2002) and *The Death of Elizabeth I: Remembering and Reconstructing the Virgin Queen* (Palgrave, 2010), and, with Sid Ray, the editor of *Shaping Shakespeare for Performance: The Bear Stage* (Fairleigh Dickinson, 2016). She has taught at the University of New Orleans, the University of North Carolina at Greensboro, and the Rochester Institute of Technology.

Dr. Christina Porter is a 2006 alumna of the Folger's Teaching Shakespeare Institute. She began her career as an English teacher and literacy coach for Revere Public Schools in Revere, Massachusetts. Currently, she is Director of Humanities for her school district. She is also a faculty member at Salem State University. She resides in Salem, Massachusetts, with her two precocious daughters.

Corinne Viglietta teaches Upper School English at The Bryn Mawr School in Baltimore, Maryland. From 2014 to 2022, Corinne was Associate Director of Education at the Folger Shakespeare Library, where she had the honor of exploring the wonders of language with thousands of amazing teachers, students, and visitors. Corinne played a key role in Folger's national teaching community and school partnerships. She has led workshops on the Folger Method for numerous organizations, including the Smithsonian,

the National Council of Teachers of English, and the American Federation of Teachers. Corinne is a lifelong Folger educator, having first discovered the power of this approach with her multilingual students in Washington, DC, and France. She has degrees in English from the University of Notre Dame and the University of Maryland.

Of Haitian American descent, **Donna Denizé** holds a BA from Stonehill College and an MA in Renaissance Drama from Howard University. She has contributed to scholarly books and journals, and she is the author of a chapbook, *The Lover's Voice* (1997), and a book, *Broken Like Job* (2005). She currently chairs the English Department at St. Albans School for boys, where she teaches Freshman English; a junior/senior elective in Shakespeare; and Crossroads in American Identity, a course she designed years ago and which affords her the opportunity to do what she most enjoys—exploring not only the cultural and intertextual crossroads of literary works but also their points of human unity.

Dr. Jocelyn A. Chadwick is a lifelong English teacher and international scholar. She was a full-time professor at Harvard Graduate School of Education and now occasionally lectures and conducts seminars there. In addition to teaching and writing, Chadwick also consults and works with teachers and with elementary, middle, and high school students around the country. Chadwick has worked with PBS, BBC Radio, and NBC News Learn and is a past president of the National Council of Teachers of English. She has written many articles and books, including *The Jim Dilemma: Reading Race in Adventures of Huckleberry Finn* and *Teaching Literature in the Context of Literacy Instruction*. Chadwick is currently working on her next book, *Writing for Life: Using Literature to Teach Writing*.

Michael LoMonico has taught Shakespeare courses and workshops for teachers and students in 40 states as well as in Canada, England, and the Bahamas. He was an assistant to the editor for the curriculum section of all three volumes of the Folger's Shakespeare Set Free series. Until 2019, he was the Senior Consultant on National Education for the Folger. He is the author of *The Shakespeare Book of Lists*, *Shakespeare 101*, and a novel, *That Shakespeare Kid*. He was the co-founder and editor of *Shakespeare*, a magazine published by Cambridge University Press and Georgetown University.

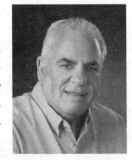

Dr. Michael Witmore is the seventh director of the Folger Shakespeare Library, the world's largest Shakespeare collection and the ultimate resource for exploring Shakespeare and his world. He was appointed to this position in July 2011; prior to leading the Folger, he was Professor of English at the University of Wisconsin–Madison and at Carnegie Mellon University. Under his leadership and across a range of programs and policies, the Folger began the process of opening up to and connecting with greater and more diverse audiences nationally, internationally, and here at home in Washington, DC. He believes deeply in the importance of teachers; also under his leadership, the Library's work in service of schoolteachers has continued to grow in breadth, depth, and accessibility.

Mya Lixian Gosling (she/her) is the artist and author of *Good Tickle Brain*, the world's foremost (and possibly only) stick-figure Shakespeare comic, which has been entertaining Shakespeare geeks around the world since 2013. Mya also draws *Keep Calm and Muslim On*, which she co-authors with Muslim American friends, and *Sketchy Beta*, an autobiographical comic documenting her misadventures as an amateur rock climber. In her so-called spare time, Mya likes to

read books on random Plantagenets, play the ukulele badly, and pretend to be one of those outdoorsy people who is in touch with nature but actually isn't. You can find her work at goodticklebrain.com.

Dr. Peggy O'Brien is a classroom teacher who founded the Folger Shakespeare Library's Education Department in 1981. She set the Library's mission for K–12 students and teachers then and began to put it in motion; among a range of other programs, she founded and directed the Library's intensive Teaching Shakespeare Institute, was instigator and general editor of the popular Shakespeare Set Free series, and expanded the Library's education work across the country. In 1994, she took a short break from the Folger—20 years—but returned to further expand the education work and to engage in the Folger's transformation under the leadership of director Michael Witmore. She is the instigator and general editor of the Folger Guides to Teaching Shakespeare series.

Roni DiGenno is a special education teacher at Calvin Coolidge Senior High School in Washington, DC. She earned her BA in Literature from Stockton University in Pomona, New Jersey, and her MA in English from Rutgers University in Camden, New Jersey. Her background in English and passion for special education led her to the educational mission of the Folger Shakespeare Library, participating in the Teaching Shakespeare Institute in 2016. She currently lives in Maryland with her husband, daughter, and two dogs.

Dr. Ruben Espinosa is Associate Professor of English at Arizona State University and Associate Director of the Arizona Center for Medieval and Renaissance Studies. He is the author of *Shakespeare on the Shades of Racism* (2021) and *Masculinity and Marian Efficacy in Shakespeare's England* (2011), and co-editor of *Shakespeare and Immigration* (2014). He was a Trustee of the Shakespeare Association of America (2018–2021), and he serves on the Editorial Boards of *Shakespeare Quarterly*, *Exemplaria: Medieval, Early Modern, Theory*, and Palgrave's "Early Modern Cultural Studies" series. He is currently at work on his next monograph, *Shakespeare on the Border: Language, Legitimacy and La Frontera*.

Stefanie Jochman teaches high school English in Oakton, Virginia. She was a participant in the Folger's 2014 Teaching Shakepeare Institute and has served on the faculty at subsequent Institutes in 2016, 2018, and 2021. In 2016, during her years of teaching in her hometown of Green Bay, Wisconsin, she earned the Golden Apple Award from the Greater Green Bay Chamber of Commerce. She is a contributing writer to the Moving Writers blog. She and her husband enjoy traveling to far-flung destinations.